Tolley's
Incorporating
a Business

A guide for accountants and business proprietors to the
taxation and other issues affecting the transfer of a
business to a company

by
Roger H Jones FTII, TEP

Senior Tax Manager
Larking Gowen, Norwich

LexisNexis™ UK

Members of the LexisNexis Group worldwide

United Kingdom	LexisNexis UK, a Division of Reed Elsevier (UK) Ltd, Halsbury House, 35 Chancery Lane, LONDON, WC2A 1EL, and 4 Hill Street, EDINBURGH EH2 3JZ
Argentina	LexisNexis Argentina, BUENOS AIRES
Australia	LexisNexis Butterworths, CHATSWOOD, New South Wales
Austria	LexisNexis Verlag ARD Orac GmbH & Co KG, VIENNA
Canada	LexisNexis Butterworths, MARKHAM, Ontario
Chile	LexisNexis Chile Ltda, SANTIAGO DE CHILE
Czech Republic	Nakladatelství Orac sro, PRAGUE
France	Editions du Juris-Classeur SA, PARIS
Germany	LexisNexis Deutschland GmbH, FRANKFURT and MUNSTER
Hong Kong	LexisNexis Butterworths, HONG KONG
Hungary	HVG-Orac, BUDAPEST
India	LexisNexis Butterworths, NEW DELHI
Ireland	Butterworths (Ireland) Ltd, DUBLIN
Italy	Giuffrè Editore, MILAN
Malaysia	Malayan Law Journal Sdn Bhd, KUALA LUMPUR
New Zealand	LexisNexis Butterworths, WELLINGTON
Poland	Wydawnictwo Prawnicze LexisNexis, WARSAW
Singapore	LexisNexis Butterworths, SINGAPORE
South Africa	LexisNexis Butterworths, Durban
Switzerland	Stämpfli Verlag AG, BERNE
USA	LexisNexis, DAYTON, Ohio

A CIP Catalogue record for this book is available from the British Library.

ISBN 0 406 965293

Typeset by Phoenix Photosetting, Chatham, Kent
Printed and bound in Great Britain by Antony Rowe Ltd, Chippenham, Wilts

Visit LexisNexis UK at www.lexisnexis.co.uk

Foreword

Gordon Brown has changed the face of British business, almost certainly by accident. A series of measures in recent Budgets has made the limited company the optimum way of operating for the vast majority of enterprises. As yet Mr Brown himself seems not to have noticed this. But any trader who is self employed or in partnership should be asking whether their current way of business remains the sensible way forward – for some it will be, for most it will not.

To move from self employment to company involves incorporation. Much has been written on this topic, some of it very good, some less so. But until now we have not had a comprehensive, authoritative book on the subject. This is it – the work we have been waiting for on incorporation.

I loved this book. Roger Jones writes with great style, smiling wryly at the idiosyncrasies of the UK tax system while explaining them with precision, clarity and humour. He writes of an area of which he has deep personal experience and he makes his subject come alive.

His breadth is wonderful – any work that deals with the plus points of a company bike scheme in incorporation has covered all the angles. He debunks some myths about his subject – after reading Roger's comments no one should still regard the proprietor's motor car as a sensible reason for not incorporating. He corrects common misunderstandings, such as how capital allowances work on the move from sole proprietor to company. He recognises the growing effect of the benefits system – in the form of tax credits – on our incorporation work. He gives us new insights, for example on the extraordinary savings that can be had from running a new property investment business through a company. He deals with the detailed yet highly important day-to-day issues of incorporation in a way that I have not seen in any other commentary. Above all, he understands how taxpayers and the Inland Revenue think and operate in the real world.

As well as being a great read this book is deeply practical. Should I myself incorporate? Roger gave me my answer early on in my reading – I worked out that in business on my own account I lose about £3,000 a year compared with being a company. But as a minefield of disorganisation could I actually cope with the administration of a company? Well, Roger's notes and checklists have given me all the ammunition I need to make it a reality – and for £3,000 a year it is well worth the effort.

What this book cannot tell you is whether the Chancellor really does dislike sole traders so much, or simply has no idea of the consequences of his measures. But in the meantime Roger gives you all you need to know about the pros and cons of incorporation and the practical way to make it a success. I thoroughly commend this book to you.

Ian Nichol
MA FCA CTA ATT

Preface

Incorporation is not a new process, though the behaviour of certain professional advisers and business proprietors in the last year or so might lead one to think that this is the case. Commercial considerations have long dictated that the corporate medium was to be preferred by certain businesses. My earliest positive recollection of advising on incorporation goes back to 1985. It was then I learned that, on a sale between connected parties, market value could not be imposed for capital allowance purposes. This simple fact can be enormously beneficial in many incorporations but, in the intervening 18 years, it seems to have escaped the attention of all but a few.

What has really changed is the tax effect of trading in the corporate medium. A combination of several apparently disparate pieces of legislation since Labour Government returned to power seems to dictate that, for tax purposes alone, the company is the preferred medium for almost all businesses.

As I surveyed a raft of potential incorporations shortly after Budget 2002, I bemoaned the continuing absence of a comprehensive book covering all aspects of the subject. Several of my colleagues suggested that I should write one. Even though I had offered advice on countless incorporations over the years, and could reasonably claim considerable practical experience, I did not then rise to the bait.

However, a number of articles written for Taxation and Tolley's Practical Tax Newsletter, and one or two other events, led to my discussing possibilities with Tolley last autumn. This led to six months of hard labour, the result of which you see before you.

Whilst there are plenty of references to the statutes, Inland Revenue Manuals etc for those who wish to dig deeper, I have tried to adopt a practical and readable style. I hope this might appeal to some business proprietors as well as professional advisers. The text is liberally sprinkled with worked examples and anecdotes and each chapter is summarised with bullet points highlighting significant planning issues.

Unless specifically stated otherwise, all income tax, capital gains tax, corporation tax, national insurance rates, allowances and bands etc are those appropriate to 2003/04 or financial year 2003.

It is based on the law and practice as understood at 6 April 2003. The Income Tax (Earnings and Pensions) Act received Royal Assent at the end of 2002/03. This stems from the tax law rewrite project and supercedes the provisions of Income and Corporation Taxes Act 1988 as regards income from employment etc. The ITEPA 2003 references are those which actually apply in 2003/04 though, for ease of comparison, the old ICTA 1988 equivalents are also included.

The 2003 Budget Speech was delivered later than has become usual, on 9 April 2003. With the exception of the demise of the nanny company (see Chapter 17), the Chancellor did nothing to inhibit the current flood of incorporations.

All commentary is based on the law in England and Wales. That applying in Scotland and Northern Ireland may occasionally be different.

Whilst I have endeavoured to make the work as comprehensive as possible, there is bound to be room for improvement. Though nothing in Budget or Finance Act 2003 will inhibit the process of incorporation, one has to be mindful of changes in practice. Possible application of the settlements legislation to husband and wife close companies is the current hot news. I should be grateful to receive any comments or suggestions, either direct or through the publishers, for possible inclusion in a second edition (should that come to pass).

Whilst every care has been taken to ensure that the contents of this work are complete and accurate, no responsibility for loss occasioned by any person acting or refraining from action as a result of any statement in it can be accepted by the author or the publishers.

My thanks must begin with a long-term friend and former colleague, Ian Nichol. He was largely responsible for convincing me to undertake this project. At least he then had the decency to review every chapter of the manuscript as it was in the making. I am very grateful for his comments along the way. Next must come my colleagues at Larking Gowen. I will not mention any by name, largely for fear of missing someone out. However, they have helped in so many ways, including suggestions for topics to include, reading parts or even all of the draft manuscript and, whether wittingly or unwittingly, providing ideas for anecdotes and examples (nothing should be read into the names of the individuals in the examples and the things they are supposed to have done!). I should also like to thank Matthew Hutton for assisting with the chapter on Stamp Duty and Paul Seal for giving the draft manuscript a final read in double quick time. Also Jill Whitelaw for her sterling efforts in turning my initial ramblings into a sensible draft. I must thank Jenny and Hannah, my wife and daughter, for putting up with so many early mornings, late nights and missing weekends during the writing process. My final thanks are due to Tolley's editorial team in bringing the process to fruition.

Roger Jones FTII, TEP
Norwich
July 2003

Contents

Contents

Contents

Contents

Abbreviations

ABA	Agricultural Buildings Allowance
ACT	Advance Corporation Tax
AGM	Annual General Meeting
AMAP	Approved Mileage Allowance Payment(s)
APR	Agricultural Property Relief
BATR	Business Asset Taper Relief
BIK	Benefit(s) in Kind
BPR	Business Property Relief
CGT	Capital Gains Tax
CIHC	Close Investment Holding Company
CIR	Commissioners of Inland Revenue
CTAP	Corporation Tax Accounting Period
CTSA	Corporation Tax Self Assessment
CVS	Corporate Venturing Scheme
CYB	Current Year Basis
EGM	Extraordinary General Meeting
EIS	Enterprise Investment Scheme
EMI	Enterprise Management Incentive
ESC	Extra Statutory Concession
ET	Earnings Threshold
FRS	Financial Reporting Standard
FURBS	Funded Unapproved Retirement Benefit Scheme
FY	Financial Year
FYA	First Year Allowance
GAAP	Generally Accepted Accounting Practice
IBA	Industrial Buildings Allowance
ICAEW	Institute of Chartered Accountants in England and Wales
IHT	Inheritance Tax
IRC	Inland Revenue Commissioners
IRNICO	Inland Revenue National Insurance Contributions Office
IRPR	Inland Revenue Press Release
LAL	Lower Annual Limit (Class 4 NIC)
LEL	Lower Earnings Limit
LET	Lower Earnings Threshold
LLP	Limited Liability Partnership
NHS	National Health Service
NIC	National Insurance Contribution(s)
NIRP	National Insurance Retirement Pension
NMW	National Minimum Wage
OLP	Original List Price
PAYE	Pay As You Earn
PET	Potentially Exempt Transfer
PLC	Public Limited Company
PPP	Personal Pension Plan
PSA	PAYE Settlement Agreement

Abbreviations

PT	Primary Threshold
PYB	Previous Year Basis
QEF	Qualifying Earnings Factor
RCA	Readily Convertible Assets
S2P	State Second Pension
SA	Self Assessment
SDRT	Stamp Duty Reserve Tax
SERPS	State Earnings Related Pension Scheme
SET	Second Earnings Threshold
SLA	Short Life Asset
SME	Small or Medium-sized Enterprise
SSCD	Simon's Special Commissioners' Decisions
ST	Secondary Threshold
STC	Simons Tax Cases
TC	Tax Cases
UAL	Upper Annual Limit (Class 4 NIC)
UEL	Upper Earnings Limit
VAT	Value Added Tax
WDA	Writing Down Allowance

Statutory Abbreviations

CA	Companies Act 1985
CAA	Capital Allowances Act 2001
FA	Finance Act (year)
ICTA	Income and Corporation Taxes Act 1988
IHTA	Inheritance Tax Act 1984
ITEPA	Income Tax (Earnings and Pensions) Act 2003
LLPA	Limited Liability Partnerships Act 2000
LPA	Limited Partnerships Act 1907
NMWA	National Minimum Wage Act 1998
SA	Stamp Act 1891
SSCBA	Social Security Contributions and Benefits Act 1992
SSCR	Social Security (Contributions) Regulations 2001
TCGA	Taxation of Chargeable Gains Act 1992
TMA	Taxes Management Act 1970

Table of Cases

Table of Statutes

Paragraph numbers in **bold** type indicate where the section is set out in part or in full.

Chapter 1

Introduction

Historical comparisons

1.1 This book is about incorporating a business, giving an automatic presumption that a business exists and wishes to switch to the corporate medium of operation. It is not about commencing business and starting from scratch as a company though, of course, many of the issues raised will be relevant in that scenario.

One might venture to suggest that a decade ago it would probably not have been written. That is not to suggest that companies set up then were never created as vehicles for the continuing operation of existing businesses. Of course they were. But on nothing like the scale which is apparent in the opening years of the 21st century. So what has changed?

Historically, why would a business proprietor have preferred to trade through a company? Reasons might include:

- 'That's how big business does it'. Big corporations prefer to trade with other companies.
- The benefit of limited liability, though that may be more perceived than real for smaller companies.
- Status. 'Managing Director' looks good on a business card.
- Future prospects for the business and the likelihood of sales.
- The comparative ease of attracting inward investment for business development etc.
- Ease of partitioning the company to facilitate the passing of the business down the generations.
- Additional scope for pension planning. Contributions to corporate pension arrangements can be far more generous than retirement annuity or personal pension policies.
- Taxation.

In the foregoing list, the concept of 'big' is deliberately first. Incorporation should be for (at least relatively) large businesses. Companies are far more strictly regimented than unincorporated businesses. The business needs to be of sufficient size to have in place the requisite administrative systems to cope, or else continuing professional assistance will be required. The author is not convinced that, if taxation implications could be ignored, trading through a company is right for the majority of small businesses. For simplicity alone, sole trader or small partnership has to be the better option.

1.2   *Introduction*

Equally, tax is (very) deliberately the last item on the list. How often have you heard the mantra 'Do not let the tax tail wag the commercial dog'. Of course, the minimisation of tax liabilities is an important factor in any commercial decision, but it should not be the overriding one. However, at least in relation to incorporation, we seem to be running rapidly to the point of view that the saving of tax is the only factor to consider. It has been suggested that failure to recommend incorporation to virtually every small business could amount to negligence for a professional adviser. That is an extreme view but it is probably true that the potential savings of the process should be drawn to the attention of most businesses.

Incorporation is not a simple process, as the following chapters will reveal. There is no single correct way to do it. All businesses are different and every issue addressed will not necessarily apply to each of them. Careful thought and planning of the individual circumstances are necessary and good professional advice is essential. Trying to cut corners and apply a 'one size fits all' approach would be a recipe for disaster. The author has lived through a good many incorporations of all the types set out below. In some instances the practical problems were learned the hard way. Hopefully, these experiences will now benefit the reader.

1.2   Companies have always enjoyed tax advantages. The author is old enough to recall that, in the early days of post-unification (the merger of income tax and surtax in 1973/74), income tax rates reached 83% on earned income and 98% on investment income. Corporation tax, on the other hand, has never been above 52%. To take advantage of this differential though, it was necessary to use the company as a moneybox and not withdraw the profits. Withdrawal meant imposition of the higher personal tax rates. For many years closely controlled companies were in any case prevented from acting as moneyboxes, so that profits suffered only lower corporation tax rates. The apportionment rules (abolished with effect from 1989/90) deemed 'excess' profits to be distributed and taxed as such in the hands of the participators whether they were actually paid out or not. So, for the typical owner-managed business, there was no great balance of advantage one way or the other for a corporate or non-corporate structure.

In so saying, one has to bear in mind the impact of National Insurance Contributions (NIC). There are powerful reasons why successive governments would prefer that we consider the payment of NIC as an insurance premium to meet the payment of contributory benefits. For most practical purposes, many of us would probably view it as a tax by another name. Until 6 October 1985, both employers' and employees' Class 1 contributions stopped at the upper earnings limit. Above that level, there was little practical difference in how additional salary or dividends were taxed (the investment income surcharge applying to dividends had already been abolished with effect from 1984/85). Although Class 1 secondary contributions are deductible in arriving at the corporate profit, a trend to favour remuneration by dividends was beginning to emerge.

1.3   This led to a popular sport. Annually, some commentators would consider the level of earnings at which incorporation could achieve some savings in the tax payable. These were carefully crafted and updated with changes in rates of tax, personal allowances etc. Initially, at least, the results may have had some meaning because the number of variables was relatively small. Things remained fairly constant until 1997 which, coincidentally or not, was the year in which a Labour Government returned to power after many years of Conservative influence. Since then, the number of (ever smaller sized) businesses looking at, and going through, the process of incorporation has grown rapidly. So what has changed?

Phasing out retirement relief

1.4   In *FA 1998*, the new Chancellor of the Exchequer decided that he was going to 'simplify' capital gains tax. With time to reflect on the changes made then, and subsequent tinkerings, this has proved to be anything but the case, but let us not start a political debate here.

The primary change was the abolition of indexation relief for non-corporate taxpayers and the introduction of taper relief. One of the consequential amendments to this fundamental change was the abolition of retirement relief. This was a very valuable relief for anybody meeting the relevant conditions and making the disposal of a business. As it stood in 1998/99, retirement relief gave total exemption on the first £250,000 of relevant gains and half of the next £750,000 of gains. Thus, a husband and wife partnership disposing of even a quite large business, realising a gain of £500,000, would pay no tax.

The substitute was business asset taper relief. This would give a maximum relief of 75% (and, as originally enacted, it took a qualifying period of ten years to reach this). So the same business disposal would attract tax of £50,000 where none was previously due. This was hardly a good deal, especially when retirement relief was phased out over five years so, when it disappeared completely, we would have only been halfway to qualifying for the maximum amount of taper relief (subsequent changes have, of course, improved this).

1.5   Immediately the hunt was on, amongst a certain class of businessmen, to find a way of retaining the value of retirement relief. Those in their 50s, meeting all conditions for retirement relief and intending to retire in the next few years, would have been sadly disappointed if they could not obtain the benefit of it. Now, the curious thing is that, in order to obtain retirement relief, the one thing you did not need to do was retire. It was sufficient to meet all the conditions (in the former *TCGA 1992, ss 163–164, Sch 6*) and make a material disposal.

How do you make a disposal qualifying for relief, whilst retaining control of the business? Ah – incorporation! The transfer of an unincorporated business to a company owned by the same proprietors would trigger a gain. That gain could be covered in whole or in part by retirement relief, uplifting the base cost of the business against the real disposal on 'proper' retirement a few years later.

In these incorporations, possible income tax advantages in the short term were an incidental benefit. The prime objective was to preserve the benefit of retirement relief and a flurry of 'let's bank retirement relief' incorporations ensued. The taxation industry responded with advice on the best time to incorporate as retirement relief was phased out and business asset taper relief was phased in, giving the optimum position (which varied according to the size of the gain).

Reduction in dividend taxation

1.6   The next significant factor had actually been announced before the end of retirement relief, but did not take effect until 6 April 1999. The last Conservative Budget in March 1997 had actually announced changes in the tax treatment of certain company distributions. So far as these still exist, they may be found in *FA 1997*. However, the first Labour Budget in June that year had even more radical proposals, including the abolition of advance corporation tax (ACT). ACT served the secondary function of forming the tax credit for the recipient of a dividend and changes to the treatment of tax credits actually appear in *F(No 2)A 1997*, though the actual death knell of ACT is in *FA 1988*.

Briefly (see **4.22–4.26** for full details), the combined effect was to reduce the rate of the tax credit from one quarter to one ninth and make it entirely notional. However, so long as the recipient was an individual taxed only at the lower rate (now starting rate) or basic rate then the notional tax credit was treated as satisfying the full income tax liability. In other words, something for nothing. The higher rate for dividend income was adjusted from 40% to 32.5%, so the higher rate taxpayer was no worse off.

The combined effect (also bearing in mind NIC) was that, at the bottom end of the market, a significant advantage arises in taking a dividend rather than a salary (see **5.20**). For the higher rate taxpayer, the advantage is harder to assess but still there for a small company.

Thus, if the business proprietor was prepared to take dividends from the company, then incorporation provided a route to increasing net spendable income.

1.7   However, this would not suit everybody – not even, it must be said at that stage, the majority. Dividends still had a very significant disadvantage. For anyone wishing to fund a private pension, dividends are not net relevant earnings for personal pension plan (PPP) purposes nor, indeed, remuneration for a relevant benefit scheme. So there remained a marked reluctance to make major use of dividends.

At least in relation to PPPs, that was about to change.

Stakeholder pension rules

1.8 *FA 2000* introduced new rules for personal pension provision in connection with what has become known as the stakeholder regime. However, the changes actually apply to all PPPs. The change took effect on 6 April 2001.

One particular aspect gives a very valuable tool to the incorporation planner. What is now *ICTA 1988, s 646B* allows the scheme member to use the net relevant earnings of a given year (the basis year) as the basis for contributions paid in that and the next five years. So we now have a means to enjoy the tax advantages of taking dividends and yet be able to fund a PPP.

This is by the simple expedient of taking a large (or at least reasonably sized) salary in one year. This then forms the basis for PPP contributions in the next five years, during which dividends are taken to reduce the tax bill. Some interesting rates of relief can arise too (see **4.38–4.39**).

Hello, the next round of incorporation. This is now well underway.

National Insurance Retirement Pension

1.9   Further, it no longer matters that dividends do not give you credits for National Insurance Retirement Pension (NIRP).

We will look at this in detail a little later (**5.23**). The self employed must pay Class 2 contributions to qualify for NIRP. An employed person (including a director of a company) must surely pay Class 1. Well, actually, no. A new *s 6A* introduced into *SSCBA 1992* with effect from 6 April 2000 allows earnings at a certain level to qualify for contributory benefits, even though no actual Class 1 contributions are paid. Look at that, something for nothing again.

Increase in National Insurance Contributions

1.10   So, we have got to the point where we do not care that the Chancellor announced a 1% increase in Class 1 (and Class 4) contributions in the 2002 Budget. This took effect from 6 April 2003 and has no upper limit.

We have already seen, however, that the director/shareholder of a private company can take dividends (in most years) and:

- enjoy a tax advantage in some instances;
- pay no NIC;
- fund a PPP, despite having no earnings;
- qualify for NIRP.

Why isn't every small business doing it? Good question – maybe the increase in NIC will push a few more that way.

What next?

1.11   If tax were the only factor, it is difficult to see why virtually every sole trader and partnership should not incorporate. There is a very powerful financial incentive to do so.

Of course, tax is not the only issue to consider. There are others, but it should now go very high on the list.

From here on in, this work assumes that serious consideration is being given to incorporation. It sets out the pros and cons along the way. It covers most (hopefully all) of the issues to be addressed in the process of incorporation.

1.12   At the risk of alienating a few readers, it does not offer a step-by-step guide to incorporation. This is both a considered and deliberate stance. Every business is different and the requirements of the owner/proprietors will diverge. Of course, there are common features in many situations, but that does not mean that every step is required in every incorporation. Neither will all the required steps necessarily be the same.

Look at the business, consider its particular features and check how to deal with them. Hopefully, you will find guidance on them all within this book.

It does conclude with an incorporation checklist, but it is stressed again that this is not so much 'how to do it' as 'have I covered all the angles?'.

Now down to business.

Chapter 2

Business Structures

2.1   Having made a decision to trade, the proprietor must first decide on an appropriate medium to use. The options are:

- Sole trader
- Partnership
- Limited liability partnership
- Company

It would be nice to say that the prime considerations are commercial ones. Tax and legal issues should follow, not lead, the decision. However, as will be seen, current tax legislation is such as to force many businesses to think about a company first and who can blame them given the possible advantages. Proportionately, the advantages are greatest at the bottom end of the market, say profits up to £40,000, precisely the area in which traditionally a company was probably the last thing to think about.

The sole trader is the archetypal small business. There is a myriad of them and this will no doubt continue to be the case. Some occupations attract a transient population of traders that come and go with the consequence that a business structure with minimal entry and exit costs would be attractive. Equally, there are many long-established businesses. Construction industry subcontractors (which have a brief special mention at **17.38–17.56**) are almost always self employed. Many professionals, e.g. doctors, lawyers, accountants, are bound by professional regulations to practice alone or in partnership. The balance may slowly begin to change as we now see, for example, accountants beginning to incorporate audit practices. There is absolutely no reason why tax practitioners cannot incorporate, although so far few have done so.

Equally, there are other businesses which are almost forced to operate through the medium of a limited company. It is often the case that large corporations prefer to trade with companies rather than individuals. This may be totally wrong, but there appears to be an inherent belief that a company is likely to be more long lived and have greater financial stability. There is a certain degree of kudos for the individual in announcing himself as a company director.

This attitude of company likes company is nowhere more apparent than in some service industries, the greatest of which is almost certainly the burgeoning information technology sector which, even 20 years ago, was almost non-existent. The large consumers of computer programmers, for whatever reasoning, did not (perhaps still do not) want to engage them as employees with attendant PAYE and employment law problems. The individual became an employee of his own one-man company which, in turn, contracted with the ultimate consumer.

Such was the perceived scale of the problem in official eyes that it spawned its own area of anti-avoidance legislation – the so called IR35 personal service company provisions. We will take a look at the effect of these later (see **17.1–17.33**).

For the time being, let's ignore any constraints which might apply and look at the basic business structures by comparing and contrasting their nature, especially the tax treatment.

Sole trader

Starting out

2.2   For simplicity alone, this has to be the preferred medium for all small businesses. Looking after one's own, it is also the major customer base of many small and medium accountancy practices. There are over two million small businesses in the UK. Even with the distorting influences of the present tax system, it seems unlikely that this will ever change. Only the well advised, administratively well organised will 'rebel' and do something more creative. Or, will the conversations in the pub have a greater influence?

Regulation of the sole trader as a business vehicle is minimal. Whilst the proprietor may have professional constraints, or encounter issues such as employment law or health and safety, fundamentally he just decides to trade and gets on with it. The start of the trade is a question of fact and he does not even need a business bank account, though it would clearly be sensible to have one.

2.3   The biggest constraints are actually imposed by the taxing authorities. Leaflet *P/SE/1, Thinking of working for yourself?* can be obtained from the Inland Revenue (for tax and NIC purposes). The registration form *CWF1*, contained within the leaflet, must be completed and returned within three months of the commencement of trade, otherwise a penalty of £100 is charged. This penalty is actually imposed by the NIC legislation [*SS(C)R, SI 2001 No 1004, Reg 87*].

2.4   It is perhaps worthwhile to take a step back and consider whether the proprietor is truly self employed. We have all heard of the company which seeks to hire workers on a 'self employed basis'. It is not a question of free choice. The true sole trader is independent of his customers; his business must have a life of its own. The status of workers is beyond the scope of this book, but a simple guide with which to start is contained in Inland Revenue leaflet *IR56, Employed or self-employed?*.

2.5   VAT registration is not required until the taxable turnover of the business has exceeded the registration limit (£56,000 as at April 2003) in the last twelve months or there are reasonable grounds for believing it will exceed the limit in the next 30 days.

2.6   If the business has any employees, even if limited to the spouse of the proprietor, there is a need to consider the operation of PAYE and register with the local tax office to deal with this where necessary.

Profits

2.7   Tax requirements apart, there is no need for a sole trader to keep financial records. Clearly it is wise to do so, but there is no mandatory requirement. There is no equivalent of statutory books for a company, no annual return is required and the proprietor can enjoy the profits of the business as they arise.

It is largely the taxman who will spoil this free and easy attitude.

2.8   Whilst not absolutely essential, for all but the very smallest of businesses, it would be wise to draw up annual accounts. Whilst the sole trader can charge any expense he likes to the profit and loss account, the final profit for tax purposes must, for all accounting periods beginning after 6 April 1999, be drawn up in accordance with Generally Accepted Accounting Practice (GAAP) [*FA 1998, s 42 as modified by FA 2002, s 103*]. This applies to all trades, professions and vocations and it often comes as a surprise to many small businesses that it applies to sole traders just as much as companies. In effect, it means that tax computations are almost always necessary to adjust the accounting profit to a figure which complies with the tax legislation.

2.9   In determining the profit, a trader may wish to claim a deduction for amounts paid to relatives, or 'wife's wages' as they were often called. To be a valid deduction for tax purposes, the amounts must be:

* Realistic in relation to the work done. See *Copeman v William Flood & Sons Ltd (1940) 24 TC 53*.
* Actually paid and not simply an accounting entry. See *Moschi v Kelly (1952) 33 TC 442 and Abbott v IRC [1996] STC (SCD) 41n*.

The mechanism is obviously to make use of the spouse's (or child's?) income tax personal allowance and lower rate/basic rate band. The downside to watch is the impact on NIC.

A developing issue might be the interplay with the new Tax Credit system, effective from 6 April 2003. The constantly changing rules in this area make effective planning difficult.

Self Assessment and payment of tax

2.10   Since 1996/97, a system of self assessment (SA) has been in place. Where so required by notice given under *TMA 1970, s 8* a taxpayer must deliver a return of his income to the Inspector of Taxes, usually by 31 January following the year of assessment. Virtually every self employed trader will need to meet this requirement.

2.11   Penalties are charged for late submission. Initially this is £100 where the return is outstanding after the due date [*TMA 1970, s 93(2)* and *Steeden v Carver [1999] STC (SCD) 283*]. A further £100 is charged where the return is still outstanding six months later (*s 93(4)*). Both amounts may be reduced where the tax liability is less than the penalty [*s 93(5)*]. In serious cases the Inspector of Taxes may seek leave from the General Commissioners to charge a daily penalty of up to £60 [*s 93(3)*].

2.12   Should a return not be issued, the taxpayer must notify that he is chargeable to income tax under *TMA 1970, s 7*. This notification must be made by 5 October following the year of assessment.

Profits from self employment

2.13   *TMA 1970, s 8(1)(a)* requires that the return contains:

> '... such accounts, statements and documents relating to information contained in the return, as may reasonably be so required.'

For the most part, this information is to be included in a series of supporting schedules to the tax return. The self employed sole trader must complete the self employment pages. These contain a pro forma profit and loss account and an extract of the balance sheet. Experience shows that, in almost all cases, detailed accounts and tax computations are required in support of the self employment pages in order to ensure that adequate disclosure is made.

2.14   There is a statutory duty to keep such records as may be necessary to deliver a complete and correct return. Where the taxpayer is in business, these records must be preserved until 31 January next, five years after the year of assessment in question [*TMA 1970, s 12B(1), (2)*]. The penalty for failure to do so can be up to £3,000 (*s 12B(5)*).

2.15   Once the figures contained therein have been adjusted as necessary to comply with *FA 1998, s 42* and specific adjustments as required by the Taxes Acts have been made, e.g. disallowance of entertaining expenditure, the assessable profit must be determined.

The current year basis (CYB) of assessment was introduced at the same time as self assessment. For once, it means what it says, for an ongoing business: the profits earned in the year of assessment form the basis of the income tax assessment for that year. Original intentions to combine SA with a move to mandatory 5 April accounting were fortunately abandoned and a free choice of accounting date is still available. Thus, profits for the accounts year ended in the year of assessment form the basis.

Example 2.15

Ian draws up accounts to 30 April annually.
His 2003/04 assessment is based on the accounts to 30 April 2003.
Danny draws up accounts to 31 March annually.
His 2003/04 assessment is based on the accounts to 31 March 2004.

It will be seen that there is a cash flow advantage in having an accounting date early in the year.

2.16 Adjustments are required when the business starts or ends:

- In Year 1, the profits assessed are on an actual basis, i.e. period from the date of commencement to the following 5 April [*TA 1988, s 61(1)*].
- In Year 2, the basis of assessment will depend on the accounting date used in that year and will normally either be the twelve months to the accounting date in Year 2 [*TA 1988, s 60(3)(a)*] or the first twelve months from commencement [*s 61(2)*].
- For Year 3, the income tax basis period will normally become aligned with the annual accounting period.

It will be seen that some profits can be assessed twice.

Example 2.16

Ian (in Example 2.15 above) started trading on 1 August 2001. He draws up accounts for nine months to 30 April 2002 and annually thereafter.

Basis periods		
2001/02	Actual to 5.4.02	8/9 (say) × ape 30.4.02
2003/04	First 12 months	9/9 (say) × ape 30.4.02
		3/12 × ape 30.4.03
2003/04	Y/E 30.4.03	

Thus, 8/9 profits for the period ended 30.4.02 and 3/12 profits for period ended 30.4.03 are assessed twice.

2.17 Unless 5 April is used as the annual accounting date, basis periods will overlap in at least one tax year. The profit of any overlap period will be identified, together with the number of days in the overlap period and carried forward. It is deducted by way of a relief on cessation of the business [*TA 1988, s 63A(2)*] or on a change of accounting date [*s 63A(1)*].

Many long-standing businesses will be carrying forward a special type of overlap relief, known as transitional relief. This arose in the year of change from the old previous year basis of assessment. Again, the relief can be given on the cessation of the business or on a change of accounting date.

2.18   Readers' attention is drawn to Inland Revenue booklet *SAT1, The new current year basis of assessment* for more explanation and extensive examples. This was originally introduced to explain the new CYB, but is equally valid today.

Payment of tax

2.19   Having delivered the required SA return, the taxpayer must then account for the tax due.

2.20   A balancing payment is normally due on 31 January following the year of assessment [*TMA 1970, s 59B(1)*]. This will reflect the tax liability calcu-lated in the self assessment for the year.

2.21   However, for established businesses or other continuing sources of income, payments on account are generally required. These are based on the liability of the previous year. Each payment on account is 50% of the relevant amount (usually the total liability of the previous year less any tax deducted at source – though de minimis amounts can be ignored) payable on:

- 31 January in the year of assessment;
- 31 July following the year of assessment.

[*TMA 1970, s 59A(2)*].

Where the payments on account are perceived to be excessive, a claim may be made to reduce or cancel them under *TMA 1970, s 59A(3), (4)*.

2.22   Interest is charged on tax paid late under *TMA 1970, s 86*. A balancing payment paid late may also attract a surcharge of 5% of the tax outstanding if it is unpaid 28 days after the due date and a further 5% if unpaid after six months [*TMA 1970, s 59C*].

2.23   Further details on submission of returns, payment of tax etc may be found in Inland Revenue booklet *SAT2, Self Assessment: the legal framework*.

Partnership

2.24   For all practical purposes, much of what has been said above concern-ing a sole trader can be repeated.

2.25   There is slightly more regulation in the form of the *Partnership Act 1890* which governs the operation of a partnership and, indeed, defines it as 'the relation which subsists between persons carrying on business in common with a view of profit'.

It is wise, in all partnership arrangements, to draw up a partnership agreement. The nature of such a document may vary enormously from that which would be appropriate for a major professional partnership to a simple agreement for a husband and wife. It should cover such issues as:

- profit sharing;
- drawings;
- dissolution;
- procedures to follow on the retirement or death of a partner;
- extent to which partners might commit the firm.

It is acknowledged that many family partnerships have no Partnership Deed and operate satisfactorily if there is evidence of an oral agreement. Partners share profits as agreed from time to time and simply demonstrate this in the annual accounts. There will be other hearsay evidence of the partnership's existence in the form of bank accounts, business stationery etc.

However, in the absence of a partnership agreement, the *Partnership Act 1890* is definitive and it is no time to find that this gives adverse consequences when there is a family dispute, divorce etc.

2.26   It should be noted that the partners are jointly and severally liable for the debts of the firm. Thus, if one partner has bound the firm to some expense and is unable to pay, the others may be required to do so.

Starting out

2.27   Partnerships should notify all the authorities in the same way as a sole trader.

The VAT registration limit applies to the partnership as a whole and not to its individual members.

Profits

2.28   Profits are to be calculated in the same way as for a sole trader.

2.29   One useful application of a husband and wife partnership is in sharing profit and thereby limiting tax liabilities. If a sole trader husband employs his wife, he may have to justify a deduction for wife's wages in his business accounts as being reasonable for the duties performed. On the other hand, if they form a partnership, they may divide the profits in whatever ratio they choose, irrespective of the amounts of work contributed. The author has never seen the Inland Revenue challenge a 50:50 profit share in a husband and wife partnership, even where virtually no work is undertaken by the second spouse.

Returns

2.30   A partnership is required to submit a single return on behalf of the partnership [*TMA 1970, s 12AA*]. This is to be completed by the representative partner who may be nominated by the Inland Revenue if one is not chosen. The penalty for late submission of a partnership tax return is £100 per partner and is not mitigable if there is no tax liability [*TMA 1970, s 93A*].

The partnership return must show not only the total taxable profit of the partnership but must also include a statement analysing this, as between the partners. One curiosity is that the profit sharing ratio cannot be applied so as to give profits to some partners and losses to others. Where necessary, in such circumstances, the profit allocations are scaled back so as to extinguish the losses nominally apportioned to other partners.

2.31   Each individual partner is then required to render a personal SA return incorporating a share of the partnership profit on the partnership pages.

2.32   The opening and closing year adjustments are not required at the partnership level, except where the whole business starts or ceases. Where a new partner joins or a current one leaves, adjustment to reach the correct CYB assessments are needed for that partner only.

Payment of tax

2.33   Settlement of tax liabilities is the exception to the general rule that partners are jointly and severally liable for the debts of the firm. For this purpose, each individual partner is deemed to be carrying on his own business and is responsible for his own tax payment in a similar fashion to a sole trader.

Limited liability partnership

2.34   This is the 'new kid on the block'. The *Limited Liability Partnerships Act 2000* received royal assent on 20 July 2000 and took effect from 6 April 2001. In some ways, it may be seen as a halfway house between a partnership and a limited company. The manner of operation is very similar to a partnership, but it offers a degree of limited liability protection otherwise afforded by a company.

The LLP should not be confused with a Limited Partnership under the *Limited Partnerships Act 1907*. This is simply a special type of partnership, rarely encountered in practice. It allows persons to participate financially in a partnership without taking an active part in the management of its affairs.

Regulation

2.35   LLPs are governed by the *Limited Liability Partnerships Act 2000*, though this is commendably short. There are extensive regulations in the *Limited Liability Partnership Regulations 2001, SI 2001/1090*, though these deal mainly with accounts and insolvency.

2.36   The LLP is a separate legal entity distinct from its members. Thus, it contrasts with an ordinary partnership which, in England and Wales at least, has no separate identity (though Scottish partnerships do). Formation of the LLP could therefore be regarded as incorporation and, like a company, the LLP must be registered at Companies House.

2.37   The limited liability partnership does have limited liability and this is the attraction of it. The liability of a member is limited to the capital which he has contributed, though members may remain personally liable for their own negligence. It is said that the major professional services firms were the drivers for creation of such an entity. If a client makes an economic loss as a result of the actions of the LLP, he may sue the firm. The negligent member may be liable for the full amount to the client, but the liability of others is limited to their capital contributions (in a serious case, this could still mean that they lose the business).

2.38   Whilst it has been suggested that small partnerships might regard a partnership agreement as optional, it is essential that the LLP has a document of constitution. Although the *Companies Act 1985* provisions apply to the LLP, the members are free to regulate their internal affairs as they see fit. However, the majority of LLPs can be expected to adopt a formal written agreement.

Profits

2.39   The accounting, disclosure requirement and audit provisions of the *Companies Act 1985* apply to LLPs and therefore all accounting standards are invoked. The result should be compatible with the requirement in *FA 1998, s 42* that the profits of a trade, profession or vocation be drawn up in accordance with GAAP.

Taxation

2.40   Where the LLP carries on a trade, profession or vocation with a view to profit, it will be treated as an ordinary partnership for income tax and capital gains tax purposes. Everything which has been said above about partnerships, including registration, returns and payment of tax applies to LLPs. The distinction between the two vehicles is essentially tax neutral.

2.41   There are restrictions on the offset of losses which flow from the limited capital contribution which a member may have made to the LLP.

2.42 Where the LLP has no trade, or trade ceases, then treatment as a partnership ends. The LLP is then taxed on profits or gains as if it were a company. The member will be taxed on gains arising from disposal of his interest in the LLP.

2.43 Transfer of an existing partnership to the LLP should have no adverse tax consequences, given the continuing tax treatment as if the LLP were a partnership. It should be noted that stamp duty exemption on creation of the LLP only applies if the members of the old partnership and the new LLP are identical.

2.44 Detailed consideration of limited liability partnerships is beyond the scope of the present work. For more detail, readers' attention is drawn to the chapter on Limited Partnerships in *Tolley's Tax Planning*.

Company

2.45 The first thing to get fixed in the mind, especially that of the small business proprietor who is heading for the first time to the corporate sector, is that the company is a completely independent entity. The shareholders may own the company, and the directors may govern the company's activities (often in a small family company, the shareholders and directors will be the same people), but its existence is independent of them. Its liabilities are not their liabilities, which may be an advantage, but it cannot be stressed too highly that its assets are not their assets.

2.46 Most companies are limited by share capital. The owners subscribe for shares. Often in small family companies, the number in issue is (relatively) small and they are all ordinary; that is to say they have full participation in assets on a winding up, the right to vote etc. The nominal value is often £1, but this does not have to be the case and does not reflect the true value. Other types of shares can be issued; the ordinaries may be split into different classes for tax planning reasons, which are explained later (see **16.60**). There may be preference shares, which have limited rights to capital but enhanced rights to dividends.

2.47 However, not all companies have share capital. Some may be limited by guarantee. These are often encountered in the charity or not-for-profit sector. The member's liability is limited to the amount guaranteed, generally £1.

2.48 Occasionally, you may encounter an unlimited company whereby the shareholders have personal unlimited liability for any debts in the company. Detailed consideration of this type of company is beyond the scope of this book, but they may sometimes be used for stamp duty planning or where the shareholders value the privacy of not putting the company's affairs on the public record at Companies House.

2.49 In addition, a company may be financed by loan capital, whether this be a simple unsecured loan account of the director or more formally constituted loan stock. Some commentators favour keeping the share capital to a minimum and financing the company largely by way of loan. The reason behind this is that surplus funds in a company may be paid out more readily by repayment of loans. Where ownership is locked into share capital, there may be legal or tax difficulties in disposing of some of this. Such a view may be excessively naive in any case. A larger share capital ensures that ownership of the company can be more readily dispersed when the time comes. Additionally, there may be problems of achieving an interest deduction for tax purposes in a company which is thinly capitalised (i.e. the debt/equity ratio is high). The UK does not (yet) have specific thin capitalisation rules, but excess interest can already be treated as a distribution in certain circumstances [*ICTA 1988, s 209(2)(da)*].

Regulation

2.50 The operation of all companies is governed by the *Companies Act 1985*.

2.51 The company must be specifically formed and registered at Companies House. Most people wanting a company will approach a company formation agent, who may be able to offer one off the shelf for £100 or so. A bespoke company, made to particular requirements, can be created within a few days, but should still cost only a few hundred pounds or much less if formed electronically.

2.52 The company must have a legal document governing its operation. This is known as the Memorandum and Articles of Association. It will set out matters, such as the size of the authorised share capital, the objects of the company, the quorum for meetings etc. Ready-made companies will come with a standard Memorandum and Articles (which can be amended). Bespoke Articles or significant amendments should be handled by a lawyer.

2.53 The company must make an annual return to Companies House.

2.54 Company accounts must be in a format specified by the *Companies Act 1985* and must show a true and fair view, whether the company is subject to audit or not. If the company's turnover exceeds £1m, or it meets certain other criteria, it is subject to a statutory audit, far more expensive than the accounts preparation and review for a smaller, audit exempt, company or unincorporated business. The accounts must be submitted to all shareholders and lodged at Companies House, where they are liable to be inspected by anyone. Some business proprietors find this aspect off-putting though smaller companies are permitted to file abbreviated accounts where the disclosure (and therefore public knowledge of the company) is limited.

2.55 The company must notify its existence to the Inland Revenue by submitting form CT41G to the Inspector of Taxes. The company will be required to register for VAT when the taxable turnover of its business has exceeded the registration limit (£56,000 as at April 2003) in the last twelve months, or there are reasonable grounds for believing it will exceed the limit in the next 30 days.

2.56   Whereas a sole trader or partnership might only have needed to register with the local tax office for the operation of PAYE where there were employees, this is likely to prove essential for a company. Its directors will be employees (or at least office holders) and, if remuneration is paid to them, then the company will need to account for income tax under PAYE and NIC.

The close company

2.57   A close company is one which is under the control of five or fewer participators, or of participators who are directors [*ICTA 1988, s 414(1)*]. When looking at a particular participator, the shareholdings of persons who are associated with him must be included so that a company with a large number of shareholders may still be 'close'. The principal exceptions are:

- a company which is not resident in the UK [*s 414(1)(a)*];
- a company which is controlled by another non-close company [*s 414(5)*];
- if the company is quoted and more than 35% of its voting power is held by the public [*s 415(1)*].

2.58   The main consequences of being a close company include an extended definition of what amounts to a distribution [*s 418*] but, more importantly, loans to participators (shareholders) are heavily penalised. The *Companies Act 1985, s 330* does not permit such loans at all, except in the very limited circumstances of *s 332–338* (e.g. small loans up to £5,000). It comes as a surprise and a shock to many that contravention of this may be a criminal act.

2.59   It would be naïve, though, to think that this prevents owner managed companies from making loans to shareholders, whether deliberately or inadvertently. The tax legislation acknowledges this and introduces a specific code to deal with it. This may be found at *ICTA 1988, s 419* et seq and is addressed in detail at **16.14–16.18**.

2.60   Close company status does have one advantage. Individual shareholders may claim relief for interest paid on borrowings used to finance the company, provided broadly that they own at least 5% of the ordinary share capital [*ICTA 1988, s 360*].

Taxation of the company

2.61   The company pays corporation tax on its basic profits chargeable to corporation tax. This will include trading income, investment income such as rents or interest and capital gains. There is less distinction between sources than is the case with income tax and, to all intents and purposes, the old schedular system of taxation has disappeared for companies. Specifically excluded from profits for this purpose is dividend income.

UK dividend income is never taxed in the hands of the company, though non-group franked investment income is included in total profits when establishing the rate of corporation tax to be applied [*ICTA 1988, s 13(7)*]. The term 'franked investment income' is somewhat archaic and anomalous, since ACT was abolished on 6 April 1999.

2.62   Trading income is established in a similar fashion to an unincorporated business, though the detailed adjustments required by the Taxes Acts vary in certain specific instances. The important thing to note is that the taxable profit is struck after deducting remuneration payable to the proprietors. This gives great scope for planning and balancing the company's liabilities against those of the individual and, to many people, is now a significant part of the rationale for incorporation. Remuneration may be taken as:

- salary/bonus;
- benefits in kind, including pension contributions;
- interest on loans.

All these items are deductible in establishing the company profit, but note that they have specific (and dissimilar) tax consequences in the hands of the recipient.

2.63   A dividend, on the other hand, is a distribution of profit after corporation tax and is not an allowable deduction.

2.64   The mainstream rate of corporation tax for FY 2003 is 30%, though only the largest companies pay this. Smaller companies pay at 19%. *FA 1999, s 28* introduced a starting rate for very small companies which *FA 2002* reduced to nil. However, the progression between bands is not smooth and produces slightly illogical results.

ICTA 1988, s 13(2) contains a formula for relieving the tax applied where profits lie in the margin between small and large companies as defined in *s 13(3)*. These limits are reduced where there are associated companies. This concept is not explored arithmetically, but is best demonstrated in the table below as marginal rates of tax which apply to profits at certain levels. *Section 13AA* has similar provisions for the company between the bands for starting rate and small companies. The combined result is that the following rates of tax apply:

Taxable profits fall in range (£)	Marginal rate of corporation tax (%)
0–10,000	0
10,001–50,000	23.75
50,001–300,000	19
300,001–1,500,000	32.75
1,500,001 +	30

2.65 A close company is a close investment holding company (CIHC) unless it falls within the exceptions listed in *ICTA 1988, s 13A(1)*, most important of which is that it exists for the purposes of carrying on a trade. Most owner managed companies will be trading and are therefore not close investment holding companies. The distinction is important because a CIHC never gets the benefit of the lower rates of corporation tax; it always pays at the mainstream 30%. A family investment company is likely to be a CIHC.

Corporation tax self assessment

2.66 Self assessment for companies was introduced for accounting periods ending 1 July 1999 or later and is not greatly dissimilar to the pay and file procedures which went before it. The detailed CTSA rules may be found in *FA 1998, Sch 18*. The CTSA return on form CT600 does though include the company's assessment of liability for the period covered.

Like the income tax provisions, the Inland Revenue will usually serve a notice under *FA 1998, Sch 18 para 3* on the company requiring submission of a return of profits. Unlike income tax, the company is actually required to provide accounts. The CT600 also includes supplementary pages requiring information on items such as loans to participators. The return must be submitted within twelve months of the end of the accounting period (with special provisions for long periods of account) [*Sch 18 para 14*].

2.67 There are penalties for late submission, starting at £100 and increasing to £1,000, depending on the actual lateness and the number of previous failures [*Sch 18 para 17*]. There are tax-geared penalties for very late submission.

2.68 Where no notice to file a return has been served and the company has taxable profits, it must notify liability [*Sch 18, para 2*].

2.69 There is a statutory duty to maintain such records as may be needed to ensure that a correct return may be submitted and these are to be preserved for six years after the period [*Sch 18 para 21*]. The penalty for failure to do this is a maximum of £3,000 [*Sch 18 para 23*].

Payment of tax

2.70 Most companies are required to pay the tax shown by the self assessment as a single lump sum nine months and one day after the year end [*TMA 1970, s 59D*].

2.71 Large companies however must make payments on account of the final liability, beginning only halfway through the accounting period. A large company for this purpose is one which is liable to pay corporation tax at the mainstream rate. Thus, it is not just companies whose income exceeds the current upper profit limit of £1.5m [*ICTA 1998, s 13(3)*] but also many smaller companies which have associates. The detailed rules are given in *TMA 1970, s 59E* and in the *Corporation Tax (Instalment Payments) Regulations, SI 1998/3175*.

The impact of instalments was phased in from 1999 to 2002, but now all instalments must be 25% of the estimated final liability payable:

- Six months and 14 days after the start of the accounting period.
- Three months after the first instalment.
- Three months after the second instalment.
- Three months and 14 days after the end of the accounting period.

The requirement to estimate current profits in order to make acceptable payments on account will place a strain on the accounting systems of many companies.

Special rules apply where the company first becomes liable to pay instalments, or the amounts otherwise due would be small.

Impact of associated companies

2.72   A nasty trap awaits!

The starting rate of corporation tax ends at £10,000 (the first relevant amount in *ICTA 1988, s 13AA(4)(a)*) and the small company's rate at £300,000 (the lower relevant maximum in *s 13(3)(a)*). Just above these figures, higher marginal rates effectively apply (see the table in **2.64**).

These figures are reduced where there are associated companies. In effect, the limits are divided by the total number of associates.

Example 2.72

Company A is associated with Company B – the limits for Company A are £5,000 and £150,000.

Company A is associated with Company B and Company C – the limits for Company A are £3,333 and £100,000.

2.73   So, what is an associate? A company is an associate of another if one of the two has control of the other, or both are under the control of the same person [*ICTA 1988, s 13(4)*] which is also invoked in *s 13AA*. Control is interpreted in accordance with *ICTA 1988, s 416* which, in turn, requires one to look at the associates of the participator.

2.74 Business Structures

Example 2.73

Alex owns 60% of the shares in Wonder Widgets Ltd, with the remaining 40% held by his wife, Rebecca. Rebecca in turn owns 75% of the shares in Dolly Dressers Ltd, with the remaining 25% held by Alex.

Alex has a controlling interest in Wonder Widgets Ltd.

He also has a controlling interest in Dolly Dressers Ltd by virtue of his personal holding of 25% plus the 75% held by his associate, Rebecca, in effect deeming him to own 100% of the company.

Wonder Widgets Ltd and Dolly Dressers Ltd are therefore associated companies for the purpose of the small companies rate limits. This much will not come as a surprise.

However, suppose that Alex owned 100% of Wonder Widgets Ltd and Rebecca owned 100% of Dolly Dressers Ltd. Neither has any direct holding in the other's company. Following the decision in *R v IRC, ex p Newfields Developments Ltd [2001] UKHL 27, [2001] STC 901*, this does not matter and the two companies will be associated.

2.74

Example 2.74

One fine morning, you have a meeting with Helen, a potential new client. She runs a successful florists shop and produces sole trader accounts showing a profit of around £30,000 last year. She wants a new accountant because she perceives that the present one never offers her any constructive advice. Instantly, you tell her that she could save around £3,800 by incorporating the business. She is impressed and instructs you to proceed.

In your haste, you fail to get enough information. In particular, you did not discover that she has just married and her husband Richard has a successful engineering company turning in profits of around £250,000. This is below the lower relevant maximum and the company pays tax at 19% amounting to some £47,500.

However, Helen's new company will be associated with Richard's company so that the lower relevant maximum is divided by two (for both companies). This does not matter for Helen's company, but Richard's engineering company will now pay tax of £61,250 (£150,000 at 19%, £100,000 at 32.75%), an increase of £13,750.

Does Helen's saving of £3,800 still look so good? Will you get a professional negligence claim?

Planning points

- An accounting date early in the tax year gives a cash flow advantage for a sole trader (or partnership) (**2.15**).
- Remember, and fix in the mind of the business proprietors, a company is a separate entity. Its assets are not their assets (**2.45**).
- When considering incorporation, note the effect of associated companies and look very carefully to find them (**2.72–2.74**).

Chapter 3

Effect of Losses

3.1   We have explored the structures available to business proprietors. It is a sign of tax liability under Schedule D case I that the activity is carried on with a view to profit. Unfortunately, though the view to profit may be there, the realisation of it may not always be the case. Losses might be incurred; indeed this is commonly the case with many business start ups.

Although it might be an indicator, the generation of a profit is not the overriding factor in determining that a business has commenced. New businesses might have initial capital costs of equipment, production costs, advertising etc., before the first sale is made. We may well have an adventure in the nature of a trade but it does not necessarily instantly produce income.

Should we therefore factor into the decision making process the possibility that losses will arise?

This work is primarily concerned with the incorporation of a business, on the presumption that there is a pre-existing sole trade or partnership business in place. It is not really intended as a guide to those first starting out in a new business venture, though many of the areas explored will be of value in deciding whether or not to trade through the corporate medium. Despite the perceived advantages of a company, this should not necessarily be taken to be the best structure to use from day one. After all, as we will continue to demonstrate, with a little care, a successful business may be readily incorporated. On the other hand, to start with a company which proves less than successful could be disastrous and far more difficult to unscramble.

So let's be pessimistic for a few moments and consider that losses may arise. In **Chapter 2**, we looked first at unincorporated structures and then the company. As far as losses are concerned, it may be more convenient to reverse the considerations.

Corporate losses

3.2   It is immediately apparent why this should come first. There is actually very little that can be done with corporate losses. Remember, a company is a completely separate entity from its owners/proprietors.

3.3 If a company incurs a trading loss, it may be set against other income [*ICTA 1988, s 393A(1)(a)*]. For the newly created company this is hardly very useful because there will almost certainly be no other income.

3.4 A corporate trading loss may also be set back against profits of the previous twelve months [*s 393A(2)*]. Again, in a start up situation, this is not going to be very helpful. Neither will the fact that terminal losses on cessation of trade can be carried back for three years.

3.5 Broadly, therefore, we are left only with the possibility that the company can carry forward its losses and set them against income from the same trade which arises in future years [*s 393(1)*].

And that, basically, is it. Start a business, which may have initial losses, in a company and those losses will be locked into the company, unused and without tax relief, until such time as the company turns in a profit. In the worst case scenario, this may mean no tax relief at all – ever.

So, stop, think carefully. Is a company the right medium in which to start a new business?

Personal losses

Early years

3.6 Losses arising from a trade, profession or vocation carried on in an individual's personal name (whether that be as a sole trader or member of a partnership) may be utilised in a number of ways, reducing other tax liabilities or, indeed, creating a repayment.

3.7 Firstly, trading losses may be set against other income arising in the year of loss or the previous year [*ICTA 1988, s 380(1), (2)*]. The relief could be against investment income or, more likely, against a salary from a previous employment.

3.8 Possibly of even more use, in the early years of a new trade, is the relief in *s 381*. Where a loss is incurred in the year of assessment in which a new trade commences, or any of the next three years, the trader may set that loss against his total income for the previous three years, taking the earliest years first. This is a very powerful relief which can generate significant tax repayments to subsidise the early costs of trading.

3.9 To obtain relief under either *s 380* or *s 381*, it is necessary to make a claim before 31 January following the year of assessment in which the loss was incurred. Where both claims are possible, the claimant is free to choose. Losses take precedence over personal allowances, which may then be unutilised.

3.10   Where losses are incurred and all income has been exhausted, there is a further relief where capital gains exist. *FA 1991, s 72* permits an extension of the *ICTA 1988, s 380* claim to capital gains. It is not an alternative. The *s 380* claim against income must come first, with relief against capital gains following next. It cannot go the other way round.

3.11   Only when all these possibilities have been exhausted, do we reach the 'standard' position equivalent to that of a company. This is that the losses are to be carried forward and set against profits arising from the same trade in future years [*ICTA 1988, s 385*].

3.12   Note one side issue. If trading losses are used against any income other than profits from a trade (not necessarily the same trade), then no relief will have been obtained against NIC liabilities. *SSCBA 1992, Sch 2 para 3* gives relief for trading losses when determining liabilities to Class 4 NIC. Therefore, having obtained income tax relief for the loss against other income, a separate record needs to be kept of such losses so that these can be carried forward and allowed against the first available trading income of a subsequent year for NIC purposes only. This means that income tax trading losses carried forward may be different from NIC losses carried forward. If immediate profitability of the business is a concern, the availability of personal loss reliefs is a strong factor in favour of starting as a sole trader (or partnership) rather than a company.

Later years

3.13   It may be that, once start up costs are out of the way, the fortunes of the business turn round quite quickly and profits begin to flow in. Possibly, all the initial losses will have been absorbed at that stage; possibly not. This could be either through continuing claims under *s 380* or *s 385*. Obviously, one route to consider is continuing the unincorporated trade until all the losses have been used up. But there is an alternative.

3.14   Where the loss making business carried by an individual (either alone or in partnership) is transferred to a company wholly or mainly for a consideration which consists of shares (and the Inland Revenue is believed to take the view that 'mainly' means 80%), any unused losses may be set against income derived from the company by it carrying on the same trade [*ICTA 1988, s 386*]. In effect, this is an extension of *s 385* so that losses are carried forward to be set against income from the company, whatever that may be. The company must still be carrying on the same trade and the individual must still own the shares acquired on incorporation, though it is understood that the Inland Revenue permits the relief where a small disposal has been made. The relief is to be given first against income assessable to income tax, usually salary first and then any interest or rents. Finally it may go against any profit distribution in the form of dividends. There is no corresponding relief against NIC liabilities.

Note that the provisions of *s 386* are very specific as to the manner of incorporation. This may inhibit the best course of action that is dictated by other factors.

Example 3.14

Anne has a sole trader business with brought forward losses of £50,000, though it is now trading profitably. She decides to incorporate and transfers the entire business to a new company which issues 80,000 £1 shares to her and a director's loan account of £20,000 is created. The company trades profitably and she takes a salary of £25,000 in each of the next two years. The losses may be set against the salary under *s 386*, but Class 1 NIC contributions are still payable.

Nicola also has a sole trader business with brought forward losses of £50,000 though it, too, is now trading profitably. She also decides to incorporate but, for personal reasons, one of the business assets is kept out of the company. The remainder of the business is transferred for a consideration that is left outstanding on loan account. The company trades profitably and she takes a salary of £25,000 in each of the next two years. Because of the manner of incorporation, the losses cannot be set against the salary and the benefit of them is effectively lost.

3.15 Even if there were no pre-existing losses, the cessation of an unincorporated trade may of itself create a loss. This can be either through utilisation of overlap/transitional relief, or through adjustments due to capital allowances etc. (see **7.2–7.13** for more details on income tax cessation computations).

All the usual provisions may be used for relieving such a loss. Additionally, a loss arising in the last twelve months of trade, a terminal loss, can be carried back and set against the profits of the same trade which arose in the previous three years. It is the loss of the last twelve months which is so treated: if the final period of account is greater or less than twelve months, it is necessary to apportion the result to establish whether a loss arose and the amount subject to the transitional loss provisions.

Capital losses

3.16 There is no business restriction relating to capital losses of either a sole trader or company. Capital losses may be set against gains realised in the same year of assessment or corporation tax accounting period (CTAP). Unused losses of an earlier year may be brought forward and set against gains of a later year or CTAP [*TCGA 1992, s 2*]. Both are irrespective of the nature of the asset on which the loss or gain arose.

Since 1996/97, personal losses must be specifically notified to the Inland Revenue [*TCGA 1992, s 16(2A)*].

3.17 There are two particular reliefs that may be of use in relation to investment in the corporate medium. Both relate to worst case scenarios and are addressed more particularly in the final chapter, *What if it all goes wrong?*, at **21.46** and **21.47**.

3.18 The first relief arises where an individual who has subscribed for shares in a qualifying unlisted trading company incurs an allowable loss on the disposal of the shares. Such a loss is computed like any other capital loss and may be set against capital gains. However, it may instead be set against income of the same year or the previous year [*ICTA 1988, s 574*]. Be careful: if the losses are set against income, only the balance of losses can then go against capital gains, but not vice versa. If the losses are set first against capital gains, the balance cannot go against income. It does not matter that the loss is incurred by the business proprietor; i.e. there is no test of connection for this purpose.

3.19 The second relief arises where a loan is made to a UK trader (including a company) and this subsequently becomes irrecoverable. The investor can then make a claim for a capital loss in respect of the amount which is irrecoverable. A similar provision applies to the guarantee of company borrowings where the guarantee is called in [*TCGA 1992, s 253*]. Note that, for this purpose, from 6 April 2003 the definition of a trading company has been tightened and now means a company which carries on only trading activities or whose other activities are not substantial (less than 20%) in relation to the total.

Schedule A losses

3.20 Losses arising from the letting of property will not usually be a significant factor in the incorporation of a business.

One inconsistency between the income tax and corporation tax rules is worthy of mention though. For an individual, Schedule A losses may normally only be carried forward and set against future income from the Schedule A business [*ICTA 1988, s 379A(1)*]. The only exception is where the loss is due to capital allowances, or the business is an agricultural estate [*s 379A(3)*] when the loss may be set against general income. There are also special rules for furnished holiday lettings [*s 503(2)(a)*].

A company on the other hand, may set a Schedule A loss against its total profits of the same CTAP whatever the nature of those profits [*s 392A*].

Planning points

- Consider the effect of losses in choosing an initial business structure (**3.5, 3.6–3.10**).
- Make optimum loss claims so that tax repayments subsidise early losses (**3.6–3.10**).
- If losses exist at the point of incorporation, the manner of incorporation may influence the relief available (**3.14**).

Chapter 4

Why Incorporate?

Level of profit for advantage

4.1   A decade ago, it was traditional for Finance Act commentaries etc. to consider the level of profits derived by a business proprietor (or partner in a partnership) at which it became advantageous to incorporate the business in order to save or defer tax. Carefully crafted examples, reflecting Budget changes in income tax rates etc. purported to demonstrate the break-even point. However, the results may have owed as much to the author's assumptions as to variations in the tax rates. Suffice it to say that, at the close of the 20th century, the optimum level of profit at which incorporation should be first considered was probably somewhere around £40,000–£45,000.

It is no longer possible to take such a simplistic view as successive Finance Acts have introduced more and more variables to the equation. These now include:

- differential tax rates as between salary and dividends;
- multiple corporation tax rates;
- the amounts to be retained within, or withdrawn from, the company.

As far as possible, these variables will be explored separately though, in any proposed incorporation, their combined effect must be applied to the circumstances in question. The many other influences, some of which are introduced later in this chapter, are considered elsewhere in this book.

Bonus v dividend

4.2   Ask most people is it better to take a bonus or a dividend and the chances are that 'dividend' will be the response. All other things being equal, there is the automatic presumption that, because there are no National Insurance Contributions (NIC) payable on a dividend, it must be the preferred option. Let's test that assumption by way of some examples.

Calculations

4.3

Example 4.3

Tax Advisers Ltd has profits of £100,000. Henry, who is the director/share-holder, wants to draw out all the profits. He is a higher rate taxpayer and the company pays corporation tax at 19%. For initial illustration, all tax and NIC rates are those applicable to 2002/03.

Bonus

Company profits		100,000
Less:	Bonus ($^{100}/_{111.8}$ × 100,000)	(89,445)
	Employer's NIC ($^{11.8}/_{111.8}$ × 100,000)	(10,555)
		nil
Corporation tax		nil
Henry's bonus		89,445
Less:	Income tax @ 40%	(35,778)
Net retained		£53,667

Dividend

Company profits		100,000
Less:	Corporation tax @ 19%	(19,000)
		81,000
Dividend paid		(81,000)
		nil
Henry's dividend		81,000
Add:	Tax credit at ⅑	9,000
		90,000
Less:	Income tax @ 32.5%	(29,250)
Net retained		£60,750

This seems to bear out the initial presumption. So a dividend is a good thing then? Not necessarily.

4.4

Example 4.4

The facts are as in Example 4.3, but Tax Advisers Ltd pays corporation tax at 30% (it has lots of associated companies).

Bonus

Company profits		100,000
Less:	Bonus (Example 1)	(89,445)
	Employer's NIC (Example 1)	(10,555)
		nil

Bonus *(continued)*

Corporation tax		nil
Henry's bonus		89,445
Less:	Income tax @ 40%	(35,778)
Net retained		£53,667

Dividend

Company profits		100,000
Less:	Corporation tax @ 30%	(30,000)
		70,000
Dividend paid		(70,000)
		nil
Henry's dividend		70,000
Add:	Tax credit at ⅑	7,778
		77,778
Less:	Income tax @ 32.5%	(25,278)
Net retained		£52,500

4.5   The result is different. The comparative efficiency of bonus v dividend actually depends on the rate of tax paid by the company. These examples demonstrate that the relevant efficiency of making withdrawal by way of dividend for a small company was reversed where the company paid corporation tax at the mainstream rate. The difference is even more pronounced if the profits lie in the marginal band so that tax is payable at an effective rate of 32.75%. Be very careful where the salary/bonus payment crosses the boundary between the company paying tax at 19% and 32.75%. You will start by relieving a bonus payment at the higher rate which is to be preferred; there will come a point though where the dividend becomes better. There is no substitute for doing the arithmetic in every case.

Of course, there is now a starting rate of corporation tax for very small companies, which is set at nil. Above this is a lower marginal rate. All of this concerns profits of less than £50,000 at which level a dividend is always to be preferred.

Consider now the position in 2003/04 when NIC surcharges have been imposed.

4.6

Example 4.6

The basic facts are as in Example 4.3, but tax and NIC rates are those applicable to 2003/04.

Bonus

Company profits		100,000
Less:	Bonus ($^{100}\!/_{112.8} \times 100,000$)	(88,652)
	Employer's NIC ($^{12.8}\!/_{112.8} \times 100,000$)	(11,348)
		nil
Corporation tax		nil
Henry's bonus		88,652
Less:	Income tax @ 40%	(35,461)
	*NIC @ 1%	(887)
Net retained		£52,304

* Assumes Henry's other salary already exceeds upper earnings limit.

Dividend

Company profits		100,000
Less:	Corporation tax @ 19%	(19,000)
		81,000
Dividend paid		(81,000)
		nil
Henry's dividend		81,000
Add:	Tax credit at $\frac{1}{9}$	9,000
		90,000
Less:	Income tax @ 32.5%	(29,250)
Net retained		£60,750

4.7

Example 4.7

The facts are as in Example 4.6, but Tax Advisers Ltd pays corporation tax at 30% (it has lots of associated companies).

Bonus

Company profits		100,000
Less:	Bonus (as Example 4.3)	(88,652)
	Employer's NIC (as Example 4.3)	(11,348)
		nil
Corporation tax		nil
Henry's bonus		88,652
Less:	Income tax @ 40%	(35,461)
	NIC @ 1%	(887)
Net retained		£52,304

Dividend

Company profits		100,000
Less:	Corporation tax @ 30%	(30,000)
		70,000
Dividend paid		(70,000)
		nil

Henry's dividend		70,000
Add:	Tax credit at $^1/_9$	7,778
		77,778
Less:	Income tax @ 32.5%	(25,278)
Net retained		£52,500

4.8 So the increase in NIC for 2003/04 enhances the benefit of dividends over salary for the small company. For the mainstream company, the balance of advantage actually switches from salary to dividend. Curiously, for the company paying tax in the marginal band of 32.75%, salary remains the best option. If you cross the margin from one band to another, there is no option but to resort to a calculator.

4.9 The following table demonstrates how the effective rate of tax on salary and dividends varies with the company's corporation tax rate.

Assume that the proprietor is in the higher rate band for income tax (and therefore the upper limit for NIC is exceeded, but 1% surcharge payable). Withdrawal of £10,000 gross will suffer effective rates of tax:

Company CT rate	Salary	Dividend
0%	47.7%	25%
23.75%	47.7%	42.8%
19%	47.7%	39.25%
32.75%	47.7%	49.6%
30%	47.7%	47.5%

The straight arithmetic gives less than the full picture.

Other factors

4.10 Apart from the straight arithmetical comparisons, there are other factors to be borne in mind in making the choice between (more) salary and taking a dividend. Set out below are a number of particular factors that one might need to bear in mind:

4.11 Who are the business proprietors? So far we have assumed a straight comparison between a sole trader (or, perhaps, husband and wife partnership) with a small company owned entirely by the same individual (or married couple). That does not have to be the case. As a business grows, diversifies or passes through the generations, the shareholdings will become more widespread.

That introduces a problem. A bonus is very specific and can be directed to reward particular individuals. A dividend is declared and paid to all shareholders. This may not matter where the shares are very closely held (say, husband and wife). However, with more diverse holdings, it may mean that dividends are directed to passive investors who contribute little to the success of the company.

4.12 Looking at the bare numbers, taking all the remuneration from a small company by way of dividend looks attractive. Tax is not the only issue though. Bear in mind NIC and the benefits to be derived. Long term there is the National Insurance Retirement Pension (NIRP). Do we want a small salary in order to preserve the NIC record and qualify for long term state benefits (even some short term ones)? Curiously, these days one does not actually have to pay any NIC. If earnings are above the lower earnings limit but below the primary threshold, no NIC is actually payable but the contributions record for NIRP etc is maintained. For this reason, always consider paying a small salary. At this level no tax is payable because the salary will be covered by the personal allowance (see **4.27**).

4.13 One very powerful reason for restricting the use of dividends in the past has been the desire to fund private pension provision. Ignoring the basic stakeholder, in order to pay personal pension premiums it is necessary to have relevant earnings. Dividends never have, and still do not, rank as earnings for this purpose. This has therefore dictated a preference for payment by way of salary if pension provision has been at the forefront of the business proprietor's mind. However, things have changed from 6 April 2001. The new rules for pension premiums mean that it is possible to nominate a basis year for personal pension purposes and use the net relevant earnings of that year to frank the premiums paid in the year and the next five years. The shareholder/director can therefore take a high salary in year 1 and dividends in years 2–6. Pension premiums can still be paid in years 2–6 by reference to the earnings of year 1 (see **4.38**).

Where there is a company occupational pension scheme in place, maximum benefits may be linked to final remuneration (see **6.45**). This may inhibit the taking of dividends as retirement approaches.

4.14 When the National Minimum Wage (NMW) first came into force, there was a brief panic as to whether its payment was relevant to private company directors. This was eventually clarified by a statement, issued by the Institute of Chartered Accountants, with the agreement of the Inland Revenue, to the effect that directors appointed under the Companies Acts were not necessarily entitled to payment of the NMW, no matter how extensive their duties or hours of work. Care needs to be taken over recently appointed directors (perhaps junior family members) who have a subsidiary contract of employment and will be entitled to the NMW (see **12.5–12.9**).

4.15   Payment of a dividend requires the company to have distributable reserves from which to declare it. If there are fluctuations in trading there may not be the reserves to meet a dividend payment. A salary is a trading deduction though, as opposed to an appropriation of profits, and can still be declared and paid even to the extent of creating a loss. Such loss could be set back against trading profits of the previous accounting period leading to a repayment of corporation tax.

4.16   Constraints which may be imposed by the personal service company legislation (see **17.13–17.25**).

4.17   It is possible that some shareholders may have obtained relief for their investment under the Enterprise Investment Scheme (EIS) (see **6.8–6.16**). This has very close constraints as to the value that may be received from the company.

4.18   Share valuation is a subject way beyond the scope of this book. However, it is often perceived (especially in regard to small minority shareholdings) that a regular dividend flow enhances their value.

4.19   Where many members of the family are involved in a close company environment, consider whether salaries are deductible. Complex shareholding structures intended to pass dividends around the family may fall foul of anti-avoidance legislation. For more on these problems, see **16.59–16.64**.

4.20   The different administrative processes involved. Payment of a salary or bonus requires the application of PAYE. Dividends require resolutions, minutes of directors' meeting and (for final dividends) approval of the members of the company in a general meeting.

4.21   Finally, a word about timing. To be deductible against profits of the relevant accounting period, a bonus must be paid within nine months of the year-end [*FA 1989, s 43*]. Income tax due under PAYE, together with any NIC, will be payable 14 days after the end of the relevant tax month. There is no especial time limit to declare and pay a dividend, provided that other reporting requirements of the Companies Acts are satisfied. Income tax will not be payable on the dividend until 31 January following the year in which it is paid. This may be a one off timing advantage if payment of dividends becomes a regular feature as most of the liability will be picked up through self assessment payments on account.

Changes in dividend taxation

4.22   *F(No2)A 1997* radically changed the former taxation treatment of dividends. Hitherto, on payment of a dividend, a company was required to account to the Inland Revenue for advance corporation tax (ACT). So far as the shareholder was concerned, this ACT franked the payment of the dividend, giving a tax credit to set against his income tax liability thereon.

These provisions were removed with effect from 6 April 1999. No longer is ACT payable. However, to prevent disadvantage to individual shareholders, two significant changes were made.

4.23 Dividends (despite the absence of any ACT payment) are now deemed to carry a tax credit at the rate of 1/9th of the amount paid (10% of the gross of dividends plus tax) [*ICTA 1988, s 231*]. This notional credit is deemed to frank the full income tax liability if the recipient's income falls in the starting rate or basic rate band [*ICTA 1988, ss 1A, 1B*]. If the shareholder has no liability to income tax, then the credit is not repayable.

So, at this level, the shareholder gets something for nothing. The company does not pay any ACT (though, it must be acknowledged, its mainstream corporation tax liability may be increased) to frank the dividend but the individual does not pay any income tax either. This may be a huge advantage in tax planning, as will be demonstrated.

4.24 The higher rate of income tax, so far as it applies to dividend income, has been reduced to 32.5% [*ICTA 1988, s 1B*]. This maintains the net income of the individual shareholder as it was before the abolition of ACT.

Example 4.24

(a) Dividend declared in 1998/99 £180. ACT rate 25%
Higher rate of income tax 40%

Shareholder's position:	
Dividend received	£180
Add: Tax credit @ 25%	45
	225
Less: Income tax @ 40%	(90)
Net spendable income	£135

(b) Dividend declared in 1999/2000 (or later) £180. No ACT
Notional tax credit @ ⅑. Higher rate of income tax 32.5%

Dividend received	£180
Add: Notional tax credit at ⅑	20
	200
Less: Income tax @ 32.5%	(65)
Net spendable income	£135

4.25 Additionally, this means that the effective rate of income tax applicable to a dividend which falls in the higher rate band of an individual is only 25%.

Example 4.25

Dividend received	£90
Add: Notional tax credit at $^1/_9$	10
	100
Higher rate tax due @ 32.5%	£32.50
Less: Tax credit	(10.00)
Tax payable	22.50
Express as percentage of dividend:	
22.50/90	25%

4.26 It follows that there are only two effective rates of income tax applicable to dividends: 0% or 25%.

Compare the rates of income tax applicable to a salary:

Covered by personal allowance	0%
Starting rate	10%
Basic rate	22%
Higher rate	40%

4.27 An immediate advantage can be seen. This factor alone may be influencing many incorporations at the bottom end of the market and this is perhaps best illustrated by an example.

Example 4.27

Carl has just incorporated Tortoise Treks Ltd and is its sole director/shareholder. The first year's profit is £14, 615.

- He draws a salary of £4,615 and pays no tax (covered by personal allowance).
- The company net profit is then £10,000 and it pays no tax (profit within nil rate starting band).
- Carl draws the whole company profit as a dividend and still pays no tax (notional 10% credit covers the liability where income falls in the starting rate or basic rate band).

Result:

Profit generated	£14,615
Tax paid	nil
Take home pay	£14,615

Last year (2002/03), Carl's unincorporated business made £14,615 (conveniently!). He paid income tax and Class 2/4 NIC leaving him with net take home pay of £11,741.

Incorporation has increased his net take home pay by 24.5%. How could he resist?

4.28   The examples at **4.3–4.7** demonstrated that a straight swap of dividends for salary will, in most cases, give an advantage for the higher rate taxpayer. Example 4.27 shows that an effective zero rate of tax on dividends and a nil starting rate of corporation tax is a huge advantage at the bottom end of the market.

4.29   What then of the many tens, or even hundreds, of thousands of middle ranking businesses? All the principles so far set out hold good, but there are so many variables that it would be impossible to provide sufficient examples here to even scratch the surface. There are basically four sets of variables:

Sole trader:	Profit taxed at nil, 10%, 22%, 40%
	NIC (Class 4) at nil, 8%, 1%
	(Plus Class 2 flat rate)
Company:	Profit taxed at nil, 23.75%, 19%, 32.75%, 30%
Director:	Salary taxed at nil, 10%, 22%, 40%
	NIC (Class 1) at nil, 11%, 1%
	(Plus company's liability at 12.8%)
Shareholder:	Dividends taxed at nil, 25%

There is no substitute for performing a detailed set of calculations based on the best estimate of the profits in each case and the proprietor's preferred balance of profit extraction from the company as between salary and dividend. Whilst a minimal salary and large dividend is likely to give the best result in the great majority of cases, there may be other factors influencing the salary level. These are explored elsewhere in this book.

To aid the process, there are many software products on the market to facilitate 'what if?' calculations.

4.30 By way of illustration only the following table demonstrates the possible savings as between a sole trader and an incorporated business where the proprietor takes a minimal salary and the balance as dividend.

Table of Net Income (£)

Profit	Sole Trader	Company	Saving
10,000	8,516	10,000	1,484
20,000	15,516	18,721	3,205
30,000	22,516	26,346	3,830
40,000	29,271	33,495	4,224
50,000	35,171	39,213	4,042

It will be noted that the savings begin to decline at the higher income levels in the table. This is the progressive influence of higher rate income tax impinging on dividends, though the impact is lessened as the corporation tax rate drops from 23.75% to 19%. Students of these statistics may care to read the article *Burning Question* in *Taxation* dated *16 May 2002* along with the rider in *Feedback in Taxation* dated *13 June 2002*.

At a profit level of about £300,000, the tax paid by an incorporated business will exceed that paid by an unincorporated business assuming that all profits are withdrawn. However, at these levels it is unlikely that all amounts will be spent as earned and the influence of retaining profits, having suffered only lower rates of corporation tax, becomes more important.

Personal pensions

4.31 Historically where the business proprietor was concerned about providing for a future pension, there was a huge disadvantage in taking dividends. They do not rank as relevant earnings against which pension premiums could be paid. However, from 6 April 2001, new tax rules were introduced. This is often referred to as the stakeholder regime and applies to all defined contribution pension schemes, most notably all personal pension plans. Old style retirement annuity contracts are not affected.

Contributions

4.32 The new rules introduced the concept of the earnings threshold (ET). For 2001/02, this was set at £3,600 and may be subject to amendment every year by Treasury order, though no change has been made for 2002/03 or 2003/04. The member (or a third party) may contribute up to the ET in each tax year to a personal pension/stakeholder scheme, regardless of his age (providing he is under 75) and of whether or not he has earnings. The £3,600 includes the basic rate tax relief on the contributions; it is equivalent to a net payment of £2,808) [*ICTA 1988, s 640(1)(a)*].

4.33 Contributions in excess of the ET are subject to the previous tests, including the earnings cap and the percentage of net relevant earnings depending on age as follows [*ICTA 1988, s 640(2)*]:

Age on 6 April	Maximum % of Earnings
35 or less	17.5
36–45	20.0
46–50	25.0
51–55	30.0
56–60	35.0
61–74	40.0

Example:	Earnings in Basis Year	Maximum Pension Contribution
Age 35	20,000	3,600 (by virtue of ET)
	30,000	5,250 (17.5% of earnings)

Earnings cap: £99,000 for 2002/03 [*ICTA 1988, s 640A*].

Basis year

4.34 No longer is it necessary for the contributions to be made by reference to the earnings of the present tax year. The member may nominate the tax year that they wish to be used as the basis year for their net relevant earnings [*ICTA 1988, s 646B*]. The year may be either the current year, or any of the previous five tax years (the nominated basis year may be earlier than 2000/01 even though the new rules did not take effect until 6 April 2001). In limited circumstances, this may be extended by a further five years. The individual need not have been a member of the personal pension scheme during the basis year. The age should be taken as at 6 April of the year of payment, as before. It can be seen then that the net relevant earnings in the basis year may be used to validate contributions over the earnings threshold not only in the basis year itself, but also in the following five tax years. If he wishes, and it is advantageous, a member may change the basis year to a subsequent year (if, for example, the net relevant earnings have increased) and this subsequent year can be used to make higher personal pension contributions in that year and the following five tax years. The Inland Revenue now accepts that, contrary to its initial opinion, the earnings cap for the year of payment (not the basis year) should be applied where relevant. See, in this respect, paragraph 4.10 of Inland Revenue booklet *IR76, Personal Pension Schemes Guidance Notes.*

Higher earnings in a subsequent year cannot be used to validate payments in an earlier year.

The ability to nominate a basis year is very important, as will be demonstrated when we move on to planning below.

Tax relief on contributions

4.35   From 6 April 2001, all contributions paid by individuals to personal pension policies are treated as paid net of basic rate tax [*ICTA 1988, s 639(3)*]. This will apply to all employees, self-employed persons, non-employed persons and minors, regardless of whether or not they are non-taxpayers, basic rate taxpayers or higher rate taxpayers. Individuals, who pay tax at the higher rate, must claim the balance of the relief from their tax office either by completing form PP120, or by completing the relevant section of their self assessment return.

Higher rate relief is given by the simple expedient of extending the basic rate band [*ICTA 1988, s 639(5A)*]. This is a change from the previous system of relief by deduction from relevant earnings. Again, this has odd effects in calculating the tax liabilities that may be exploited in planning.

Payments to old style retirement annuity policies are still paid gross and the full tax relief is obtained through the self assessment.

Carry-back of contributions

4.36   From 6 April 2001, any pension contributions paid will be subject to new carry-back rules. Under these, a contribution that is to be carried back to the previous tax year must be made no later than 31 January following the end of the tax year to which it is to be carried back [*ICTA 1988, s 641A*]. The rules for achieving this are complex and caused endless problems in respect of 31 January 2002. For 2002/03 onwards, the Inland Revenue has notified rather more relaxed administrative procedures in its May 2002 *Working Together* Bulletin.

- After 6 April 2001, only contributions made between 6 April and the following 31 January can be carried back and can only be carried back to the previous year.
- A carry-back election must be made to the scheme administrator on or before the time of payment and, once made, it is irrevocable.

- The election to carry back all or part of the contribution to the previous year should be made to the scheme administrator on a form PP43(New), or in a letter, by fax, or e-mail, or even by telephone. In the case of the latter, the scheme administrator should confirm the details in writing and must include the date of the actual election, date of payment and the amount to be carried back.
- The above should not be confused with making claims to higher rate relief. Such claims should be made on the self assessment tax return or, if that has already been submitted, in a stand-alone claim, i.e. a letter to the Tax Office.
- The letter would be accepted by the Revenue, without supporting documentation from the scheme administrator, so long as it contains all the necessary details, such as the date of election, date of payment and amount to be carried back. However, it is recommended that the claim is made on a form PP120 or PP43(New). The latter may be the original or a copy where the scheme administrator has retained the original.
- The actual claim to higher rate relief can be made after the payment and election have taken place and could be after 31 January. The scheme administrator could have the payment and the election to carry back just a few days before 31 January. They would then send the scheme member a form PP43(New) for completion to claim higher rate relief. The member may not then be able to send the copy of the completed form to the Tax Office until after 31 January and, in these circumstances, although the form was completed and dated after 31 January, that in itself will not invalidate the claim.

Concurrent membership with occupational scheme

4.37 An employee who is a member of an occupational pension scheme may make an election to pay up to the ET (£3,600 gross) each tax year to a personal pension scheme, while continuing as a member of the occupational scheme [*ICTA 1988, s 632B*]. Certain conditions apply:

- He must not have been a controlling director of a company, either in the tax year when commencing such payments, or in any of the five immediately preceding tax years. (Controlling director means that either on his own, or with one or more associates, he is the beneficial owner, directly or indirectly, of 20% or more of the ordinary share capital of the company) [*ICTA 1988, s 417(5)*].
- He must have had earnings from his pensionable employment of less than the remuneration limit (initially set at £30,000 for 2001/02 and, as at April 2003, not revised) for at least one of the last five tax years, commencing 2000/01. (Contrast the basic rule for nominating a basis year.)
- An individual wishing to take advantage of this will need to provide the personal pension scheme administrator with a certificate, identifying the qualifying year in which the member has earnings of no more than the remuneration limit, confirming his earnings for that year, and confirming his total contributions will not exceed £3,600 gross. Once a qualifying year has been nominated in the certificate, contributions up to the earnings threshold can be made for the five tax years following the qualifying year, after which a new qualifying year will need to be certified.

It is interesting to note that remuneration from employment appears to exclude P11D benefits in kind.

Dividend v remuneration

4.38   It may no longer be necessary for directors/shareholders to withdraw funds from their companies as salary in each year in order to establish net relevant earnings for pension contribution purposes. There will be greater flexibility to choose to withdraw funds as dividends, with lower National Insurance consequences, once a basis year for pension contribution purposes has been established. Thus a pattern might be:

Example: Individual aged 51

	Salary	**Dividend**	**Maximum Pension Contribution**
	£	**£**	**£^{1}**
Year 1	50,000	0	15,000
Year 2		50,000	15,000
Year 3		50,000	15,000
Year 4		50,000	15,000
Year 5		50,000	15,000
Year 6		50,000	17,500
Year 7	50,000	0	17,500
Year 8		50,000	17,500

[1]   Note this is the contribution gross of basic rate tax.

The maximum amount that could be paid to personal pension schemes will be established by reference to the salary in the basis year. Note that basic rate tax relief will be obtained by the scheme administrator adding this to the pension fund. A higher rate taxpaying contributor, whose main source of income for the year is dividends, will receive tax relief at a marginal rate of 44.5%.

4.39   Yes, that did say 44.5%.

Example 4.39

Brian is the sole working director of Universal Widgets Ltd. He owns 99% of the issued shares (his wife has the rest). The company is profitable (and pays tax at 19%) and he has been taking a salary of around £50,000 p.a. He is aged 37 and wants to put around £10,000 into a personal pension plan.

What tax (and NIC) relief can he get?

4.39   Why Incorporate?

YEAR 1 – Assume that he has taken a salary of £50,000 and the company is left with profits of £100,000.

Company

Profit	100,000
Tax @ 19%	(19,000)
Retained earnings	£81,000

Individual

Salary	50,000	
Less: PA	(4,615)	
	45,385	
£1,960 @ 10%	196.00	**196.00**
£28,540 @ 22%	6,278.80	
£38,540 @ 22%		**8,478.80**
£14,885 @ 40%	5,954.00	
£4,885 @ 40%		**1,954.00**
	12,428.80	**10,628.80**
Class 1 NIC	3,086.35	**3,086.35**
(30,940 – 4,615) × 11%		
19,060 × 1%		
	15,515.15	**13,715.15**
Saving £15,515.15 less £13,715.15		**1,800.00**
BR tax retained £10,000 @ 22%		**2,200.00**
		£4,000.00 (40%)

NOTE: Plain type –Tax liability before PPP relief
       Bold type –Tax liability/saving after PPP relief

YEAR 2 – He takes a salary of only £4,000 and a dividend of £41,000 net to restore similar total gross income of £50,000.

Company

Profit	100,000
Add: Salary	46,000
Class 1 NIC	5,809
	151,809
Tax @ 19%	(28,844)
	122,965
Dividend	(41,400)
Retained earnings	£81,565

Individual

Salary		4,000	
Less: PA		(4,000)	
Dividend	41,400		
Tax Credit	4,600	46,000	
£615 @ 10%		61.50	**61.50**
£1,960 @ 10%		196.00	**196.00**
£28,540 @ 10%		2,854.00	
£38,540 @ 10%			**3,854.00**
£14,885 @ 32.5%		4,837.62	
£4,885 @ 32.5%			**1,587.62**
		7,949.12	**5,699.12**
Saving in year £7,949.12 less £5,699.12			**2,250.00**
BR tax retained £10,000 @ 22%			**2,200.00**
			£4,450.00 (44.5%)

NOTE: Plain type – Tax liability before PPP relief
Bold type – Tax liability/saving after PPP relief

Employer contributions

4.40   This is where the fun really starts.

At the outset of the new rules, the Inland Revenue took the view that employer contributions to an employee's personal pension plan must be based on the earnings from that employment in the current year only. The limit, as a percentage of net relevant earnings, applies to the total of employer and employee contributions. In February 2002, an Update from the Pension Schemes Office notified a whole host of revisions to the guidance notes contained in Inland Revenue booklet *IR76*. Possibly the most significant change was acceptance that employer contributions may be made by reference to the net relevant earnings of the employee's nominated basis year. In some ways this is curious; the employee may not even have been in that employment in the basis year.

4.41

Example 4.41

If the employee wishes to make a contribution of £1,000 to his personal pension scheme, then the cost to the company of providing the salary to do this is £916, thus:

Salary	1,000
Employer's NIC	128
	1,118
CT relief at 19%	(214)
	£914

At this stage, the employee's tax rate is irrelevant as full tax relief is available by deduction or reduction in the self assessment. Assume that the employee is above NIC upper earnings limit.

However, if the employer pays the premium direct into the employee's pension scheme, the net cost is only £810, thus:

Salary	1,000
CT relief at 19%	(190)
	810

The premium paid is not a benefit in the employee's hands and is specifically excluded from NIC liability [*ICTA 1988, s 643; SS(C)R 2001, SI2001/1004 Sch 3 Part VI Reg 2*].

The difference is more marked if the employee has a NIC liability as, again, this cannot be relieved by payment of a personal pension premium out of net salary.

4.42   The story does not end there, because:

- employer contributions cannot be carried back;
- it is impossible to take advantage of the 44.5% tax relief which the employee can obtain on dividends.

The calculations become very complex because there are so many variables but the following would appear to be correct for a 40% taxpayer:

Marginal rate of CT	Most efficient way of funding PPP
0%	Dividend
23.75%	Employer contribution
19%	Dividend
32.75%	Employer contribution
30%	Employer contribution

There is no real solution, other than to perform the detailed calculation in every case.

National Insurance Contributions

4.43   So far, the computations have merely stated that NIC are payable as a foregone conclusion. The Government would prefer that we did not consider NIC to be a tax though, in all but name, that is effectively what it is.

The Budget of 2002 imposed a surcharge on NIC. The impact of NIC will be explored more closely in the next chapter, but the increase is to all intents and purposes an additional tax. Critics of present government policy have even called it a stealth tax.

Incorporation may provide a facility to reduce the impact of the new charge in certain circumstances. Examples at **4.4** and **4.7** demonstrate that additional NIC does, in some cases, tip the balance of advantage between salary and dividend. A flood of small incorporations is anticipated solely for this reason and experience so far suggests that this is beginning to happen.

Planning points

- In most cases, extraction of profit by way of dividend has less tax cost than bonus/salary (**4.3**, **4.4**, **4.6**, **4.7**).
- The dividend/salary choice may be complicated by other factors (**4.10–4.20**).
- A business earning nearly £15,000 need pay no tax at all (**4.27**).
- Where making personal pension contributions, nominate a basis year to facilitate remuneration by way of dividend (**4.34**).
- A personal pension contribution set against dividends may get tax relief at up to 44.5% (**4.39**).
- Consider employer (the company) contributions to a PPP (**4.41**).

Chapter 5

National Insurance Contributions

5.1 So far, we have seen the impact of differential tax rates on the method of withdrawing profits from a company. Successive governments insist that NIC is not a tax, though, for all practical purposes, one might regard it as such. Certainly, its impact must be taken into account in any consideration of incorporation. Indeed, NIC alone may be the driver to the next round of incorporations, given that the Budget of 2002 effectively introduced a 1% surcharge without limit on NI contributions (or should it be 2% for the family company/director unit?).

In some ways, it may seem paradoxical that one should want to move from self employment where the 'mainstream' rate (Class 4) is now 8% to employment where the mainstream rate (Class 1 primary and secondary) is now 23.8%.

One must also consider the impact of contributions on benefits which might be received at a later date.

Class 2 and Class 4 contributions

Class 2

5.2 Every self employed earner, over the age of 16 and under pensionable age, is liable to pay Class 2 contributions at a flat rate [*SSCBA 1992, s 11(1)*]. The liability is measured in complete weeks and includes periods of inactivity, for example holidays, until the earner is no longer gainfully engaged in self employment.

The current weekly rate is £2.

5.3 A person who would otherwise be liable to pay Class 2 contributions may be excepted from liability where the earnings do not exceed a specified amount, £4,095 for 2003/04 [*SSCBA 1992, s 11(4)*]. A claim is required and exception generally commences on the date of application, though limited backdating is permitted. The certificate of exception from liability may be granted for some time forward, typically three years, even though earnings may rise to such an extent that contributions are required. If these circumstances prevail, the individual should carefully consider the impact on future benefits if contributions are not made. Given that the amount otherwise payable is only £2 per week, applying for exception is now taking penny pinching to the extreme.

5.4   Class 2 contributions are most conveniently paid by monthly or quarterly direct debit.

Class 4

5.5   Class 4 contributions are payable in respect of profits or gains derived from a trade, profession or vocation. Essentially, they are a further levy on any profits chargeable to income tax under case I or II of Schedule D [*SSCBA 1992, s 15(1)*].

Class 4 contributions are payable in respect of earnings above the lower annual limit (LAL) and below the upper annual limit (UAL). For 2003/04:

* The lower annual limit is £4,615
* The upper annual limit is £30,940

[*SSCBA 1992, s 15(3)*].

The percentage rate is 8%.

Since 6 April 2003, a 1% charge is applied to all profits in excess of the UAL (without any limit).

5.6   Class 4 contributions are included in the income tax self assessment on profits and the usual income tax provisions apply to payment.

Class 1 contributions

Primary

5.7   A person who is categorised as an employed earner (and, for the purposes of this work, that will encompass the person who holds the office of director in a company) is liable to pay Class 1 contributions in respect of earnings from the employment. The person must be aged over 16 and below retirement age.

Class 1 contributions are payable on earnings above the primary threshold (PT) and below the upper earnings limit (UEL). Since 2001/02, PT has been equalised with the single person's income tax personal allowance. For 2003/04:

* PT is £89 per week
* UEL is £595 per week

[*SSCBA 1992, ss 5(1) and 6(1)*].

The percentage rate is 11%.

Since 6 April 2003, a 1% charge has applied to all earnings in excess of UEL (without limit).

5.8 Do not confuse PT with the lower earnings limit (LEL) [*SSCBA 1992, s 5(1)(a)(i)*]. LEL is the level of weekly earnings at which entitlement to contributory benefits begins. Until 5 April 2000, PT and LEL were numerically the same. This is no longer the case.

Secondary

5.9 The employer is also liable to pay secondary Class 1 contributions in respect of employed earners' earnings above the secondary threshold (ST) [*SSCBA 1992, s 6(2)*].

There is no UEL for secondary contributions. They are also payable in respect of earnings of an employed earner where there are no primary Class 1 contributions (e.g. because the employee is above retirement age).

For 2001/02 onwards, ST has been aligned with PT and the income tax personal allowance. Therefore, for 2003/04:

- ST is £89 per week

The percentage rate is 12.8% and contributions continue at this level without any upper limit.

5.10 Unlike primary contributions where the employee gets no tax relief, secondary contributions are deductible in arriving at the taxable profits of the employer's business.

5.11 Curiously, the employer is not only liable to account for the secondary contributions but, initially at least, for the primary contributions as well. Both contributions are to be paid to the Inland Revenue (with income tax deductions under PAYE) by the 19th of the month following the payment of the relevant earnings. Smaller employers may make quarterly payments, where the total amount due (income tax and NIC) is less than £1,500 per month. Class 1 contributions are treated as if they were income tax and the provisions of the *Income Tax (Employments) Regulations1993, SI 1993/744* apply.

The employer may recover the primary contributions paid when making payment of the relevant remuneration to the employee.

Class 1A contributions

5.12 Class 1A contributions were originally introduced on 6 April 1991 specifically in relation to the provision of a company car to an employee as an employment benefit. Otherwise there was no NIC on payments in kind. During the 1990s, an ever more esoteric range of assets was used to provide payments in kind to employees which were nevertheless almost instantly convertible to cash.

5.13 To counter the perceived loss of contributions to the Treasury, Class 1A contributions were extended on 6 April 2000 to apply to most taxable payments in kind [*SSCBA 1992, s 10(1)*]. Class 1A is, so far at least, an employer only charge. The rate is the same as Class 1 secondary contributions, i.e. 12.8% for 2003/04.

5.14 A return on form P11D(b) is required by 6 July following the year of assessment in which the benefit is provided and payment of contributions is to be made by 19 July.

5.15 Class 1A contributions are deductible in arriving at the taxable profit of the employer.

5.16 Class 1A contributions do not apply to:

- Benefits in kind which are exempt from income tax either by statute (e.g. mobile telephones) or extra statutory concession (e.g. Christmas parties costing less than £75 per head in 2002/03). This will be rationalised in 2003/04 as *ITEPA 2003* enacts many former concessions.
- Benefits in kind covered by a dispensation. Employer companies should ensure that a dispensation is obtained wherever possible. Not only does this ease administration for the company, but should ensure that there is no NIC. Whilst a claim under *ITEPA 2003, s 336; ICTA 1988, s 198* may alleviate the income tax charge in respect of reported benefits in kind and expenses, this is a tax provision and does not necessarily apply to NIC.

Class 1A contributions may be payable in respect of the gross amount. E.g. A company employs a chauffeur to drive the director around. The chauffeur's salary is £25,000 and the split of journeys is 70:30 business:private. The income tax benefit is £7,500. The Class 1A liability is based on £25,000. If a dispensation could be obtained for business travel, the Class 1A liability would be on £7,500.

Payment of home telephone bills without due care and deliberate thought in advance can prove to be a disaster.

- Items already attracting Class 1 NIC e.g. non-cash vouchers.
- Items included in a PAYE Settlement Agreement (PSA).
- Items otherwise specifically exempt by virtue of *Social Security (Contributions) Regulations 2001, SI 2001/1004, Reg 40* of which, so far, there appears to be only one, namely childcare (but not the payment of school fees).
- Certain other minor items.

5.17 In planning the overall remuneration package, some business proprietors may wish to take remuneration by way of benefits in kind and in certain instances, this can be tax efficient. However, in assessing the overall impact, the payment of Class 1A NIC must be borne in mind.

5.18 For the sake of completeness, one should also mention Class 1B contributions. In certain circumstances, an employer may agree to settle the employees' income tax liabilities in respect of certain minor or irregular benefits. This is known as a PAYE Settlement Agreement or PSA. Where a PSA is in force, Class 1B contributions are included. Where relevant, these take precedence over Class 1 or Class 1A.

Combined effect

5.19 In an owner managed company, it can therefore be seen that where earnings fall between PT and UEL, the total NIC now payable is at a rate of 23.8%, a not inconsiderable sum. It is well in excess of the 8% NIC payable by a self employed person. To avoid the disadvantage, one must be prepared to withdraw funds other than by way of salary.

5.20 At this level, of course, the employee will be paying only basic rate income tax so that the total impost is not as great as that for a higher rate taxpayer. Nevertheless a dividend is still to be preferred.

Example 5.20

Gary wishes to draw £10,000 from his family company which has profits of £40,000 after deduction of a salary of £15,000 already paid to him.

Bonus

Company profit to be withdrawn	10,000
Less: Bonus ($^{100}/_{112.8} \times 10{,}000$)	(8,865)
Employer's NIC ($^{12.8}/_{112.8} \times 10{,}000$)	(1,135)
	nil
Corporation tax	nil
Gary's bonus	8,865
Less: Income tax @ 22%	(1,950)
NIC @ 11%	(975)
Net retained	5,940

Dividend

Company profit to be withdrawn	10,000
Less: Corporation tax @ 23.75%	(2,375)
	7,625
Dividend paid	(7,625)
	nil
Gary's dividend	7,625
No tax as falls in BR band	
Net retained	7,625
Effective rate of tax on:	
Bonus	40.6%
Dividend	23.7%

Note particularly how close the effective rate on the bonus is to a higher rate taxpayer (see **4.9**) and the huge saving he can make by taking a dividend.

The effect on benefits

National Insurance Retirement Pension

5.21   One might call this the strangest insurance policy in the world! The theory is that an employed person (whether self employed or an employee) pays NIC during his working life and generates a contribution record against which the basic National Insurance Retirement Pension (NIRP) is paid after retirement age. The first anomaly is that it is today's contributors who actually pay for today's pensions. There is no question that an individual's own pension contributions are 'invested' to provide his pension. The second anomaly is that individuals in certain circumstances don't actually have to pay anything anymore.

5.22   There are two contribution conditions:

- The first is that the NIRP claimant must actually have paid Class 1 contributions of at least 52 times the weekly LEL in a tax year since 6 April 1978 (or the equivalent payment of Class 2 contributions).
- The second is that a claimant must show a minimum number of qualifying years in his working life. From 1978/79, a qualifying year is one in which he paid (or was credited with) contributions on at least 52 times LEL (or paid the equivalent number of Class 2 contributions). The rules for working life and the number of qualifying years to establish full pension entitlement can be found in *SSCBA 1992, Sch 3 para 5*. Modified rules apply for years before 1978/79.

5.23   Remember though that we said earlier (see **5.8**) that LEL is no longer significant in relation to the payment of contributions. These start at PT (which is a higher figure). From 6 April 2000, 'payment of contributions' includes receipt of earnings equal to or exceeding LEL but on which no contributions are paid [*SSCBA 1992, s 6A(2)*].

For 2003/04, LEL is set at £77 per week and we have already seen that PT is £89 per week. So, on earnings lying between these two figures, a credit is available in order to establish a contribution record for NIRP but no contributions are actually due.

This is a very useful planning tool in remunerating small company directors. Note that the company must still have a PAYE scheme in operation and submit an annual return in order to record the earnings for this purposes, even if no income tax or NIC is actually payable.

State second pension

5.24 What about the state second pension (S2P) which replaced the state earnings related pension scheme (SERPS) from 6 April 2002? Whilst many readers will know the basic parameters of NIRP qualification, the understanding of S2P seems at best sketchy. It does not help that S2P will initially give rise to an earnings related pension which will continue for older contributors. After an interim period, which may be as little as five years, it is proposed that S2P should change to provide an additional flat rate pension for contributors born after a specified date.

5.25 If you have stuck with this chapter, you will already have met LEL, PT and UEL. You will know that until 6 April 2000, LEL and PT were the same. Since then, they have diverged and it is now possible to establish a contribution record for NIRP without actually paying any NIC. Thus, where a policy of taking remuneration largely by way of dividends is adopted (to take advantage of lower tax rates and no NIC), it is recommended that a salary of around £4,615 should be taken – it establishes a contribution record but no income tax or NIC is payable.

For completeness, there is actually a fourth limit. This is the secondary threshold (ST), which is the point at which the employer starts paying secondary Class 1 contributions. Historically this has always been the same as PT, frozen for 2003/04 at 2002/03 levels, currently £89 per week. We could have some serious fun when Gordon Brown decides that PT and ST should be different. In some ways, we are moving to that with the additional 1% NIC charge for 2003/04.

5.26 Having got that fixed, we need to layer on the rules for establishing entitlement to S2P. For this purpose the band of earnings between LEL and UEL is sub-divided into three further bands by two intervening thresholds. These are conveniently named the low earnings threshold (LET) and the second earning threshold (SET) – ripe for confusion with LEL and ST.

LET was initially set in 1999/2000 at £9,500 p.a., but may be increased annually in line with inflation, including for the period before S2P came into operation. The *Social Security Pensions (Low Earnings Threshold) Order 2003, SI 2003/324*, has fixed LET at £11,200 for 2003/04.

SET is fixed formulaically by reference to LET and QEF (which is the annual value of LEL), thus:

$$SET = 3 \times LET - 2 \times QEF$$

(and there are rules for rounding).

This makes SET for 2003/04, £25,600.

5.27   Lost yet? Do you recall the meaning of LEL, PT, UEL, ST, LET, SET and QEF?

5.28   Next, how to qualify for S2P. There are formulaic calculations which are different for the three bands between LEL and UEL which were established above. Comments here are confined to the first of these.

Eventually (for an employee reaching state pension age on or after 6 April 2009) the band 1 (LEL to LET) qualifier will be 40% of earnings. There are transitional provisions for employees reaching state pension age before 6 April 2009, but let's not complicate matters excessively.

There is a statutory presumption that an employee earning between LEL and LET has earnings for S2P purposes of LET. Actual earnings in that band seem relevant only for calculating the residual entitlement to S2P for a contracted out employee [*SSCBA 1992, s 44A*].

5.29   So, if we look at a small company director (or the employed wife of a sole trader), the sensible advice would say to pay a salary of £4,615 (disregarding other factors). This ensures no tax, no NIC and satisfaction of the contribution condition for NIRP.

However, the figure of £4,615 is above LEL but below LET. Therefore, the statutory presumption for S2P purposes is that the salary is £11,200. Dependent on the employee's age, the rights to S2P will be based on 40% of this latter figure.

So it is better than we first supposed. The salary of £4,615 gives not only qualification for NIRP but also S2P at a rate as if the earnings were actually £11,200. This gives an additional pension of around £2 per week per year of contributions.

5.30   Taking a higher salary and payment of NIC does not enhance NIRP – this is a flat rate benefit. However, payment of additional contributions will increase the S2P record and therefore the amount ultimately payable but only once the salary exceeds LET. This factor is unlikely to give a significant influence over decisions on incorporation of a business.

Planning points

- A dispensation eases administration of expense payments/benefits and can reduce Class 1A NIC liability (**5.16**).
- Know and understand the meaning and function of LEL, PT, UEL, ST, LET, SET and QEF (**5.22–5.26**).
- Remember that earnings between LEL and PT attract no tax or NIC but do qualify for contributory benefits (**5.23**).
- Ensure all qualifying earnings are recorded. This may mean opening a PAYE scheme even where no tax is due (**5.23**).

Chapter 6

Other Advantages of a Company

6.1 The author remains to be convinced that the corporate medium is right for almost all small businesses (see **1.1**), though it does have to be admitted that the tax savings do provide a compelling reason for going in that direction. The present Government seems to take the view that all small businesses already trade as companies. How many times have you heard the Chancellor of the Exchequer in recent years say that he is introducing new measures to reward enterprise. Then you find that the particular incentive is only available to a company. The 2003 Budget Speech contains the words:

'I will today back up the cut to 19p in small business tax . . .'

To arrive at 19p, small business must equal company. Is there some sort of hidden agenda to promote the company as the preferred business medium for all?

Apart from the direct tax advantages of incorporation, there are now a number of other issues to consider: reliefs and incentives which are available only to companies. If you want to take advantage of them, you have to have a company. These include relief for intangibles, research and development tax credits and exempt gains.

6.2 Do not forget the immediate advantage that incorporation may separate control and management of the business. Sole traders and partners are all things to their businesses, owners, managers and workers. The shareholders of a company have the ultimate voting control and can take a dividend as a return on their investment. However, they can do this without raising a finger in the day-to-day management. The directors, on the other hand, have the delegated duty of management as well as some onerous liabilities. In many private companies, especially family ones, there will be significant overlap of the individuals who are the shareholders and those who are the directors. Often they are identical. They must understand their two differing roles and the responsibilities these impose.

This chapter will explore a mixture of additional items to consider in making the decision to incorporate. To maintain a sense of balance, it will also reflect on some possible disadvantages.

Corporate moneybox

6.3   Why would one want to withdraw money from a company at all? The first advantage has to be freedom of choice. Suppose you ran a developing business. The profit does not have to be very high, around £35,000, before the marginal tax rate becomes 40% (no, on second thoughts, make that 41% with the recently imposed NIC surcharge).

Example 6.3A

In order to invest £10,000 in developing the business, you actually need to earn £16,950, thus:

Profit		16,950
Less:	Tax at 40%	(6,780)
	NIC at 1%	(170)
		£10,000

The problem with being a sole trader or partner is that you have to pay tax on everything you earn, whether you want to draw it out and spend it, or plough it back into developing the business.

Suppose the business is incorporated. Say its profits are a little higher than the onset of higher rate income tax for the individual. At £50,000, it will be paying corporation tax at a marginal rate of 19%.

Example 6.3B

In order to invest £10,000 in business development, the business now only needs to earn £12,346, thus:

Profit		12,346
Less:	Tax at 19%	(2,346)
		£10,000

So the same effect is achieved by the company with profits a whopping 27% lower. How about that for an incentive to incorporate?

This is the first degree of flexibility. There is no need to suffer high rates of personal tax unless there is a necessity to withdraw profits from the company.

Clearly the proprietor will need something to live on and a successful businessman is likely to want to enjoy the fruits of his labour. There is every likelihood that a significant part of the profits will be withdrawn and much of this will be required as cash (this leads to the salary/dividend comparisons of **4.3–4.9**). But, until the cash is needed, why bother?

6.4   If there are no business requirements for the company to retain realised profits, be wary of ever-growing investments in the company. In time they could prejudice:

- Business asset taper relief in respect of a capital gain later realised on disposal of the company shares. A trading company must not have non-trading activities which exceed 20% of the total (see **18.26**).
- Business property relief. Shares in a company whose activities are wholly or mainly investment orientated will cease to qualify (see **13.12**).
- The small companies' rate of corporation tax. Assuming that the company is closely controlled then, unless it exists mainly for the purpose of carrying on a trade or one of several other precisely defined reasons, it will be deemed to be a close investment holding company and liable to tax at the mainstream corporate rate of 30%.
- Close company apportionment has been used in the past to prevent company shareholders and directors from retaining excessive profits (see **1.2**). Many commentators perceive reintroduction of similar provisions as a way in which the Government may limit the present incorporation jamboree.

Also, keep an eye on the ultimate disposal of the company. There is, in effect, a double tax charge on retained corporate profits. The first is the corporation tax applied when they are earned (which is acknowledged to be low). However, when retained, they may enhance the share value and increase the capital gains tax charge on sale or liquidation. Do not be discouraged though. So long as business asset taper relief is not prejudiced, the total should still be less than taking out a bonus with its attendant income tax and NIC costs.

6.5   Note also though that the proprietors can influence the timing of profit withdrawal. It is not necessary to take cash out as the company earns it. Profits may fluctuate. The proprietors can choose when to make withdrawals and thereby smooth the flow of personal income to minimise their liability.

There could be an unexpected side effect to this. The new tax credits, working tax credit and child tax credit, payable from 6 April 2003, are income dependent. Not many business proprietors will be concerned about the working tax credit which does run out at fairly modest income levels (difficult to exemplify because the benefit is dependent on personal circumstances as well as income). However, the family element of the child tax credit is not tapered away until income exceeds £50,000 per annum. If there is an opportunity to smooth the flow of income by timing withdrawals from the company, then entitlement to tax credits might also be maximised.

Limited liability

6.6   This is what incorporation is supposed to be all about, is it not?

A sole trader or partner is totally exposed to:

- claims from creditors in the event of the business suffering financial failure;
- claims from affected parties in respect of loss, injury etc arising from poor workmanship.

In theory, trading through a company ring-fences the liability. The loss of the proprietor is limited to his investment in the share capital of the company. This may be true for large established public limited companies. However, it is probably not the case for small private companies where individuals will almost certainly be required to give personal guarantees and charge assets to secure the company activities.

In the family company or owner managed company, the benefit of limited liability may be largely illusory.

Raising finance

Bank borrowings

6.7   Many businesses rely on borrowings to finance their operations. A sole trader or partner must almost always rely on secured or unsecured loans from a bank, often backed by personal guarantees and with charges over personal assets.

There is no reason why a family company or owner managed company should not operate in the same fashion, though personal guarantees may still be a prerequisite. Assuming that sufficient assets have been transferred on incorporation, the company may give a floating charge over assets generally, an option not available to a sole trader or partnership.

What happens though when the company wants to 'move up a gear' and expand? Banks may be unwilling to lend sufficiently large amounts, or invest in what they perceive to be risky ventures. Enter the venture capitalist or 'business angel'.

Enterprise Investment Scheme

6.8   The aim of the Enterprise Investment Scheme (EIS) is to provide encouragement for new equity investment in small(ish) unquoted trading companies. Most family or owner managed companies are precisely that. The scheme has been around for nearly ten years as successor to the former Business Expansion Scheme but is still not terribly widely used. There might be two particular reasons for this:

- at least so far as income tax relief is concerned, it is difficult for proprietorial investors to qualify;
- the legislation governing the scheme is desperately complicated, to the extent that it will deter all but the most committed.

However, it has to be considered an advantage of incorporation as there is no similar means of investing in a sole trader or partnership business.

6.9 EIS offers the possibility of three separate tax reliefs:

- income tax relief on the initial investment;
- CGT exemption on disposal of EIS shares;
- CGT deferral of existing gains where EIS shares are acquired.

Full consideration of this scheme is well beyond the scope of this book (and investors intending to use it, or companies seeking to obtain funds by this means, must seek specialist advice). Very broadly, the income tax relief (and CGT exemption) require that a qualifying individual makes an investment in a qualifying company which is carrying on a qualifying trade and that certain conditions are satisfied throughout the relevant period.

6.10 A qualifying investor is an individual who is liable to UK income tax and who is not connected with the company during a period usually beginning two years before the share issue and ending three years after [*ICTA 1988, ss 291, 312(1)*]. He will be connected with the company if, together with his associates, he possesses, or is entitled to possess, over 30% of the issued ordinary shares in the company, loan capital and ordinary shares or voting power in the company [*s 291B*].

Normally, a person who is a director of the company would be regarded as connected with it irrespective of any shareholding. However, to encourage the business angel investor, this rule is overridden provided that he is not connected with the company as an employee or director before the subscription for shares and, when appointed, receives only reasonable remuneration for services provided [*s 291A*].

6.11 The acquisition must be by way of subscription for new ordinary shares for cash [*s 289*]. Relief is given on a minimum subscription of £500 up to a maximum subscription of £150,000 in any tax year [*s 290*]. Relief is given at the lower rate of income tax [*s 289A*]. It reduces the tax liability, not income, so for maximum relief the income tax liability must otherwise be at least £30,000. There are very particular rules as regards the making of claims [*s 306*].

6.12 A qualifying company must be an unquoted trading company and remain so throughout the relevant period, usually until three years after the share issue or commencement of trade if later [*ss 293, 312(1)*]. The gross assets of the company must not exceed £15m before the share issue and £16m after [*s 293*].

It must employ the funds raised by the share issue for the purposes of a trade carried on by it within specified time limits; usually 80% within 12 months and the balance within 12 months thereafter, but take especial care if the company is not trading at the time of the share issue [*s 289*]. The company's trade must be carried on mainly in the UK [*s 289(2)*] though curiously it does not seem to have to be a UK company. The company must not be under the control of another company [*s 293(8)*]; this means that it is unsuitable for a company which may have extensive institutional finance as it might then be technically controlled by the venture capital company.

6.13   The company must carry on a qualifying trade. All trades qualify except those that don't! The prohibited trades are listed in [*s 297*] and are not repeated here. They are broadly those perceived to be relatively less risky because of major asset backing or essentially financial services.

Beware the two-tier test. The company must exist wholly for the purposes of carrying on a qualifying trade [*s 293(2)*]. Its non-trading activities must not be 'significant' (which is undefined) which should be taken as very minimal. The trade itself must not consist to a substantial extent of prohibited activities [*s 297(2)*]. 'Substantial' is not defined but taken to be 20% – see Inland Revenue *Inspectors Manual para 6584*. This does not mean that the company can have activities outside its trade which are less than substantial.

6.14   There are very significant anti-avoidance measures dotted throughout the EIS legislation in *ICTA 1988, Part VII, Chapter III*. Great care must be taken to ensure that the conditions for relief are not only satisfied at the time of investment but also throughout the relevant period.

6.15   Where EIS income tax relief is given in respect of a share subscription, and not withdrawn, then any gain arising on disposal of the shares is exempt from CGT [*TCGA 1992, s 150A*]. This is potentially a far more valuable relief to the investor if the company trades successfully. Care needs to be taken with share identification where there are two or more holdings of the same share. Disposals are matched with acquisitions on a first-in first-out basis, not last-in first-out which is the usual position with share disposals.

6.16   CGT deferral operates in a similar way, except that there is a separate code governing it. This is contained in *TCGA 1992, Sch 5B* which, whilst bearing heavily on the income tax rules, is subtly different. Therefore, there are further pitfalls for the unwary. One significant and beneficial difference is that the investor may be connected with the company so far as this relief is concerned. A qualifying investment can defer pre-existing capital gains. This is explored as a possible means of incorporation in **9.40–9.47**.

6.17   For the sake of completeness it should be mentioned that there is also a Corporate Venturing Scheme (CVS). This might be considered broadly as a corporate form of EIS, though it has its own code of operation to be found in *FA 2000, Sch 15*. Whilst it is broadly similar to EIS, again, there are subtle distinctions which may trap the unwary. An investing company may get relief at 20% on an investment comprising up to 30% of the ordinary share capital in an unquoted trading company.

Relief for intangibles

6.18   *FA 2002, Sch 29* introduced a major reform to the taxation of intangible assets, but only for companies. Yet again it is an area where, if you wish to take advantage, it is essential to be trading in the corporate medium.

Hitherto, intangible assets have fallen within the chargeable gains regime. The effect of the new legislation is to take specified intangible assets out of this and into the normal trading rules. Thus a tax deduction may be obtained for expenditure and receipts from disposal are taxed as income. This applies only to expenditure on or after 1 April 2002; earlier expenditure still falls in the old regime.

6.19   Intangible assets for this purpose are defined as those created or acquired by the company for use on a continuing basis in the course of the company's activities. The term 'intangible assets' has the same meaning as for accounting purposes (see *FRS 10*). The legislation specifically includes intellectual property and, importantly, goodwill. Intellectual property is defined to include:

* patents, trademarks, registered design, copyright or design rights;
* plant breeders' rights;
* rights under foreign law relating to the above;
* information or techniques not protected but having industrial, commercial or economic value;
* any licence or other right relating to the above.

6.20   Where expenditure on such items is incurred on or after 1 April 2002, then a tax deduction may be claimed. This may be in one of five ways:

* written off as incurred;
* amortisation (this may be in accordance with accounting standards or, alternatively, the company may elect for a fixed rate of 4% of cost);
* a write down as a result of an impairment review;
* loss on realisation;
* reversal of a previous tax credit.

6.21   The corollary is that most income and gains will give rise to a credit for tax purposes, e.g.:

* receipts recognised in the profit and loss account;
* upward revaluations;
* credits in respect of negative goodwill;
* reversals of previous accounting losses and tax debits;
* gains on realisations.

Perhaps the last point here is the most important one to note. Whilst most commentators enthuse about the ability to get a tax deduction for purchased intangibles such as goodwill, less comment is made about the corollary effect.

On sale, having written off the cost, the full proceeds will be chargeable to corporation tax.

6.22 Gains arising on disposal of intangible fixed assets (including goodwill) falling within this legislation may be deferred. This has been achieved by introducing a mechanism for rollover relief. This is similar to the relief of that name for CGT purposes. Broadly, a profit on disposal of one intangible asset can be postponed if the proceeds are reinvested in another intangible asset. Clearly companies may be holding assets acquired before 1 April 2002 which remain within the chargeable gains rules. It is not possible to mix and match the old and the new. So, a gain on an old asset cannot be deferred by acquiring a new one falling within the *FA 2002* regime.

6.23 Finally, before you get too excited, there are rules to prohibit relief in respect of expenditure on transactions between related parties [*Sch 29 paras 95, 118*]. Thus it is not possible to incorporate an existing business, have the company make a payment for goodwill acquired from the former sole trader or partnership and then promptly write off the expenditure in the new company. If only the rules were that accommodating.

Research and development tax credits

6.24 Any business can claim a deduction for the revenue costs of research and development in arriving at its profit for tax purposes. However, in yet another of his gestures to the corporate business, the Chancellor has introduced a research and development tax credit.

These first appeared in *FA 2000, Sch 20* for companies which are small or medium-sized enterprises (SMEs). The application was extended to large companies (i.e. non-SMEs) by *FA 2002, Sch 12*.

A 'SME' is taken for this purpose from Commission Recommendation 96/280/EC [*FA 2000, Sch 20, para 2*] as one:

- with less than 250 employees; and
- turnover not exceeding €40m; or
- a balance sheet total not exceeding €27m.

From 1 April 2000, a corporate SME may claim tax relief on 150% of qualifying research and development expenditure. From 1 April 2002, a large company may claim tax relief on 125% of qualifying research and development expenditure though the schemes for differing sized companies are subtly different. The minimum amount spent in an accounting period must be more than £25,000 before a claim is possible. *Finance Act 2003, s 168, Sch 31 para 2* reduces the minimum figure to £10,000 though the operative date is not clear.

6.25 Brilliant! Tax relief on more than you spend. But, do not get too excited. The author has yet to see a valid claim. He cannot be alone. In the late autumn of 2002, the Inland Revenue was actively campaigning to 'sell' the relief having received far fewer claims than were anticipated at the consultation stage. Indeed, December 2002 saw publication of a Special Edition of the *Tax Bulletin* devoted solely to this topic. This seems to be actively campaigning for claims even to the extent of offering prior discussions with the relevant Inspector.

6.26 The snag lies in what is qualifying research and development for this purpose. It is defined in *ICTA 1988, s 837A* as activities to be treated as research and development in accordance with generally accepted accounting practice. *Research and Development (Prescribed Activities) Regulations 2000, SI 2000/2081* imports the text of 'Guidelines on the Meaning of Research and Development (R&D) for Tax Purposes' issued by the Department of Trade and Industry on 28 July 2000. Broadly it is work that contains an appreciable element of innovation or creativity in the fields of science and technology. It should aim to break new ground or to resolve scientific or technological uncertainties. It is often described as 'blue skies' research.

And therein lies the problem. It does not encompass ordinary commercial development. It is a nice idea but few companies seem to qualify.

6.27 Oh; and why tax credit? In certain circumstances (insufficiency of income etc.) the company may create a loss which is immediately unrelievable. In those circumstances it may choose instead to take a payable tax credit.

Substantial shareholding exemption

6.28 Relief for expenditure on intangibles was not the only benefit for companies to be derived from *FA 2002*. *Sch 8* introduced a new *TCGA 1992, s 192A* and *Sch 7AC*. This gives a total relief from taxation where a trading company disposes of all or part of a substantial shareholding in another trading company.

In some ways, this may mirror parts of the EIS scheme available to individuals and by which exemption from CGT on disposal of qualifying shares may be achieved. However, it goes rather further in that shares for this relief may be in any trading company, not simply one which is small and growing. Apparently the rationale was to match similar reliefs available in other European companies and thereby dissuade multinational corporates from investing elsewhere, other than the UK. It is, though, another example of the Government favouring a company against any other trading medium.

6.29 Whilst it might be in the mind's eye of the business proprietor looking to incorporate, it is very much a long-term benefit and not a means of disposing of a single trade without payment of tax. Since both the investing company and the investee company need to trade, it will take some time to set up an appropriate structure and it suggests some diversity of operation. Where a group structure is intended, this relief should be borne in mind when it is established.

Broadly the relief is total exemption from tax on a gain realised where a trading company makes a disposal out of a substantial shareholding in another trading company. It follows that a loss realised in these circumstances is not an allowable loss. The relief commenced on 1 April 2002 but can apply to holdings acquired before that date.

6.30   The definition of a 'trading company' is modelled on the CGT taper relief definition as modified by *FA 2002* (see **18.28**). It is a company carrying on trading activities, whose activities do not include, to a substantial extent, activities other than trading activities.

6.31   A substantial shareholding is an interest in shares which must give the beneficial entitlement to not less than 10% of:

- the ordinary share capital; and
- the profits available on a winding up; and
- the assets available for distribution to equity holders.

The 10% measure is peculiar to this relief and without prejudice to the meaning of 'substantial' elsewhere in the *Taxes Acts*.

6.32   The investing company must have held a substantial shareholding in the company invested in throughout a twelve-month period beginning not more than two years before the day on which the disposal takes place.

Both companies must satisfy the trading company test throughout the qualifying period which begins with the start of the latest twelve-month period for the substantial shareholding test and ends with the time of disposal.

In the present context this is a brief summary of the relief which is far more extensive and, as ever, contains various anti-avoidance provisions.

Rewarding key employees

6.33   In all but the smallest of businesses, there will come a stage in development at which the proprietor becomes increasingly dependent on one or more key employees. Their contribution will become such as to be an integral part of the business operation.

In tightly controlled family businesses, these may be other family members, perhaps the adult children of the proprietor. Their ultimate reward may well be the ownership of the business once the 'elder statesman' retires.

In other cases, there may be no such obvious succession. Either there are no direct successors to the business or potential candidates do not wish to assume the responsibility. The key employee(s) may then be independent parties whose contribution is to be valued. Hopefully they are adequately rewarded by means of salary and benefits in the short term. However, this may not be enough. To ensure their continued participation and loyalty to the business rather more may be required. Something to enhance a sense of belonging.

To the unincorporated business, the solution may be partnership. This may prove less than satisfactory from both sides though. The employee may still desire a significant salary prior to a profit share. He may not relish the prospect of being exposed to losses or the risk of joint and several liability. From the proprietor's point of view, he may not wish to give away a significant slice of the business in the early stages. The difficulties may be compounded if there is more than one key employee.

6.34   What is needed is a means of carving off small bits of the business, the ability to gear the reward to the performance of the individual and a gradual development.

How to do that? Incorporate of course. What is a share but a small slice of the company. Ensure that there is adequate authorised share capital and shares may be issued to key employees in progressive portions, rewarding their service and giving them an increasing stake in the business. Additionally, with care and forethought to the structure, it may prove possible to reward key employees by dividends, giving the benefits of incorporation to them as well.

It may come as a culture shock to some business proprietors. The company is their baby. They created it, developed it and made it grow through their own efforts. The last thing they may want to do is to give part of it away. On the other hand, it may become a necessary evil to ensure the continued existence of the company.

6.35   How are advantages best achieved? The simplest may be a straight gift of shares to the favoured employees, or a new share issue by the company. This may have a downside problem straightaway for the employee. Why did he get the shares? Because of his employment, of course. They therefore represent a taxable benefit of the employment. Indeed, their value is probably basic earnings chargeable under *ITEPA 2003, s 62: ICTA 1988, s 19,* following the decision in *Weight v Salmon (1935) 19 TC 174.* However, provided that the shares are not readily convertible assets within *ITEPA 2003, s 696; ICTA 1988, s 203F* (which most private company shares will not be), PAYE does not need to be applied. If these circumstances prevail, there is no NIC charge. Depending on the value of the shares, the tax liability could be large giving a significant disincentive to the employee; quite the opposite of what was intended.

6.36   Enter the world of share option and share incentive schemes. This can be a complex and fairly specialist area. However, never fear, there is probably only one scheme which is really suitable for the private company.

6.37 *Other Advantages of a Company*

To be fair, *FA 2000* actually introduced two new share schemes:

- The first governed by *ITEPA 2003, ss 488–515, Sch 2; FA 2000, Sch 8,* was known originally as the all Employee Share Ownership Plan, later changed to Share Incentive Plan. It provides tax incentives to enable all employees to participate in the share capital of their employer company.
- The second is governed by *ITEPA 2003, Sch 5; FA 2000, Sch 14,* and is known as the Enterprise Management Incentive. This provides a tax efficient means of rewarding key employees in small and growing trading companies.

The Government's intention is that, between them, these two schemes should satisfy most of the need for employee participation in employer companies, though earlier savings-related and executive option schemes still exist. Back to the business proprietor's point of view that the last thing he might want to do is to give away part of his company, the share incentive plan is unlikely to find a place in the overall arrangements for a private company. The particular disadvantage is that it is an all employee scheme and, for that reason alone, is unlikely ever to find favour with a small private company. The enterprise management incentive on the other hand could be just what is needed.

Enterprise Management Incentive

6.37   Formed as part of a range of reliefs to encourage enterprise, the Enterprise Management Incentive (EMI) has restrictions on the individuals who may participate and the companies which may be involved. The rules are similar, but not identical, to EIS (see **6.10–6.14**).

Broadly, a qualifying company may grant a qualifying share option to an eligible employee.

6.38   A 'qualifying company' is one:

- which is independent;
- whose gross assets do not exceed £30m;
- which exists wholly for the purpose of carrying on a trade; and
- whose trading activities do not include to a substantial extent excluded activities. These are largely asset-backed or financial trades and therefore inherently less risky.

[*ITEPA 2003, Sch 5, Part 3; FA 2000, Sch 14 paras 12–26*].

6.39   An 'eligible employee':

- must work at least 25 hours per week in the business of the company. If less time than this is devoted to the company, it must be at least 75% of the individual's total working time;

- must not have a material interest in the company. 'Material interest' is broadly the ability to control 30% of the ordinary share capital of the company.

[*ITEPA 2003, Sch 5, Part 4: FA 2000 Sch 14 paras 27–36*].

6.40   Qualifying options:

- cannot cover shares with a value in excess of £3m at any one time;
- cannot be granted as to more than £100,000 to any one employee at any time;
- will usually be granted at market value. They can be granted at less than market value though, in that case, will not enjoy the full tax benefits;
- must be over ordinary shares;
- must be capable of exercise within ten years.

[*ITEPA 2003 Sch 5 paras 5–6, Part 5; FA 2000 Sch 14, paras 10, 11, 37–41*].

6.41   If all the conditions are met:

- if, as is usually the case, the option is granted at market value, there is no income tax payable either on the grant or the exercise of the option;
- if the option is granted at less than market value, an income tax charge will arise under *ITEPA 2003, s 476; ICTA 1988, s 135* on the exercise of the option;
- when the shares are subsequently disposed of, only CGT is payable. Business asset taper relief is available and, unusually, the qualifying holding period runs from the date of grant of the option, not the acquisition of the shares.

[*ITEPA 2003, ss 528–531; TCGA 1992, Sch 7D paras 14–15; FA 2000 Sch 14 paras 42–45, 56–57*].

6.42   This is necessarily a very brief summary of the scheme and readers intending to employ it must consider the detailed rules (which contain the inevitable anti-avoidance provisions and claw back arrangements in certain circumstances) carefully before proceeding. The general lack of restrictions on the shares used in EMI (the ability to have pre-emption rights etc) adds to the attractiveness.

Overall, EMI seems to achieve the objectives required:

- the business proprietor can provide an incentive in the form of share ownership;
- the employee must pay for the shares but not now. He could be granted options now at £1. In five years time the shares could be worth £10 and he decides to exercise the option. He still pays £1 and has an immediate paper profit of £9 per share.

There are no adverse upfront income tax charges.

Pensions

6.43   The sole trader or business partner has no choice if he wishes to make private provision for a pension. There is no alternative to the personal pension plan (unless a retirement annuity policy has been in place since before the rules changed in 1988).

Incorporation though can open up a whole new world of pension provision. There is the opportunity to move away from personal provision and into the realms of employer (or company) schemes. Whilst many company directors will stick with PPPs (see **4.31–4.42**), employer based schemes offer the opportunity to save far more and accrue higher benefits far more swiftly.

6.44   Approved occupational schemes (governed by *ICTA 1988, Part XIV, Chap I*) are broadly of two types:

- Money purchase or defined contribution. This is a direct parallel for the PPP. There is no guarantee of the pension to be paid. The contributions paid by the company (and possibly the employee) go to an earmarked fund for the individual and are broadly used to purchase an annuity on retirement.
- Final salary or defined benefit. The pension is based on the employee's final salary and length of service. It is paid out of a central fund rather than a designated fund for the employee. It cannot exceed two-thirds of final salary. This type of arrangement is distinctly unfashionable because of the high and indeterminate cost of providing the benefit.

Given that the permitted maximum benefits may accrue over as little as 20 years, the possible contributions may be enormous, certainly well in excess of the percentage limited contributions by an individual to a PPP. Where the employee has control over a profitable company, this can prove to be a very beneficial use of funds.

6.45   In making the decision to go for a company scheme, the proprietor should consider:

- the company gets tax relief for normal contributions actually paid in the accounting period. There may be some spreading of large (greater than £500,000) special contributions;
- there is no limit on employer contributions (except actuarially to provide the maximum benefits);
- employer contributions are not a benefit for the employee for income tax or NIC;
- the employee can contribute up to 15% of emoluments;
- the maximum pension is two-thirds of final salary, subject to the earnings cap (£99,000 for 2003/04) where the scheme was established after 17 March 1987.

Final salary is more correctly termed 'final remuneration' as it may include not only salary but also bonuses etc. and taxable benefits in kind. For an ordinary employee, the measure is taken in any one of the five years preceding the normal retirement date. There is an alternative, available to the ordinary employee, which must be used for controlling directors. It is the average of remuneration for three consecutive years ending not more than ten years before the normal retirement date. A controlling director for this purpose is one who (together with certain associates; spouse, minor children and trustees of settlements made by the individual or spouse) can control more than 20% of the voting rights in the company. This will clearly inhibit flexible remuneration planning techniques as retirement comes nearer. There is no option but to take salary (rather than dividend) with attendant NIC costs.

6.46   The company may go for a fully insured scheme, where the contributions are simply passed to an insurance company for independent management. Alternatively, if the proprietor is prepared to take a hands on approach, the scheme may be self administered. Indeed small self administered schemes are very popular with proprietors of many small companies. Small is in respect of the number of members (maximum eleven) rather than the sums contained which are unlimited. The real advantages are that the funds within the pension scheme may be used to benefit the company (though in so doing the primary objective of paying the pension must not be forgotten).

One popular use is for the pension fund to purchase business premises which are then leased to the (sponsoring) trading company. This is seen as an effective use of capital and payment of rent (which must be at a market rate) gives the pension fund income. This goes untaxed within the fund notwithstanding the availability of a deduction to the company. Another alternative is to make a loan back to the company; this must be on commercial terms and not exceed 50% of the available fund.

All self administered schemes must have a pensioner trustee appointed to ensure all regulations are complied with.

6.47   Many rules govern the operation of all types of occupational pension scheme but there is remarkably little primary legislation. The ultimate governors of pension schemes are the Inland Revenue Pension Schemes Office, now part of Inland Revenue Savings, Pensions and Share Schemes Business Stream, and the Occupational Pensions Regulatory Authority who have wide discretionary powers to ensure funds are not misused.

6.48   For the sake of completeness, a company might also consider an unapproved scheme such as a funded unapproved retirement benefit scheme (FURBS). Their primary use nowadays is to top up other schemes where the pension cap presents a problem as regards the size of the fund.

- Contributions to a FURBS are deductible for the employer, but represent a benefit in kind on which the employee must pay income tax and, since 6 April 1999 (in the view of the Inland Revenue at least), NIC.
- The income of the fund is taxed at 22% and gains at 34%. Consequently many FURBS are established overseas in order to accumulate funds more quickly.

- There is total flexibility of investment since a FURBS is not dependent on Inland Revenue approval.
- The pension when received is taxable as income. A lump sum from a UK-based FURBS is tax free but an overseas FURBS will be taxable.

Some disadvantages

6.49 Lest the reader should be lulled into a false sense of security, it should not necessarily be thought that everything is rosy on the corporate side of the fence. There are disadvantages to the process, many of which will seem to be proportionately bigger to the typical small businessman looking to incorporate solely for tax savings.

6.50 There is, it has to be said, substantially more administration in running a company than any other form of business. A lot of this stems from the fact that the company is an entirely separate entity. It is governed in operation by the *Companies Acts* which place certain obligations on the owners. These include requirements for meetings, maintenance of statutory books, the submission of an annual return etc. Just to put the frighteners on, some breaches of *Companies Act* requirements are criminal offences.

Additionally, an acceptable minimum of accounting is required (sorry, incorporation does mean the end of brown paper bag accounts).

All of these require a business sufficiently well developed to have administrative systems in place to cope with such niceties. The alternative must be the acceptance of the need for continuing professional help which is an expense to set against the tax savings of incorporation.

6.51 Although many small companies will not require an audit of their accounts, the accounting procedures to be adopted are often more stringent. In theory, *FA 1998, s 42*, requires the accounts of all businesses to follow UK GAAP but, in practice, small unincorporated businesses may not be quite so enthusiastic in its application.

6.52 Incorporation will lead some small businesses to the operation of PAYE procedures for the first time. Whilst many sole traders and partnership will have employees necessitating such mechanisms to be in place, at the smaller end of the market this may not necessarily be the case. The pure sole trader or husband and wife partnership may not have encountered it before. On incorporation though, such individuals will become directors and/or employees of the company. Any remuneration paid to them by the company must be under deduction of tax through PAYE. This is a further administrative burden. Elsewhere in this book it is suggested that salaries to be paid in such circumstances might be quite small to such an extent that no income tax or NIC is due. There may nevertheless remain a requirement to have a PAYE scheme and maintain the necessary records for benefit purposes.

6.53 Mention of PAYE brings us back to NIC. Why, some people will question, do we want to head for the corporate medium where the mainstream rate of NIC is an eye-watering 23.8% (Class 1 primary 11% plus Class 1 secondary 12.8%). On the face of it, this does compare badly with Class 4 at 8% (plus the nominal Class 2). The difference is that Class 4 is virtually impossible to avoid. If the business proprietor is prepared to be more creative in ways of taking remuneration though, payment of Class 1 almost becomes optional.

6.54 The proprietors of many unincorporated businesses will make private use of assets used in the business. This may be as simple as a car which is used for both business and personal travel. Depending on the nature of the business, it can be far more extensive, e.g. the farmer who uses the farmhouse as the centre of business operations and charges all expenses to his trading account; at the same time, it is his private home. In the Schedule D regime, it is simply necessary to apportion the costs between business and private use. The former is an allowable deduction in determining the trading profit. The latter is disallowed in the tax computation. Switch to the corporate medium and such simplicity is lost. Remember again, the company is a separate entity. It may deduct all costs of using an asset; these will either be in respect of its business use or in respect of provision of remuneration to an employee (the director). The individual is now treated separately and employment income rules apply. The measure of his benefit is the cost to the company of providing it, though many items have particular rules especially the company car which has a fixed scale benefit bearing no relation to actual costs (see **15.1–15.23** for extensive commentary on company cars). Many regard the benefits code rules as a retrograde step when used to the relative freedom of Schedule D. Remember also that employment expense rules are notoriously restrictive. There is that additional word 'necessarily' in *ITEPA 2003, s 336; ICTA 1988, s 198,* which is not to be found in *ICTA 1988, s 74* which merely requires an expense to be incurred wholly and exclusively for business purposes. This may trouble the small businessman who operates from home and is used to charging a proportion of heating, lighting etc. in his business accounts. This may not be so easy once he becomes a company director.

6.55 Particular trades have particular rules and it seems that the farming fraternity can come off badly when incorporating. Indeed, whilst many farming companies are long established providing a satisfactory trading medium, it is questionable whether now is the time to indulge in incorporation in this sector. There are especial trading difficulties in the early years of the 21st century. Incorporation should never be taken lightly – this is especially the case with farmers. Particular issues include the loss of farmers averaging. Sole trader farmers and partners in agricultural partnerships may elect to relieve fluctuating profits [*ICTA1988, s 96*] to smooth the tax charges where profits can vary widely. This option is simply not available to a company. Other more obscure issues may involve agricultural quotas. For example, sugar beet contract tonnage (not strictly a quota, but a right to production) may reduce by as much as 30% when ownership is changed. This could be a major disincentive to incorporation.

Additionally, the Common Agricultural Policy is in the throes of a Mid-Term Review (summer 2003) which may result in the loss of subsidy if there is a change in occupier of the land. This could well be the case with incorporation. Since agricultural subsidies can be around £100 per acre, these are clearly far more important than saving a few thousand pounds in income tax. Farmers may therefore be best advised not to consider incorporation until the Mid-Term Review is complete.

6.56   When considering the trading medium and development of a business, possibly the last thing to spring to mind is what happens when it comes to an end. Some businesses have a finite existence and can be sold or passed down within the family. Others may only be as good as the proprietor. When he decides to retire, the business may end. There strikes what has been called the penalty of double CGT. If the company ceases to trade, it may realise its assets and will pay corporation tax on any profit. This leaves the company with a pile of cash; if the proprietor seeks to extract this, even by liquidation, there will be further tax chargeable. These days, given the influence of 75% business asset taper relief, the latter may not be the disincentive it once was, but must still be borne in mind in long-term planning.

Planning points

- A company offers a cheaper way of reinvesting profits (**6.3**).
- The Enterprise Investment Scheme offers tax incentives for the investor into a company (**6.9–6.16**).
- A company can now get tax relief on purchase of intangible assets including goodwill (**6.18–6.22**).
- The research and development tax credit can give companies tax relief on more than actual expenditure (**6.24–6.26**).
- A company can make certain share disposals and pay no tax (**6.28–6.32**).
- A company can offer key employees a tax efficient stake in the business (**6.37–6.41**).
- A company may have more flexible pension arrangements (**6.43–6.47**).
- The seven advantages listed above are *only* available to a company.

Chapter 7

Income Tax Cessations

7.1 It is axiomatic that incorporation of a business must involve the cessation of a former sole trade or partnership. Whilst some might regard the change as a continuation of trade, it must be remembered that the company is a totally separate entity, chargeable to corporation tax and not income tax. It is therefore necessary to apply appropriate cessation adjustments to the unincorporated business.

We have looked briefly at the calculation of taxable profits under the current year basis of taxation for income tax (see **2.12–2.18**). It is now necessary to study far more closely the adjustments which arise on cessation and which may influence the act of incorporation. Far too often this seems to be treated as a tidying up process after the event when, in reality, it should be part of the advance planning.

The cessation will, of itself, cause certain adjustments to the tax computation especially as regards stock and capital allowances. The latter is so important that the whole of **Chapter 8** is devoted to it.

Cessation computation

7.2 The general position under current year basis (CYB) is that the income tax assessment for a given year is based on the profits of the accounting period ended in that year. Adjustments are needed in the opening years to get to this position (see **2.16**).

7.3 Similar adjustments are necessary when a business ceases. There is no gap between the basis periods at cessation. The profits forming the basis of the assessment for the final tax year will be those earned in the period beginning immediately after the end of the basis period for the preceding year and ending on the date of cessation [*ICTA 1988, s 63*]. Depending on the accounting date and date of cessation, this could be a period of more or less than twelve months.

7.4 The tidy minded may seek to incorporate a business on its established accounting date. This may prove to be a false presumption and we go on to explore the parameters for establishing what might be a better date to choose. Unless the incorporation does take place on the usual accounting date, the accounts to cessation of the sole trade (or partnership) will be for a period other than twelve months. Use of a different date for the final accounting period will not normally trigger the change of basis period rules. It is inevitable that a different accounting date is required, but there is no intention that the new date becomes a new annual accounting date. The cessation rules of *ICTA 1988, s 63* automatically take priority over *s 62* for the year of cessation.

7.5

Example 7.5

Ian (see **2.16**) draws up his annual accounts to 30 April in each year. He decides to incorporate on 1 August 2005. He will have drawn up accounts to 30 April 2004 which form the basis of the assessment for 2004/05.

He may then draw up accounts for 12 months to 30 April 2005, followed by 3 months to 31 July 2005, or simply 15 months to 31 July 2005.

The 2005/06 assessment must be on profits from 1 May 2004 (immediately after the 2004/05 accounting date) to 31 July 2005 (the date of cessation).

On the first alternative that is:

*   Accounts to 30 April 2005, plus
*   Accounts to 31 July 2005.

On the second alternative that is:

*   Accounts to 31 July 2005.

At first sight, this might appear to make no difference, but there is a huge importance for capital allowances (see **8.16**).

Overlap relief

7.6   Where 5 April has been used as the annual accounting date of a business, the total profits assessed will automatically equal the total profits earned. There will be no overlap between any income tax basis periods. In practice, the Inland Revenue will accept that accounts drawn up to 31 March may be treated as coterminous with the tax year end (see para 1.99 of Inland Revenue booklet *SAT1, The New Current Year Basis of Assessment*).

Drawing up accounts to 5 April (or 31 March) has the advantage of simplicity. The profit earned during a tax year suffers income tax in that same year. No basis period adjustments are necessary. For this reason alone, many small sole traders will choose this accounting date.

7.7   It may not be the optimum though. It may be preferable for a seasonal trade to choose an accounting date such as 30 September or 31 December.

Equally, many businesses may choose an accounting date which is twelve months from commencement of business and keep to this annually thereafter. In dispassionate tax terms, 30 April is probably the best accounting date in giving the maximum period of time between earning a profit and paying tax thereon. There is a particular advantage when profits are rising. Occasionally other factors, such as the IR35 personal service company legislation, may dictate that a particular date is to be preferred – in this case, 5 April.

However, in using an accounting date other than one coterminous with the tax year end, there will be one or more years in which the basis periods for two adjacent tax years overlap. This usually occurs in years two or three of a new business, at which time the CYB basis periods and accounting periods are brought into alignment. This has already been demonstrated at **2.16**. In addition, an adjustment may be made on a change of accounting date during the life of the business. The logic to creation and use of overlap relief is that the profits earned throughout the life of a business are all subject to tax once, and once only. If the business has a long life, inflation if nothing else destroys this theory. Overlap relief created 20 years ago (say) is proportionately far less valuable when the business ceases trading today. There were many changes of accounting date in the early days of CYB in order to use up overlap relief before its value depreciated.

Any remaining overlap relief can be useful in the tax year in which the business ceases. It is given as if it were an additional trading deduction incurred in that period [*ICTA 1988, s 63A(3)*]. In most instances, the use of overlap relief simply reduces the assessable profit in the final year. Depending on the relative size of the profit and the overlap relief, a loss may be created. Equally, if a loss already arose in the period of cessation, the overlap relief will augment that loss. A loss created or enhanced by overlap relief is treated in exactly the same fashion as any other trading loss. The usual loss relief claims demonstrated in **3.13–3.15** may be made.

Transitional relief

7.8   Many long standing unincorporated businesses will have started trading before the switch to CYB in 1996/97. Overlap relief will be irrelevant to them.

1995/96 was the last year of the old previous year basis (PYB) of assessment. 1997/98 was the first 'proper' year of CYB. In 1996/97, a system of profit averaging was used to get from the old system to the new. This ensured that all relevant accounting periods figured in income tax assessments; without the averaging, some profits may have escaped.

PYB required opening and closing years' adjustments, just as much as the new CYB, though the effects were somewhat different. With PYB, the application of the closing year rules was such that there was nearly always a gap between the basis periods used and profit arising in that gap escaped tax. That is not the case with CYB. A corollary of the 1996/97 averaging is the loss of the closing year's gap. To a certain extent this is reinstated by transitional relief. The amount of transitional relief is equal to the profit in the period between the end of the basis period for 1996/97 and 6 April 1997. This period lies before the date on which the CYB rules came into full force but the profits of that period are taxed under the new rules [*FA 1994, Sch 20 para 2(4)*].

For all practical purposes, transitional relief is treated like overlap relief. Therefore it reduces the profit or can create or augment a loss of the final period.

Examples

7.9

Example 7.9

Chris is a sole trader and his profits are rising steadily. When should he incorporate?

Profit	Year ended	30.6.01		£48,000	
	Year ended	30.6.02		£54,000	
	Year ending	30.6.03		£60,000	(accruing evenly)
(a)	Incorporation	31.3.03			
	Assessments	2001/02	Y/e 30.6.01		£48,000
		2002/03	Y/e 30.6.02		£54,000
			9/12 × y/e 30.6.03		£45,000
					£99,000
(b)	Incorporation	30.4.03			
	Assessments	2001/02	Y/e 30.6.01		£48,000
		2002/03	Y/e 30.6.02		£54,000
		2003/04	10/12 × y/e 30.6.03		£50,000
(c)	Incorporation	30.6.03			
	Assessments	2001/02	Y/e 30.6.01		£48,000
		2002/03	Y/e 30.6.02		£54,000
		2003/04	Y/e 30.6.03		£60,000

For all practical purposes, there is no difference between (b) and (c). Two months additional trading have given £10,000 more profit but the tax thereon is paid at a similar time (31 January 2005).

Note the distinction between (a) and (b). One month's additional trading has given £5,000 more profit but the tax in respect of profits earned in the part period to 30.6.03 is payable on 31 January 2005. Advancing the cessation by one month has brought forward the tax payment in respect of the profits for the part period to 30.6.03 by a whole year to 31 January 2004. A substantial cash flow disadvantage.

7.10

Example 7.10

Now bring in overlap relief. Martin also considers an appropriate date to incorporate. He has overlap relief carried forward of £25,000.

Profit	Year ended	28.2.02	£42,000	
	Year ended	28.2.03	£48,000	
	Year ending	29.2.04	£54,000	(accruing evenly)

(a)	Incorporation	31.3.03		
	Assessments	2001/02	Y/e 28.2.02	£42,000
		2002/03	Y/e 28.2.03	48,000
			1/12 × y/e 29.2.04	4,500
				52,500
			Less overlap	(25,000)
				£27,500

(b)	Incorporation	30.4.03		
	Assessments	2001/02	Y/e 28.2.02	£42,000
		2002/03	Y/e 28.2.03	£48,000
		2003/04	2/12 × y/e 29.2.04	9,000
			Less overlap	(25,000)
				£(16,000)

In (b) the assessments are £4,500 higher in total reflecting the additional one month of trading. The result for 2003/04 is a loss; if this is carried back and set against the 2002/03 profits the distinction is less marked than in Example 7.9 and there is no cash flow disadvantage.

7.11 So far we have seen the impact of two influences:

• the timing of tax payments;
• overlap relief.

It will be noted that, in 7.10(b), there is no assessable profit in 2003/04 so personal allowances are wasted. The presumption is that a company later trades profitably and a salary is drawn to use personal allowances. Is there an alternative?

7.12

Example 7.12

As in Example 7.10 but Martin keeps trading until profits absorb overlap relief and personal allowance (30 November 2003).

7.13 *Income Tax Cessations*

(a)	Assessments	2001/02	Y/e 28.2.02	£42,000
		2002/03	Y/e 28.2.03	£48,000
		2003/04	7/12 × y/e 29.2.04	31,500
			Less overlap	(25,000)
				£6,500

The 2001/02 and 2002/03 assessments are in line with 7.10 (or indeed a continuing sole trade).

Tax payable by Martin in 2003/04 is £188.50. If the company then earns profits at the same rate and accounts to 29 February 2004, its tax liability is just under £3,000.

(b) Had Martin incorporated at 30 April 2003, the company would have earned £49,500 to 29 February 2004. Martin might take a salary of £27,000 to put his drawings back as (a) above. This leaves the company with a tax liability of nearly £6,000 (including NIC). Martin would pay tax and NIC of £7,150. So the total additional liability is more than £10,000. Against this is the absence of terminal loss relief, say £16,000 at 40% (though some would be relieved at 22% only) or £6,400. Being over-enthusiastic about incorporating has cost over £4,000 in additional tax.

7.13 One could go on forever, but examples remain just that, examples. It is at this point that you wish that the client had chosen a 31 March accounting date when, at least, there is no need to consider the impact of overlap relief. In any other case, there is no substitute for looking at the realised profits, projected future profits, amount of overlap relief and dates in each case. A wrong decision can result in a substantial additional income tax liability on cessation or, at least, a cash flow disadvantage. The proprietor is not going to welcome that as a penalty for incorporation.

7.14 Even then, we can disrupt the whole issue by adjustments which vary the profits. Particular issues here include:

- stock valuation;
- capital allowances.

The latter is of sufficient importance to merit its own chapter. Before we go on to address stock, do not forget:

Payment of tax

7.15 In the author's experience, virtually no sole traders (and very few partnerships) make any provision for tax in their business accounts. For the most part, tax liabilities falling due now are paid out of profits earned now.

Example 7.15

In Example 7.9, Chris drew up accounts to 30 June each year. Ignoring incorporation, the tax due for 2002/03 would be payable by two payments on account on 31 January 2003 and 31 July 2003, with a balancing payment on 31 January 2004. He will quite probably meet the 31 January 2004 bill out of incoming funds at the end of 2003, despite the fact that he began earning the relevant profits as long ago as 1 July 2001 (the basis period for 2002/03 is 1 July 2001 to 30 June 2002).

Had he taken the 30 April 2003 option for incorporation, the inflow of funds to the sole trader business would have stopped on this date. But he still has the 31 July 2003 and 31 January 2004 tax payments to make.

7.16   Pre-incorporation planning must therefore involve estimating the outstanding tax liabilities of the sole trader business and making adequate provision for them in the final accounts. If this is not done, the business proprietor will find himself having to fund these liabilities from income earned by the company. Since the company's income is not his, the extraction of a sufficient amount (whether by way of salary or dividend) will have its own attendant liabilities – which can so easily be avoided with adequate forethought.

7.17   The proprietor also needs to be warned in advance of the change in timing of tax payments which is occasioned by incorporation:

- Chris's sole trader assessment for 2002/03 was based on profits earned in the period 1 July 2001 to 30 June 2002. Tax is payable in instalments falling due between 31 January 2003 and 31 January 2004. Payment of the tax therefore falls more than 1½ years after the inflow of the corresponding funds.
- If the incorporated business draws up accounts to 30 June 2004, tax is payable on 1 April 2005, a delay of only nine months.
- If Chris draws a taxable salary from the company, income tax and NIC is payable only 14 days after the month of payment.

Treatment of stock and work in progress

Stock

7.18   Historically, stock and work in progress could be sold by an unincorporated business to a company for whatever price the parties agreed. That price would determine the respective tax liabilities of the parties. One exception would be the case where a business was transferred to a company in exchange for shares. In those circumstances, the value of the shares issued must reflect the value of assets transferred to the company as that would be a transfer between connected persons. It would seem that *ICTA 1988, s 100(1)(a)* then requires market value to be applied.

7.19 To prevent manipulation in this fashion, the matter has been concluded for transactions after 28 November 1994 by the inclusion of *subsections 1A–1G* in *s 100* by *FA 1995, s 140*. There is extensive commentary on these anti-avoidance provisions in the Inland Revenue *Inspector's Manual paras 570a–k*.

The basic position now seems to given by *sub-s 1(a)* and *1A* such that stock is always deemed to pass between connected persons at market value. The meaning of 'connected persons' is defined in *sub-s 1F* and is rather wider than the usual Taxes Act definition in *ICTA 1988, s 839*.

7.20 However, the transferor and transferee (sole trader or partner and new company) may jointly elect under *sub 1C* that the stock is instead to be treated as transferred at the higher of cost or the amount actually paid. Since the sale price or market value must be included in the cessation accounts of the unincorporated business to determine the final profit, but is also deductible in arriving at the profits of the company, there is scope for planning. If the unincorporated business pays tax at 40% but the company at only 19% (say), the stock should be transferred at a low value to reduce the income tax profits at the expense of corporate tax profits increasing but taxed at lower rate. The choice of transfer value is not infinitely variable though. It seems that it must either be market value or cost (net realisable value if lower).

7.21 Where an election is appropriate, it must be made within two years of the end of the chargeable period in which the transfer occurs.

7.22 Note that such an election is only permissible where stock is 'sold or transferred for valuable consideration'. It appears that if the stock is gifted to the company (which is not an impossible position in certain types of incorporation) then market value must prevail with no option available.

7.23 Some commentators question whether such an election would be valid where the business is transferred in exchange for shares, so that the basic provision in *ICTA 1988, s 100(1)(a)* applies. The writer is not aware of the Inland Revenue taking this point, but it may be worth bearing in mind where the stock is valuable and has appreciated significantly since acquisition.

7.24 Given that *ICTA 1988, s 100* normally permits the transfer of value to be only market value or, on election, historic cost the scope for manipulation by adjusting the proceeds seems minimal. However, in relation to transactions on or after 24 July 2002, where stock is sold or transferred with other assets, the consideration must be apportioned on a just and reasonable basis to each of the assets. Whilst this may inhibit transactions between unconnected parties, it does not override the existing connected party rules [*FA 2002, s 106(1)*].

Work in progress

7.25 For the vast majority of businesses, everything so far said about stock applies equally to work in progress. There are, though, distinct rules concerning the valuation of work in progress on discontinuance of a profession or vocation. These are to be found in *ICTA 1988, s 101*.

The basic position remains as for stock before the introduction of the *FA 1995* anti-avoidance provisions. That is to say, where there is valuable consideration, e.g. on a business transfer in exchange for shares, the work in progress is taken to have that value. As before, this must be the market value. On a gift, market value must prevail.

7.26   The Inland Revenue is normally prepared to accept whatever value is attributed to work in progress, unless it is blatantly unreasonable. The Revenue will not seek to make any adjustment so long as the value attributed to work in progress follows the basis consistently used for accounting purposes. Should you have occasion to deal with the incorporation of a professional partnership, *ICAEW Technical Release TAX 7/95*, 15 February 1995, includes a guidance note on the taxation implications of transfers of work in progress and debtors on the incorporation of such a business.

7.27   There is a further curious provision relating to the cessation of a profession or vocation in that the taxpayer may elect for the closing work in progress on cessation to be taken as having its cost value [*ICTA 1988, s101(2)*]. Any realised excess is then treated as a post-cessation receipt under *s 103*.

Planning points

- Always check the income tax assessments arising on cessation of the unincorporated business and choose a suitable date for incorporation to minimise the effect (**7.9, 7.10, 7.12**).
- Always provide for outstanding income tax liabilities in the cessation accounts (**7.16**).
- Make sure the business proprietor is aware of the advance in timing of tax payments on incorporation (**7.17**).
- Ensure that a payment is made for stock on incorporation. This gives the option to elect for transfer at cost (**7.20**). If there is no payment, market value must be used (**7.22**).

Chapter 8

Capital Allowances

Plant and machinery

Writing down allowances

8.1   When a person acquires capital assets for use in his business, he will usually charge a depreciation allowance in the annual accounts. This is not an allowable deduction for tax purposes and will be added back in the tax computation. A comprehensive code of capital allowances governs the reliefs which are available for such expenditure.

8.2   So far as plant and machinery are concerned, a system of pooling is in place. In essence, all expenditure on such items is added together and any person carrying on a qualifying activity, which includes a trade, profession or vocation [*CAA 2001, s 15(1)*] may claim an allowance in calculating taxable profits. There are exceptions which, so far as relevant, will be mentioned below.

There is an enormous body of case law defining what is 'plant and machinery'. Detailed consideration of this is beyond the scope of the present work. However, it is assumed to include machinery and equipment, motor vehicles, fixtures and fittings in buildings etc., all of which might be employed by a business proprietor in carrying out profit generating activities.

Most expenditure will fall into the general or main pool [*CAA 2001, ss 53, 54(1)*]. Exclusions include:

- expensive cars;
- short life assets;
- plant or machinery used partly for purposes other than a qualifying activity;
- long life assets.

[*CAA 2001, s 54*].

There are, however, other minor ones.

The qualifying expenditure on which writing down allowances (WDA) may be claimed is the total of expenditure in the chargeable period less proceeds of any disposal plus unused expenditure brought forward.

8.3   A WDA at 25% is available on the pooled expenditure in the chargeable period. The allowance must be claimed [*CAA 2001, s 3*], usually in a tax return.

8.4 Capital Allowances

The claim does not have to be for the full amount of the allowance nominally available. A lower amount may be specified [*CAA 2001, s 55(5)*].

8.4 Note particularly that WDAs are given for a chargeable period, not a year of assessment or even an income tax basis period. The chargeable period for capital allowances may coincide with the income tax basis period but it does not have to. A chargeable period is for income tax purposes, a period of account or, for corporation tax purposes, an accounting period of the company [*CAA 2001, s 6*].

Where the chargeable period is longer than a year, the 25% allowance is proportionately increased. Where the chargeable period is less than a year, or the qualifying activity is only carried on during part of it, the allowance is proportionately reduced.

The concept of a chargeable period is very important on incorporation.

8.5 After deducting the WDA, the residue of available qualifying expenditure, usually known as the written down value, is carried forward to the next chargeable period.

8.6 'Expensive cars' [*CAA 2001, Part 2, Chapter 8*], now something of a misnomer as the limit is £12,000, are not pooled. They are dealt with singly. The writing down allowance is still 25% but limited to a maximum of £3,000 in any chargeable period.

8.7 Plant and machinery used for purposes other than a qualifying activity is also treated separately. This might typically be a car or van used by the proprietor of an unincorporated business for private travelling as well as for business use. The WDA is available as before at 25%, but the allowance so calculated is then apportioned between the private and business proportion, with a deduction taken in the tax computation for the business part only [*CAA 2001, s 207*]. At least in theory, the disallowed proportion might reflect not only private use but also personal choice. This follows the principle established in *G H Chambers (Northiam Farms) Ltd v Watmough (1956) 36 TC 711*. The author has not seen this point taken by an Inspector of Taxes for many years, though Inland Revenue *Capital Allowances Manual, para 2422* sets out the circumstances in which it might be considered.

8.8 Expenditure on short life assets (SLA) [*CAA 2001, Part 2, Chapter 9*] may, on election under *CAA 2001, s 85* made within two years of the end of the relevant chargeable period, be left out of the main pool. Instead, the expenditure goes to a separate SLA pool. WDAs may be claimed at 25% as before. 'Short life' is not actually defined, but there is no advantage in making an election if the asset will be held for more than four years. The rationale for doing it is to get an early balancing allowance on items expected to have a short useful life.

8.9 Expenditure on long life assets [*CAA 2001, Part 2, Chapter 10*] must also be excluded from the main pool where expenditure on this type of asset exceeds £100,000 in a chargeable period. Therefore, it is not commonly encountered in small businesses. A 'long life' asset is one with an anticipated economic life, when first brought into use, of 25 years or more. WDAs are at 6% only [*CAA 2001, s 102*].

First year allowances

8.10   Enhanced allowances for the year in which expenditure is first incurred have come and gone over a long period. Such allowances are currently available in a variety of forms to differing businesses provided that they are carrying on a qualifying activity [*CAA 2001, s 15(1)*]. A company can never get first year allowances (FYA) on a purchase from a connected party, notably in the current context, the proprietor of the former unincorporated business [*CAA 2001, s 217*].

8.11   Expenditure incurred by a small or medium-sized enterprise on most types of plant and machinery qualifies for FYA [*CAA 2001, s 44*]. 'Small or medium-sized enterprise' (SME) is defined by reference to *CA 1985, s 247* imported for this purpose by *CAA 2001, s 47*. Although it is a Companies Act definition, it applies here to all businesses whether incorporated or not. Broadly a small or medium-sized enterprise is a business which satisfies at least two of the following:

- turnover not exceeding £11.2m;
- assets not exceeding £5.6m;
- employees not exceeding 250.

In his 2003 Budget Speech, the Chancellor of the Exchequer said that he intended to align the definition of SME with that applying in Europe. That could mean an increased turnover limit of £20m, depending on the approval of the European Parliament in summer 2003. New UK legislation will then be required to extend the range of businesses qualifying for FYA.

The rate of allowance is currently 40% [*CAA 2001,s 52(3)*]. This is deducted from the first year qualifying expenditure before addition to the pool for later year WDAs.

Certain types of expenditure are excluded from availability for FYAs. A comprehensive list is contained in *CAA 2001, s 46*, but most notable are:

- motor cars (though see **8.14**);
- long life assets;
- assets previously used privately by the business proprietor;
- assets used for leasing.

8.12   Expenditure incurred by a small enterprise on information and communications technology qualified for FYA up to 31 March 2003. *Finance Act 2003, s 165* extends this by one year to 31 March 2004. Again, a *Companies*

Act definition is imported to define 'small', but applies equally to a company or an unincorporated business. For this purpose, a small enterprise must satisfy at least two of the following:

- turnover not exceeding £2.8m;
- assets not exceeding £1.4m;
- employees not exceeding 50.

The position is not clear though these limits could well be increased in line with the general definition of SME (see **8.11** above). A business that is just above the present limits might wish to defer this type of expenditure until late 2003 to see whether a full tax write off of costs may be possible.

Information and communications technology expenditure is defined in *CAA 2001, s 45* and includes:

- computers and associated equipment which will include peripheral devices for computers (printers, scanners etc.), equipment for providing a data connection between computers and dedicated electrical systems for computers;
- other qualifying equipment, including WAP telephones, third generation mobile telephones and devices designed to be used for receiving and transmitting information to and from data networks by being connected to a television set or similar device;
- software for the purposes of the equipment in the first two bullet points above.

The rate of allowance is 100%, i.e. a total write off of the expenditure in the year in which it is incurred.

8.13   Expenditure incurred by any business on providing energy saving plant or machinery is eligible for FYA [*CAA 2001, s 45A*]. Qualifying expenditure is on plant and machinery of a type specified by Treasury Order [*CAA 2001, s 45A(3)*]. A list of items currently qualifying is contained in an Energy Technology Product List issued jointly by the Department for the Environment, Food & Rural Affairs (DEFRA) and the Inland Revenue. Initially, it has been limited to items within the following technology classes: boilers, combined heat and power, lighting, motors and drive, pipework insulation, refrigeration and thermal screens.

The 2003 Budget announced that, from 1 April 2003, similar relief is available for expenditure on designated plant and machinery to reduce water consumption and improve water quality. The *Finance Act* reference is unclear but it seems to fall within *FA 2003, s 167, Sch 30*.

The simplest way to establish whether a particular product qualifies is to look at the list on the enhanced capital allowances website at www.eca.gov.uk.

The rate of allowance is 100% [*CAA 2001 s 52(3)*].

8.14 Expenditure incurred by any business on acquiring low emission motor cars between 17 April 2002 and 31 March 2008 qualifies for FYA [*FA 2002, s 59, Sch 19*]. A 'low emission' car is one emitting 120 grams per kilometre (g/km) of carbon dioxide (CO_2) or less. The number of cars available on the market meeting this fairly exacting criterion is increasingly rapidly. A reasonable choice is now available and it is a factor which should be seriously considered in providing a vehicle for business use.

The rate of allowance is 100% [*FA 2002, Sch 19 para 5*].

8.15 In all cases, a claim for FYA is required and, as with WDAs, can be for a specified sum less than the full amount due [*CAA 2001, s 52(4)*].

Cessation of qualifying activity

8.16 Neither WDA nor FYA are available in the final chargeable period.

The final chargeable period is (for the main pool or long-life asset pool) the chargeable period in which the qualifying activity is permanently discontinued [*CAA 2001, s 65(1)*].

WDA is prohibited by *CAA 2001, s 55(4)*.

FYA is prohibited by *CAA 2001, s 46(2) General Exclusion 1*.

Remember that a company is a totally separate entity from its proprietor. Incorporation therefore involves cessation of the trade carried on by a sole trader or partnership and the commencement of a trade in the company. Any thoughts of continuation must be discounted. We are moving from an income tax environment to a corporation tax environment. Immediately before incorporation therefore there is a chargeable period in which the trade is permanently discontinued for capital allowance purposes, and some WDA or FYA may be lost.

8.17 In virtually every case, the new company will be connected with the proprietors of the unincorporated business. In most cases, the company's shareholders and directors will be identical to the sole trader or business partners. Connection follows under *ICTA 1988, s 839 (6), (7)*. Thoughts of capital gains tax might naively lead to the conclusion that market value should be brought into account. That may, or may not, be correct. The disposal value of plant and machinery is to be interpreted in accordance with the table in *CAA 2001, s 61*. This bears careful consideration because there may be important planning advantages.

The result, almost incidentally, is that there will be a balancing allowance or balancing charge. A balancing allowance occurs when the disposal value is less than the written down value of the pool [*CAA 2001, s 55(2)*] and is given as a deduction in the income tax computation in a similar fashion to a WDA or FYA.

A balancing charge occurs when the disposal value is more than the written down value of the pool [*CAA 2001, s 55(3)*] and is treated as an addition to profit.

Incorporation by share issue

8.18   We have not yet dealt with capital gains tax, but the main incorporation relief for the purposes of this tax requires that the whole business is transferred to a company in exchange for an issue of shares by the company.

In this case, the shares passing one way are consideration for the assets passing the other. As this is a connected party transaction, the shares must have a value equal to the market value of the assets transferred in. In effect therefore market value has been paid for the plant and machinery.

The effect of this can be demonstrated:

Example 8.18

Tim draws up accounts to 31 March. He incorporates on 31 December 2003. The written down value of the plant and machinery on 31 March 2003 was £8,000. A new machine was bought for £2,000 on 1 November 2003. The market value of all items in the pool at 31 December 2003 was £9,000. The company sold a machine for £200 on 1 March 2004 and replaced it with a new one costing £3,000.

Sole Trader

WDV b/f 31/3/03		£8,000
Addition (no FYA as trade discontinued in period)		2,000
		10,000
Market value 31/12/03		(9,000)
Balancing allowance		£1,000

Company

Market value 31/12/03		9,000
Sale		(200)
		8,800
WDA 25% × 3/12		(550)
		8,250
Addition	3,000	
FYA 40%	(1,200)	1,800
WDV c/f 31/3/04		10,250
Total allowances: Sole trader and company		£2,750

8.19 The parties do not necessarily have to suffer the balancing allowance or charge. Instead the transferor and transferee (the previous sole trader and the company) may make a joint election under *CAA 2001, s 266* that the plant and machinery are transferred at a price which gives rise to neither a balancing allowance nor a balancing charge. So what does that really mean? It has been suggested (including by some that ought to know better) that the computation proceeds as follows:

Example 8.19

The facts are as in Example 8.18 but a joint election is made under *CAA 2001, s 266*. There is an *incorrect* presumption that Tim gets writing down allowances in the final period of trading.

Sole Trader

WDV b/f 31/3/03		£8,000
Addition (no FYA as trade discontinued in period)		2,000
		10,000
WDA 25% × 9/12		(1,875)
WDV c/f 31/12/03		8,125

Company

WDV b/f 31/12/03		8,125
Sale		(200)
		7,925
WDA 25% × 3/12		(495)
		7,430
Addition	3,000	
FYA 40%	(1,200)	1,800
WDV c/f 31/3/04		9,230
Total allowances: Sole trader and company		£3,570

In other words, there has been an attempt to give a writing down allowance right up to the date of incorporation. This is wrong.

8.20 There is nothing in *CAA 2001, s 267* to override the rules in *CAA 2001, ss 46, 55* that prohibit a WDA or FYA in the final chargeable period. And the trade of the former sole trader *is* discontinued at the point of incorporation. So, the plant and machinery is actually transferred at the tax written down value at the *start* of the final period of account of the sole trade. The true capital allowance position is thus:

Example 8.20

The facts are as in Example 8.18 but a joint election is made under *CAA 2001, s 266*. Correctly, Tim gets no writing down allowances in the final period of trading.

8.21   *Capital Allowances*

Sole Trader

WDV b/f 31/3/03	£8,000
Addition (no FYA as trade discontinued in period)	2,000
WDV c/f 31/12/03	10,000

Company

WDV b/f 31/12/03		10,000
Sale		(200)
		9,800
WDA 25% × 3/12		(613)
		9,187
Addition	3,000	
	(1,200)	1,800
FYA 40%		
WDV c/f 31/3/04		10,987
Total allowances: Sole trader and company		£1,813

So, in the circumstances given, the true allowances are only about half what the naive might have thought. Indeed, it would be better not to make the election under *CAA 2001, s 266* at all since the available allowances are actually reduced. Yet, it is surprising how many advisers elect for transfer at written down value as a matter of course without giving it a second thought.

Timing of incorporation

8.21   The absence of any capital allowances at all in the final period of account means that great care should be taken in selecting the date on which to incorporate. In Example 8.20, there is a nine-month period of account in which Tim gets no capital allowances. A tidy minded adviser may favour incorporation at the traditional accounting date and make a *CAA 2001, s 266* election 'because it's easier'. So, Tim gets no capital allowances in the last period when, perhaps, there are substantial profits taxed at 40%. The pay off, of course, is that the company gets a higher writing down allowance in its first period of trade but it pays tax at only 19%. Is this good planning, especially if the client bought a large piece of equipment just before incorporation in anticipation of first year allowances to mitigate the tax on the profits? When there might be 100% FYA on computer equipment or a low emission car one needs to be very careful that this is not prejudiced by the act of incorporation. Pre-incorporation planning must encompass the effect on capital allowances.

8.22   Remember that capital allowances are given for a period of account (not a year of assessment). Where accounts have traditionally been drawn up to 31 March, incorporation on that date will mean the loss of FYA or WDA for a full accounting period. How about incorporating at 30 April instead? The final period of account in which no capital allowances can be given is therefore only one month – a far more acceptable proposition. The author is often asked how short the final period might be. In theory at least perhaps as little as a day, though this might be unduly provocative to the Inspector of Taxes. A month is probably realistic.

8.23 It has been suggested that, as an alternative, accounts could be drawn up to just before the date of the incorporation, say 28 February in the examples considered here, then further accounts drawn up at the date of the incorporation (31 March). The first would be a change of accounting date and would have to meet the various conditions of *TA 1988, s 62A*. The second would presumably be a compulsory end of basis period, so it would not have to meet the conditions. If the tax return is filed with the notice of change of accounting date in it, the date is effective unless the Revenue objects within 60 days of receiving the return, even if it is done for tax-avoidance reasons within five years of a previous change. It appears unusual for the Revenue to create a time limit that would count against it so heavily, especially as it seems a time limit that it would be unlikely to meet.

A better way?

8.24 If capital allowances are important on incorporation, and it has to be said that major savings can be made this way, then there is a better way to do it.

All of the foregoing flows from incorporation by the *TCGA 1992, s 162* route. There is an alternative. This is to ignore the incorporation relief in that section and go for the alternative afforded by *TCGA 1992, s 165*. This relates to a gift of business assets though payment of some proceeds is possible and has been popular in the last few years with business proprietors keen to 'bank' retirement relief. An election under *CAA 2001, s 266* is still possible if this means of incorporation is preferred and it would leave us in the position demonstrated by Example 8.20.

8.25 Instead though, the company should actually pay the sole trader for the plant and machinery. Where there are actual proceeds, then they are taken as the disposal value under *CAA 2001, s 61(2), Table Item 1*. Market value is not substituted even where the vendor and purchaser are connected. So, Tim could sell his plant and machinery to the company for, say, £200. This gives a large balancing allowance relievable against final year profits taxable at 40% with an immediate reduction in the liability:

Example 8.25

The facts are as in Example 8.18 but plant and machinery are sold to the company for £200.

8.26   *Capital Allowances*

Sole Trader

WDV b/f 31/3/03	£8,000
Addition (no FYA as trade discontinued in period)	2,000
	10,000
Sales proceeds	(200)
Balancing allowance	9,800

Company

Purchase price		200
Sale		(200)
		nil
WDA 25% × 3/12		(nil)
		nil
Addition	3,000	
	(1,200)	1,800
FYA 40%		
WDV c/f 31/3/04		1,800
Total allowances: Sole trader and company		£11,000

The trade off is that the company has precious little expenditure on which to claim allowances but then its profits are taxed solely at 19%. So there is a permanent saving of 21% of the balancing allowance as well as a cash flow advantage.

8.26   Many people seem surprised at the assertion that *Item 1* of the table in *CAA 2001, s 61* is appropriate. They point to *Item 2* which begins 'sale of plant or machinery where the sale is at less than market value' which is undoubtedly the case here and there follows an automatic presumption that market value must prevail so that a large balancing allowance is not possible. This is incorrect. *Item 1* can be overridden by *Item 2*, but only where the specified conditions are met:

'sale of the plant or machinery where –

(a) the sale is at less than market value,
(b) there is no charge to tax under ITEPA 2003, and
(c) the condition in sub section (4)[of s 61] is met by the buyer.

[then the disposal value is] the market value of the plant or machinery at the time of sale.'

(a) is satisfied, as is (b). So, do we meet the condition in sub section (4)? This is:

'The condition referred to in *item 2* of the table is met by the buyer if –
the buyer's expenditure on the acquisition of the plant or machinery cannot be qualifying expenditure under this part or part 6 (research and development allowances) or

the buyer is a dual resident investing company which is connected with the seller.'

This condition is not met (watch the double negative) because the company's expenditure is qualifying expenditure for the purposes of capital allowances on plant and machinery. So, market value cannot be substituted for the actual proceeds.

All of this is confirmed in the Inland Revenue *Capital Allowances Manual* at *para 23250*.

Note: there must be some proceeds even if only £1 or so. If there are no proceeds at all, so there is a pure gift, then market value prevails [*CAA 2001, s 61(2), Table Item 7*].

8.27 It is perhaps inevitable that the variables do not end there. An alternative to Example 8.25 might be to forego the advantages of a large balancing allowance (if we are considering a very small business with an income tax rate of 22%, it is very comparable to the small companies corporation tax rate of 19%). If the plant and machinery were to be sold to the company at market value (say, £16,000 left outstanding on loan account), the choices are:

- no election under *CAA 2001, s 266*: balancing charge on vendor of £6,000, capital allowances to purchaser on £16,000, loan account £16,000;
- election under *CAA 2001, s 266*: no balancing charge or allowance on vendor, capital allowances to purchaser on £10,000, loan account £16,000.

The ability to elect to transfer at written down value, even though the loan account is based on market value (which must be justifiable, of course), seems very favourable.

The proprietor can then draw down on the loan account at a later date without further tax charge.

8.28 A final word of caution. Do not attempt these price manipulations in order to get preferential balancing allowances with any sort of plant and machinery. It generally only works with the main pool.

8.29 If an expensive car is transferred between connected persons (within *ICTA 1988, s 839* for this purpose) then the combined effect of *CAA 2001, ss 79, 213* appears to be to introduce market value to the transaction. This was certainly the case with the former *CAA 1990, s 34(4)*, though the wording of the new legislation would seem to require market value on any transaction (whether between connected persons or not). Therefore, if an expensive car is transferred on incorporation there will be a balancing allowance or balancing charge for the unincorporated business calculated by reference to the market value (or first cost if lower); the company gets future WDAs based on that market value.

8.30   If, before the four year cut off date for short life asset treatment, an asset subject to such an election is transferred to a connected person, the vendor and purchaser may make an election. The effect of this fresh election under *CAA 2001, s 89(6)* is that the original SLA election continues with the purchaser and the transfer is deemed to take place at tax written down value. If no such election is made, the purchaser is still treated as having made the original SLA election with its original terminal date – see *CAA 2001, s 89(4)*. The transfer is treated as taking place at the lower of original cost or market value. Thus, unless the market value of any SLA item is below original cost (and written down value), no balancing allowance arises.

Industrial buildings

8.31   Very broadly, an industrial building is a building or structure used for the purposes of a qualifying trade [*CAA 2001, s 271*]. A qualifying trade is defined in *CAA 2001, s 274* and generally amounts to productive manufacturing or processing though some ancillary activities, and one or two oddities, are included.

Also included is a qualifying hotel [*CAA 2001, s 79*]. Broadly, this must have accommodation in a permanent building, be open for at least four months in the period April to October, have at least ten bedrooms available for letting and provide services which include breakfast and an evening meal.

8.32   The schemes of allowance have varied over the years but currently an annual allowance of 4% is available to a person who incurs expenditure on a qualifying building [*CAA 2001, ss 309, 310*]. The allowance continues on a straight line basis for 25 years from the date on which the building was first used. Enhanced allowances are still available in enterprise zones and previous initial allowances may have reduced the expenditure further than would otherwise be apparent. A claim is required and this may be for a lesser amount than the full allowance which is available.

8.33   The allowance available is in respect of the actual cost of constructing a building. The claimant must have a relevant interest in the building [*CAA 2001, s 286*]. This will usually be the freehold or a long lease. There are rules for dealing with the situation where the building was originally constructed by a property developer and is then acquired by the end user. Broadly the relevant interest is the same interest in the property which was held by the person originally incurring the expenditure. However, where a long lease (greater than 50 years) is granted over the building, both lessor and lessee may jointly elect that the lease becomes the relevant interest for the purposes of industrial buildings allowances (IBAs) [*CAA 2001, ss 290, 291*].

8.34   As with plant and machinery, WDAs for industrial buildings are given for a chargeable period. This is broadly a period of account and WDA can be proportionately increased or decreased for a period longer or shorter than twelve months. Apart from the conditions stated earlier, a building must be in use at the end of the period as an industrial building [*CAA 2001, s 309*].

8.35 Unlike plant and machinery, there is no requirement that the claimant should be carrying on a qualifying activity. Basically, all that is needed is:

- qualifying expenditure on a building;
- ownership of the relevant interest;
- the building to be in use as an industrial building.

Therefore, the person holding the relevant interest need not necessarily be the occupier and user of the building. This is important on incorporation.

8.36 IBAs are generally allowed as an expense in arriving at the profits of the trade, where the owner of the relevant interest occupies the building [*CAA 2001, s 352*]. If the owner of the relevant interest lets someone else use the building, then the IBAs are set against the rents received in establishing the profit of a Schedule A business [*CAA 2001, s 353*].

Position on incorporation

8.37 A sole trader or partnership using an industrial building (or qualifying hotel) will get WDAs on qualifying expenditure. Because of the rules set out above, those WDAs need not cease when the trade of the unincorporated business ends.

A balancing adjustment for IBAs is only required on the happening of a balancing event [*CAA 2001, s 314*]. The main balancing events are:

- sale of the relevant interest;
- if the relevant interest is a lease, the ending of the lease except where the person entitled to it acquires the reversionary interest;
- the building is demolished or destroyed;
- the building ceases altogether to be used.

[*CAA 2001, s 315*].

8.38 On incorporation, we are primarily concerned with the sale (or not) of the building to a company. This should not be taken as a foregone conclusion. In some incorporations, the whole assets of the business will go to the company. However, it is far from uncommon that buildings are retained outside. Three alternatives therefore arise:

- the building is sold to the company;
- the building is retained by one (or more) business proprietors and a long lease is granted to the company;
- the building is retained by the proprietors and a short lease or mere licence to occupy is granted to the company.

8.39   Where there is a sale of the relevant interest, proceeds from the balancing event will primarily be the proceeds of sale [*CAA 2001, s 316, Table Item 1*]. Where the parties to the transaction are connected, which will almost invariably be the case on incorporation, market value is substituted [*CAA 2001, ss 567, 568*]. If the transfer should be by way of gift, then market value is imposed [*CAA 2001, s 573*]. For this purpose, the sale proceeds or market value cannot exceed the first cost of the building; where they do, the capital gains tax position must be considered.

Accordingly, a balancing adjustment is calculated. Where the (deemed) proceeds exceed the residue of qualifying expenditure, this will be a balancing charge to be added to the profits of the unincorporated business. Where the proceeds are less than the residue, a balancing allowance is given as an expense [*CAA 2001, s 318*]. A further adjustment may be necessary if the building has not been an industrial building throughout its life.

8.40   The position of the purchaser (the company) is somewhat different. It will take on the residue of qualifying expenditure which is effectively the amount of the sale proceeds. WDAs are available to it, calculated by apportioning this amount rateably over the remaining chargeable periods to the 25th anniversary of first use of the building [*CAA 2001, ss 311, 313*].

8.41   The vendor and purchaser may override the need for a balancing adjustment by joint election under *CAA 2001, s 569* that the transaction be deemed to take place at a value equal to the residue of qualifying expenditure at that time. Such an election must be made within two years of the end of the chargeable period.

8.42   Where the former business proprietor retains the relevant interest in the industrial building, he may grant a long lease (greater than 50 years) to the company. The prime position remains that IBAs stay with the owner. Prima facie no balancing adjustment is required. However, the parties may jointly elect that the relevant interest should pass with the leasehold interest [*CAA 2001, s 290*]. The effect is to treat the grant of the long lease as if it were a sale of the relevant interest and like consequences flow as in **8.39–8.40** above.

8.43   Where the former business proprietor retains the relevant interest and a long lease is not granted, then the rights to IBAs remain with him. Consideration must then be given to payment of rent (see **14.23** et seq and **15.49**).

8.44   Because of a general imposition of market value to the transaction, the scope for tax planning with IBAs is more limited. However, dependent on respective values and the likely profits at the end of the sole trade and beginning of the corporate trade, some modest advantage may be taken by choosing between market value or written down value where an industrial building is transferred to the company.

Agricultural buildings

8.45   An agricultural building is a building such as a farmhouse, farm building or cottage, fence or other works [*CAA 2001, s 361*].

Where expenditure is incurred by a person having a freehold or leasehold interest in land in the UK occupied for the purposes of husbandry in constructing such a building, then agricultural buildings allowances (ABA) may be available [*CAA 2001, ss 361, 362*].

8.46   Currently, an allowance of 4% is available. This is given on a straight line basis for chargeable periods throughout a 25-year period starting on the first day of the chargeable period in which the expenditure was incurred [*CAA 2001, ss 372, 373*]. A claimant may reduce his claim for ABA to an amount less than that nominally available.

8.47   As with IBAs, the claimant of ABAs must have a relevant interest in land. This is usually the freehold or leasehold interest held when the expenditure was incurred. Qualifying expenditure will normally be the cost of constructing a building though, again, there are rules for dealing with buildings bought unused [*CAA 2001, s 370*].

As with IBAs, and unlike plant and machinery, there is no requirement that the owner of the relevant interest should also occupy and use the building. What is needed is:

- qualifying expenditure on a building;
- ownership of the relevant interest;
- the building being used and occupied as an agricultural building.

8.48   Where it is the owner of the relevant interest who occupies and uses the building, ABAs are generally allowed as an expense in arriving at the profits of trade. If the building is let, then the owner of the relevant interest will generally set ABAs against the rents received in establishing the profit of a Schedule A business.

Position on incorporation

8.49   As previously noted for IBAs, some incorporations will proceed with the transfer of all assets of the business including the buildings. Equally, many do not and the buildings are held outside the company. This leaves two choices for ABAs:

- the building is sold to the company;
- the building is retained and let or informally licensed to the company.

8.50   Unlike IBAs, a balancing adjustment does not automatically arise on the sale of the relevant interest in an agricultural building. The basic position is that the residue of allowances simply passes to the purchaser [*CAA 2001, s 375*]. That is to say, the former business proprietor gets WDAs up to the date of incorporation. The company gets WDAs of the same amount for the remainder of the chargeable periods throughout the original 25-year life of the building. If the incorporation takes place in the middle of a chargeable period, the allowance is apportioned for that period between the transferor and transferee.

8.51   There can be a balancing event, but only where both parties to the transaction specifically elect for one. The timing of such election is odd because it may be different for the two parties. For income tax purposes, it must be given on or before the normal time limit for amending a tax return for the tax year in which the relevant chargeable period ends. For corporation tax purposes, it must be given no later than two years after the end of the relevant chargeable period [*CAA 2001, s 382*]. In that event, a balancing adjustment arises for the vendor where the proceeds (equal to market value, or first cost if lower, since the parties are connected) is less than the residue of qualifying expenditure or a balancing charge where the proceeds are greater than the residue of qualifying expenditure. The acquiring company may write off its expenditure (i.e. the amount used in the computation of the balancing adjustment) over the remainder of the writing down period.

Election for a balancing adjustment for ABAs is very unusual but, depending on valuations and profits, some modest advantage might be obtained on incorporation.

8.52   Where a former business proprietor retains the relevant interest in the business, the rights to ABAs remain with him. Consideration must then be given to payment of rent (see **14.23** et seq and **15.49**).

Planning points

- WDA and FYA on plant and machinery are not available in the final chargeable period of the unincorporated business (**8.16**).
- Election for transfer of plant and machinery at written down value does not override the general rule on WDA and FYA (**8.20**).
- Choose a date for incorporation that minimises the loss of allowances (**8.22, 8.23**).
- Consider selling plant and machinery to the company for a price which gives a predictable balancing allowance (**8.25, 8.27**).

Chapter 9

Capital Gains Tax

9.1 This really is a 'begin at the beginning' chapter. What is a business? There is no satisfactory definition in the Taxes Acts. At *Capital Gains Manual paras 65712–65715*, the Inland Revenue analyses some court decisions and concludes that a business is somewhat wider than a trade. However, the passive holding of investments or an investment property would not be a business.

Going further back to basics and, having tried several dictionaries, the best on offer was:

- one's occupation or affairs;
- what keeps one busy or concerns one;
- trade, profession or occupation.

None of which really help. The author therefore offers his own definition:

> Business (n) – a collection of assets, actively managed with a view to deriving income therefrom.

The important bit here is the assets. There cannot be many businesses (any at all?) which do not need assets of some kind in order to operate.

If we have a sole trader, he will own them personally. If we have a partnership, they will either be:

- Partnership property (in which case, in England and Wales at least, each partner will be deemed to own his proportionate share in them). See Inland Revenue *SP D12* as regards the CGT treatment of partnership assets; or
- Held by one partner outside the business and rented to, or informally licensed to, the partners.

When the business is incorporated, the assets must be transferred to the company. If they are not, how will the company carry on the business? It may not be necessary to transfer all the assets but if some are left outside, a degree of flexibility may be lost in the incorporation process. The position of assets held outside the company is covered in detail in **Chapter 14**.

Chargeable assets to transfer

9.2 What assets might the business own? There could be stock, tools and equipment, land and buildings, goodwill and investments. If it has been going for some time, there will also be work in progress and debtors.

Therefore we have got to get some or all of these into the company. And what does the *Taxation of Chargeable Gains Act* tell us in this context: 'All forms of property shall be assets for the purposes of this Act'.

There are exempt assets, of course, but we will not go into a detailed exposition here.

The fundamental point is that, in all but the smallest businesses, there will be CGT considerations on the transfer of a business to a company. It is surprising how many people do not think about this.

The position of stock is generally dealt with under income tax rules (see **7.18–7.24**).

Many items of tools and equipment (including motor vehicles), fixtures and fittings in buildings etc. will have attracted capital allowances as plant and machinery. Income tax adjustments will be necessary (see **8.16–8.17**). This does not stop assets of this type being chargeable to CGT (though chattels having a value of £6,000 or less and motor cars are exempt [*TCGA 1992, ss 262, 263*]). However, *TCGA 1992, s 37* excludes from the CGT computation any consideration taken into account as a receipt in computing income. An actual gain in respect of this type of asset will therefore only arise where it is transferred for a value greater than original cost (which will be rare).

There may be income tax consequences to certain buildings too (hotels, industrial buildings and agricultural buildings – again see **8.37–8.42**, **8.49–8.51**) but, in most instances, we need to consider the CGT aspects on transfer of land and buildings.

Goodwill. Ah – goodwill! What is it? Can it be transferred? This is a subject in itself (see **14.4–14.10**). Don't forget that, in many instances, it will not appear on the balance sheet of an unincorporated business. Ensure that it is of a type which is transferable.

Deferred gains

9.3 Capital gains are generally realised on the disposal of assets. But what if the gain does not relate to the (current) disposal of an asset? Is this a riddle you ask yourself? Well, no not really – just a nasty trap for the unwary.

9.4 There are various instances in the *Taxation of Chargeable Gains Act* where tax on realised gains may be deferred until the happening of some later event. The one of especial significance here concerns a particular form of rollover relief.

The basics of rollover relief are addressed at **14.11–14.19**. In the present context though, note especially **14.18–14.19**. A gain realised on the disposal of one asset, which has been used in a trade, may be deferred against the acquisition of a second asset where the new asset is a wasting asset, also used in a trade [*TCGA 1992, s 154*]. In that case, no adjustment is made to the base cost of the second asset. The gain on the first asset is calculated according to normal rules and simply deferred until the earliest of:

- the disposal of asset number two;
- the cessation of use of asset number two in a trade;
- the expiry of ten years from the acquisition of asset number two.

If an asset carrying a deferred gain is transferred to a company on incorporation, that will be a disposal. The original deferred gain comes back into charge. And, there is nothing you can do about it. None of the reliefs examined below cope with this.

The deferred gain now chargeable arose on an earlier disposal and cannot be expunged by the incorporation reliefs. The tax will be due and payable.

9.5   So, in your preparations to incorporate a business, always check whether there have been previous claims to rollover chargeable gains on business assets within the last ten years. Especially note whether any such gains were merely deferred and not 'properly' rolled.

Sale proceeds

9.6   Back to basics again. The transfer of assets from an unincorporated business to a company is a disposal for the purposes of CGT.

Further, it is a disposal between connected persons. For this purpose, a company is connected with another person, if that person has control of it or if that person and persons connected with him together have control of it [*TCGA 1992, s 286(6)*].

It will be extremely rare that the proprietors of the former unincorporated business are different to the controlling shareholders of a company. In most instances they will be identical.

Where there are transactions between connected persons, the rules of *TCGA 1992, s 18* prevail, in particular that the transaction is to be treated as a bargain not made at arm's length. This in turn brings *TCGA 1992, s 17* into play, to the extent that:

- the consideration for the business proprietor(s) disposal of the assets is to be treated as their market value;
- the company's corresponding acquisition value is also to be treated as market value.

[*TCGA 1992, s 17(1)*].

So, for the purposes of the CGT computation, the chargeable assets of a business are treated as passing at market value.

9.7 However, the actual consideration may be:

- shares in the company, which may be of more than one class;
- loan stock in the form of a debenture or similar though, in the writer's experience of small private companies, this is rare;
- cash, often left outstanding on a director's loan account;
- nothing, it being quite common to gift the assets of a business to the company.

9.8 If there were to be a large chargeable gain, with tax payable, this would amount to a significant disincentive to incorporation. Various reliefs exist to alleviate this problem and the rest of this chapter explores them:

- the first is in *TCGA 1992, s 162* headed 'Rollover Relief on Transfer of Business';
- the second is in *TCGA 1992, s 165* headed 'Relief for Gifts of Business Assets'.

These two are the most used and, as will be seen, the latter is more flexible. Do not forget, however, the EIS CGT deferral relief in *TCGA 1992, Sch 5B*, sometimes referred to as 'The Third Way'.

9.9 Finally, to play devil's advocate, given the flurry of activity to incorporate many very small businesses, do we need a CGT incorporation relief at all? Would taper relief and the annual exemption alone be enough?

Relief in section 162

9.10 The prime incorporation relief is contained in *TCGA 1992, s 162* headed 'Rollover Relief on Transfer of Business'. The relief is mandatory if specified conditions are met and does not require a claim. *Subsection (2)* simply says that [the cost of the new assets, i.e. the company shares] shall be deducted from the chargeable gain. Correspondingly, *subsection (3)* gives the base cost of the new assets as reduced by the amount left out of the CGT computation on incorporation. There are provisions for apportionment where the consideration is not wholly in shares.

9.11 The relief applies where three conditions are satisfied:

- that a person who is not a company (i.e. sole trader, partner) transfers to a company a business as a going concern,
- together with the whole assets of the business, possibly excluding cash, and
- the business is so transferred wholly or partly in exchange for shares issued by the company to the person transferring the business.

[*TCGA 1992 s 162(1)*].

The relief is therefore very specific. All of the assets of the business (apart from cash which is, of course, not a chargeable asset) must be transferred to the company and this must be done wholly or partly in exchange for shares. In fact, cash is not the only item which may be left out. Inland Revenue *ESC D32* indicates that relief under s 162 is not precluded by the fact that some or all of the liabilities of the business are not taken over by the company.

It may be a fine distinction but does cash mean cash? Does it extend to bank accounts? The author has seen evidence to suggest that the Inland Revenue may seek to challenge the relief under *s 162* where a bank account is omitted from the transaction. Such a fear seems unfounded as the Inland Revenue *Capital Gains Manual at para 65719* does mention cash 'including sums held by the business in a bank deposit or current account'.

Notwithstanding this comfort, to prevent such a challenge, would it be wise to clear out and close unwanted bank accounts before the incorporation transaction proceeds?

Note also that the shares must be issued to the transferor (of the business). This is not the time to do remuneration or inheritance tax planning. It is not uncommon that a sole trader, on incorporation, wishes the spouse to take shares in the new company. To ensure that relief under *s 162* is obtained, the shares should be issued to the business proprietor who might later transfer some to the spouse. Failure to do this would seem to preclude relief.

On the face of it, so far, it all seems simple enough.

9.12

Example 9.12

Janine decides to incorporate her retail gift shop. A very simplified balance sheet shows the assets to be stock £30,000, shop premises £100,000 (cost £80,000) and goodwill £20,000 (cost nil). The entire business is transferred to a newly formed company Super Gifts Ltd and 1,000 ordinary £1 shares are issued to her.

(a) The market value of the 1,000 shares is £150,000 being the total value of the assets transferred in (market value applies as this is a connected persons transaction).

(b) The consideration (shares issued) is apportioned in a just and reasonable manner, thus:

Stock	£30,000
Shop premises	£100,000
Goodwill	£20,000

(c) The chargeable gains are:

9.13   *Capital Gains Tax*

Shop, consideration	100,000	
Less: Cost	(80,000)	20,000
Goodwill, consideration	20,000	
Less: Cost	nil	20,000
Total gain		£40,000

The whole of this gain will be rolled over under *s 162*.

(d) The CGT base cost of the shares, for a future computation on disposal is:

Market value	150,000
Less: Gain rolled over *s 162*	(40,000)
Base cost	£110,000

9.13   However, it may not always be this easy.

Quite possibly on the day of incorporation neither the business proprietor nor any of his advisers will know what is the value of the business assets to be transferred. In Example 9.12 above, we are assuming that 1,000 ordinary £1 shares are issued at a premium of £149 each. Equally, the company could have issued 150,000 shares at par or any variation in between the two extremes. Private companies often try to keep the share capital relatively low. Combine this with the unknown value of the assets going in and it is inevitable that a share premium will arise. Consider then that incorporation is the date of contract and completion is when all valuations etc. are complete and the final book entries can be made.

Date of contract? What contract? Far too often, a transaction of this type is purported to have taken place but there is often no evidence that it actually has. To avoid a challenge by the Inspector of Taxes and the risk of a taxable gain, as well as to demonstrate title to the assets on a later sale, a document of transfer is strongly advised (see **11.31**).

9.14   Do not be fooled into thinking that the gain will always be fully relieved. The business must be transferred as a going concern and must therefore reflect liabilities to be satisfied by the company. An undertaking to satisfy these liabilities amounts to further consideration. *ESC D32* prevents the assumption of liabilities from being treated as consideration for the purposes of the *s 162* computation. However, this does not mean that the liabilities can be ignored in determining the market value of the assets transferred. Where the liabilities are relatively high, the net asset value of the business (which equals the value of the shares issued) may be low. If the chargeable assets have large inherent capital gains (watch for goodwill off the balance sheet) then it may be impossible to roll all of the gain – the base cost of the shares cannot go below zero.

Example 9.14

Colin is a sole trader publican at the Railway Tavern. The balance sheet is thus:

Freehold property	300,000
Fixtures and fittings	25,000
Stock	25,000
	350,000
Less: Bank loan	(225,000)
Creditors	(50,000)
	£75,000
Represented by:	
Capital account	£75,000

The property originally cost £200,000 and there is goodwill off balance sheet of £75,000 for which Colin paid nothing.

He forms the Railway Tavern Ltd and 1,000 ordinary £1 shares are issued to him.

(a) The market value of the shares issued is £150,000 being the total net value of the assets transferred in.

(b) The chargeable gains are:

Property:	Consideration (market value)	300,000	
	Less: Cost	(200,000)	100,000
Goodwill:	Consideration (market value)	75,000	
	Less: Cost	nil	75,000
			175,000
Less:	Rolled over under *s 162*		(150,000)
Chargeable gain			£25,000

Subject to taper relief and annual exemption, this gain is immediately taxable.

(c) The CGT base cost of the shares is:

Market value	150,000
Less: Gain rolled over *s 162*	(150,000)
	£nil

So, we can get a situation where all the assets are transferred, only shares are issued and yet a chargeable gain still arises.

9.15   The consideration given is commonly entirely represented by an issue of shares. They may be ordinary shares, or there could be some preference shares. It is increasingly common that the ordinary share class is split into A shares, B shares, C shares etc and this is to facilitate later remuneration planning, but a degree of circumspection should be taken with this approach. The potential problems of an unusual share structure are covered at **16.60–16.64**.

111

The author has even seen suggested that some of the shares might be redeemable. The idea is to realise smaller gains (which might be covered by losses, taper relief and the annual exemption) on redemption of the shares in small tranches in later years. This would seem to be tempting fate and an almost certain charge under the anti-avoidance provisions of *ICTA 1988, s 703* et seq. A clearance application under *s 707* is strongly advised if this route is contemplated.

9.16   Occasionally, though, other consideration might be taken. This could be in the form of loan stock issued by the company or more simply the creation of a director's loan account with a credit balance. In these circumstances, the gain which may be rolled over is limited to:

the fraction A/B of the amount of the gain on the old assets where:

- A is the cost of the new assets (shares); and
- B is the value of the whole consideration received by the transferor in exchange for the business.

[*TCGA 1992, s 162(4)*].

Example 9.16

Linda runs a grocery business as a sole trader and decides to incorporate. The net asset value of her business is as follows:

Freehold property	200,000	(cost 100,000)
Fixtures and fittings	4,000	(cost 10,000)
Stock	6,000	(cost 6,000)
Goodwill	30,000	(cost nil)
Debtor	5,000	
	245,000	
Less: Trade creditors	(20,000)	
	£225,000	

Linda transfers the business to The Corner Shop Ltd which issues 1,000 ordinary £1 shares to her and a director's loan account of £40,000 is created.

(a) The market value of the shares issued is £185,000 being the net asset value of the business transferred in, less the loan account.
(b) The chargeable gains are:

Property:	Consideration	200,000	
	Less: Cost	(100,000)	100,000
Goodwill:	Consideration	30,000	
	Less: Cost	nil	30,000
			130,000

Amount rolled over under *s 162*

A/B × 130,000 =

$\dfrac{185,000 \times 130,000 =}{225,000}$ (106,889)

Chargeable gain   £23,111

Subject to taper relief and annual exemption.

(c) The CGT base cost of the shares is:

Market value	185,000
Less: Gain rolled over *s 162*	(106,889)
	£78,111

9.17   The application of *s 162* is somewhat intractable. First, because it requires the transfer of all the business assets (with very limited exceptions) to the company. Second, most of the inherent value of the business is locked into the share capital of the company and cannot readily be extracted.

Could we therefore extract something from the business before the incorporation, or be more careful in the consideration we choose?

Some commentators recommend that, if there is a substantial capital account in the unincorporated business, then the proprietors should be advised to draw down on it before incorporation. Presumably such a capital account is there in the first place in order to fund continuing trading operations. If this is the case, then there is every likelihood that the funds withdrawn will be reintroduced into the company shortly afterwards by means of a credit to a director's loan account.

Perceived challenges to this process are often said to stem from *Furniss v Dawson [1984] STC 153*, in that the transactions are preordained and the intermediate one has no real purpose. The net effect of which is to re-characterise the transaction as if the business had been transferred for a consideration partly in the issue of shares and partly in cash (as in **9.16**). A counter-argument might be demonstrated by the incorporation agreement (we do have one, don't we? – see **9.13**) showing the intention to transfer the entire assets of the business in return for shares. In which case, the withdrawal of cash from the capital account must be part of the net business assets and is therefore now encapsulated in the share capital.

Could a similar challenge stem from the principle in *W T Ramsay Ltd v IRC [1981] STC 174*, notably that there is a circular series of transactions leaving the business in the same position as before it started? It is better not to risk it by being too provocative.

A major asset retained from the business (commonly property) certainly prejudices the application of *s 162*. What about a minor one though? It is not unusual that a business proprietor would wish to retain personal ownership of a private car outside the company. Although used in the business, it may not have been on the balance sheet anyway. Though the author has never encountered it, some evidence is reported that certain Inspectors of Taxes have tried it on as a reason to deny *s 162* relief. Of course, it may be necessary to remove and retain part of the pre-incorporation capital account, for example to meet the tax liabilities of the unincorporated business. Provided that the final accounts of the unincorporated business have made full provision for outstanding tax liabilities, this should not be a problem.

9.18   A better solution might be to think more carefully about the consideration to be given by the company. If it is entirely the issue of shares, then the whole gain on the transfer of the business assets is (usually) deferred but then their full value is locked into the company. If some other consideration is given, there will be a chargeable gain, but does it need to be a taxable gain? Let's go back to Example 9.16 and rework it.

Example 9.18

The facts are as before in Example 9.16.

The net asset value of Linda's business is £225,000.

The gross chargeable gains are £130,000.

Would Linda be better advised to create a loan account of £54,000 as well as taking 1,000 ordinary shares?

(a) The market value of the shares is £171,000 being the net asset value of the business transferred in, less the loan account.

(b) Chargeable gains (gross), as before   130,000

Amount rolled over under *s 162*

A/B × 130,000 =

$$\frac{171,000 \times 130,000}{225,000} = \qquad (98,800)$$

Chargeable gain	31,200
Business asset taper relief (75%)	(23,400)
	7,800
Annual exemption (to cover)	(7,800)
Taxable gain	£nil

Linda has therefore created a director's loan account of £54,000 on which she is later free to draw with no additional tax liability.

(c) The CGT base cost of the shares is:

Market value	171,000
Less: Gain rolled over *s 162*	(98,800)
	£72,200

This is only £5,911 below Example 9.16 but Linda has an additional credit of £14,000 to her loan account.

9.19 Historically then, when following the *s 162* route to incorporation, the consideration given by the company might have been an issue by the company of its own shares and nothing else. At the present time, we need to think more creatively. If there is some non-share consideration, then a chargeable gain may arise but, if there is no tax due, then we have another way of taking tax free profits from the company.

Indeed, do we want the relief in *s 162* at all? The Government seems to think that we might not.

Override in Finance Act 2002

9.20 As we have already seen, the prime CGT incorporation relief in *s 162* is mandatory. No claim is required. If the individual making the disposal of chargeable assets to the company meets the conditions laid down, then the relief is given.

The only exception to this was retirement relief (now repealed) which was also available without claim where the relevant conditions were satisfied. On incorporation, the Inland Revenue accepted that where both retirement relief and incorporation relief were due then retirement relief took precedence. This had the advantage of giving the proprietor a tax free uplift in the base cost of the shares due to the availability of retirement relief. In all other instances, incorporation relief had to be taken. As we have seen, this makes the relief somewhat intractable. If, for some reason, the relief was not required then the transferor would need to take deliberate action to breach the conditions for its application.

9.21 Things have changed from 6 April 2002. *FA 2002, s 49* introduced a new *TCGA 1992, s 162A* which permits a specific claim to disapply *s 162*. The reason for this is a perceived anomaly with taper relief though changes to taper at the same time lead one to question just how serious an anomaly that would be for the future.

The perceived problem was that, where *s 162* applies on incorporation, the chargeable gain on the business assets transferred to the company is deducted from the cost of the shares. As we have seen above (**9.12**) that cost is actually their market value. Taper relief on the other hand is a deduction from the chargeable gain. As there is no chargeable gain in these circumstances (because it is deducted from the cost of the shares) it follows that entitlement to taper relief on the assets transferred to the company is lost.

The shares in the company issued on incorporation are a new asset and the qualifying holding period for taper relief must begin again. If these shares are sold shortly after incorporation then any previously earned entitlement to business asset taper relief on the assets transferred would be lost. It is questionable just how serious a problem this now is as the qualifying holding period for maximum business asset taper relief was also reduced by *FA 2002, s 146* to just two years.

The circumstance of selling a business within two years after incorporation is probably quite rare, unless the incorporation was a deliberate manoeuvre to facilitate its disposal. The problem is therefore more perceived than real. Whatever the rights and wrongs, the facility to disapply *s 162* is now in place.

9.22   The basic position is still that *s 162* applies without claim. If it is to be overridden, then the business proprietor making the disposal to the company must make a claim usually by the second anniversary of 31 January following the year of assessment in which the disposal took place. This is shortened to the first anniversary if the shares are sold before the end of the year following incorporation. If the business was transferred from a partnership to a company, each individual partner may separately choose whether or not to make a claim under *s 165A* [*TCGA 1992, s 165A(3), (4), (7)*].

The effect of the election is that the gain on disposal of business assets to the company is calculated in the usual way, taking the benefit of taper relief. There is no deferral and tax is payable on the net gain. The base cost of the shares issued on incorporation is therefore market value. Presumably a disposal within two years will not show a huge gain so that the tax payable on a share disposal would be minimal. Clearly the alternatives should be explored before incorporation if it is thought likely that an early sale will occur. A comparative example is offered at **19.6–19.8**.

9.23   If there will be no sale until more than two years from incorporation, maximum business asset taper relief still becomes due. In that event, it is probably better to take *s 162* deferral and taper the gain on the share disposal but, so far as one's crystal ball can predict future events, a comparison of examples ought to be considered.

9.24   If, having made a claim under *s 162A*, there is a transfer of shares between spouses, that is ignored. The sale of shares by the recipient spouse is treated as made by the donor spouse [*TCGA 1992, s 162A(5)*].

Relief in section 165

9.25   Many incorporations use instead the relief in *TCGA 1992, s 165* headed 'Relief for Gifts of Business Assets'. From the outset, this is something of a misnomer; it does not simply apply to gifts. It would be better termed a relief for transfers at under value, but this does not have quite the same ring to it.

9.26   A business asset for this purpose is defined in *subsection 2*. Most of the categories set out there are irrelevant here, but it does include:

- An asset, or interest in, an asset used for the purposes of a trade, profession or vocation carried on by the transferor.

[*TCGA 1992, s 165(2)(a)(i)*].

Any chargeable asset used in a sole trade or partnership by the asset owner is therefore encompassed.

9.27   The relief applies where the asset owner disposes of it by a bargain which is not at arm's length [*TCGA 1992, s 165(1)(a)*]. We have already established (see **9.6**) that the transfer of assets from an unincorporated business proprietor to the company will be such because it is a connected party transaction.

9.28   What follows is that:

- a chargeable gain otherwise arising is reduced by the 'held over gain'; and
- the amount of the company's CGT base cost is also reduced by the held over gain.

[*TCGA 1992, s 165(4)*].

The held over gain will be demonstrated by example shortly.

9.29   Unlike *s 162*, application of which is mandatory in the relevant circumstances, a specific claim is required for the gift relief to apply [*TCGA 1992, s 165(1)(b)*]. The claim must be made jointly by both the individual making the transfer and the company. The Inland Revenue require the claim to be made on the form contained in helpsheet *IR295* to the self assessment tax return. No shorter time limit is specified, so the general time limit of five years following 31 January following the year of assessment in which the transfer takes place applies. In practice, claims will always be made long before this, otherwise CGT on the gain would become payable.

9.30   Note that *s 165* contains no requirement that the transfer shall be the whole of the business or even all of the assets used in the business. It is simply 'an asset' used in a trade, profession or vocation. Thus it is totally flexible and we can cherry pick which assets a *s 165* claim might apply to. Indeed, we can select certain assets from the unincorporated business and pass them to the company, leaving others behind. A *section 165* claim is quite in order to cover the gains on those transferred. So we have a flexibility which is absent from the *s 162* process.

9.31   The amount of the gain which can be held over is:

- in the case of a pure gift (no proceeds at all), the gain which would otherwise arise in deeming the proceeds to be market value [*TCGA 1992, s 165(6)*], or

- in the case of a transfer at under value, the amount by which the deemed gain exceeds the excess of the actual consideration over the costs deductible in the CGT computation [*TCGA 1992, s 165(7)*].

For the most part, CGT computations in this chapter ignore the indexation allowance in *TCGA 1992, s 53*. Here we must not. The costs deductible are those given by *TCGA 1992, s 38* only and, therefore, specifically exclude indexation.

Example 9.31

Paul runs a golfing supplies business. He decides to incorporate it but wishes to retain a number of assets personally. He will however transfer to the company the business premises now valued at £180,000. The CGT base cost is £75,000.

(a) Capital gain arising:

Consideration (market value)	180,000
Less: Cost	(75,000)
	£105,000

(b) If Paul gifts the property to the company the whole of the gain is held over.

The base cost of the property for the company is:

Market value	180,000
Less: Held over gain	(105,000)
Base cost for future disposal	£75,000

(c) If Paul sells the property to the company for £50,000.

Actual proceeds	50,000
Less: Allowable cost	(75,000)
Excess	£nil

The result is as in (b) above. This is probably not a realistic option as Paul is missing the opportunity to take a further £25,000 tax free; the proceeds might as well be £75,000 – the result is similar.

(d) If Paul sells the property to the company for £125,000.

Actual proceeds	125,000
Less: Allowable cost	(75,000)
Excess	£50,000
Gross gain	105,000
Less: Excess	(50,000)
Gain held over	£55,000

The excess is also the chargeable gain subject to taper relief and annual exemption.

The base cost of the property for the company is:

Market value	180,000
Less: Held over gain	(55,000)
Base cost for future disposal	£125,000

9.32   Unlike *s 162*, there is no fixed process to follow. A typical scheme might therefore be:

- Form the company (or acquire a shelf company) and issue shares by cash subscription. Typically, the number of shares will be small.
- Sometime later, on incorporation, transfer the required assets to the company either by pure gift or by sale for proceeds of a personally determined amount. Note that the company's undertaking to satisfy any liabilities of the unincorporated business will amount to proceeds for this purpose.
- At the outset, the company is unlikely to have substantial cash, so the proceeds are often left outstanding on loan account.
- Sometime later, when the company is trading profitably, the proprietor may draw down from the loan account effectively taking the proceeds without further tax cost.

9.33   There is perhaps less need in these circumstances for a formal incorporation agreement (which is essential for the *s 162* process). Any property transfer will be evidenced by a conveyance. However, because of its intangible nature, there ought to be a document evidencing the transfer of goodwill. Do not forget also that other items, such as stock and plant and machinery attracting capital allowances, may need to be sold to the company at particular prices. All in all, some sort of document is still a sensible requirement.

What section 165 cannot do

9.34   This may seem obvious but, before you claim a CGT relief, make sure that you have a capital gain.

9.35   If you have a creative artist, author, playwright, composer etc., any sum received for exploitation of their talent is deemed to be income, even if there is a total disposal of the copyright.

If you try to incorporate such a profession by the route in *s 162*, then the deemed market value payment will be chargeable to income tax. This flows from the decision in *MacKenzie v Arnold (1952) 33 TC 363* which established that all receipts from copyright, even lump sums for total disposal, are income. Further *Mason v Innes (1967) 44 TC 326* established that an author has no stock so market value cannot be imputed for income tax purposes on a gift of copyright. At this point, you may be thinking that it sounds ripe for a *s 165* claim on a gift of assets to a company.

Enter the new rules for intangible assets in *FA 2002, Sch 29*. In particular *para 92* deems a transfer of intangible assets between related parties as taking place at market value where one of the parties is a company. So a gift of copyright now takes place at market value, leading back to the original income tax charge. It follows that there is no chargeable gain because the proceeds charged to income tax will be excluded by *TCGA 1992, s 37* and the *s 165* claim is impossible. Fortunately, though, this is limited to copyrights created on or after 1 April 2002.

Section 162 and section 165 compared

Section 162

9.36
1. Mandatory. If certain conditions are satisfied the relief is given automatically.
2. Requires a fixed method of incorporation:
   * form company, issue a few shares;
   * transfer entire business and assets to company;
   * company issues more shares (and loan/cash) to the transferor of the business as consideration.
3. CGT base cost of shares – market value less gain rolled over.
4. Base cost of assets in company – market value. Incorporation was a connected party transaction; *s 162* depresses the share base cost, not that of the assets.
5. Can be overridden by a claim under *s 162A*. Partners in a partnership can separately choose to make this claim or not.
6. Value of assets locked into share capital of company unless cash/loan note issued. Amount which can be withdrawn relatively low.
7. Other assets, such as debtors, must go into the company.
8. Permits the carry forward of losses under *ICTA 1988, s 386* (see **3.14**).

Section 165

9.37
1. Optional. Claim required.
2. Method of incorporation more flexible:
   * form company, issue required number of shares;
   * transfer only assets required to company;
   * company may pay for assets; price flexible.
3. CGT base cost of shares – subscription price, minimal.
4. Base cost of assets in company – market value less gain held over.

5. Claim may cover all assets or selected ones. Partners in partnership may make different claims to suit personal circumstances.
6. Shareholder/director free to draw on loan account created as consideration for asset transfer. The amount may be quite high.
7. Debtors may be left out of company. Care though if creditors exceed debtors and both are excluded from the transfer. The company's satisfaction of the creditors amounts to consideration for other assets transferred.
8. Cannot carry forward losses under *ICTA 1988, s 386* (see **3.14**).

Mix and match?

9.38   For the most part, there is a straight choice between incorporation by the *s 162* route or the *s 165* route. There is no right or wrong answer. All the circumstances of the business, its asset values etc. must be considered along with the future intentions of the proprietors. An appropriate decision must be made.

Whilst *s 162* is the prime incorporation relief, it is probably true to say that, at the present time, it is less used. *Section 165* is preferred because of the greater flexibility which it affords. The only real downside risk to the use of *s 165* is a possible challenge by the Inspector of Taxes as regards the apportionment of consideration. Whilst this may have been agreed by the vendor and the company, it is not binding on the Inland Revenue. It will cover not only chargeable assets but also items such as stock, plant and machinery etc. There may be very valid tax planning reasons for the figures attributed to various items. Success is more likely with a proper documentary record of the transactions, which is less open to challenge than an unrecorded global figure of proceeds intended to cover all items and arbitrarily split at a later date.

9.39   What you cannot do is to pick the best bits of *s 162* and *s 165* and use them both. We have seen that there may be circumstances in which *s 162* can leave a residual chargeable gain. This is not eligible for a claim under *s 165* because there are actual market value proceeds (the shares). Equally, there was a well known pitfall where retirement relief applied to the gain but an amount was left in charge. The rules for retirement relief and gift relief did not necessarily coincide so, again, a taxable gain could be left. This latter problem disappeared with the repeal of retirement relief.

Enterprise Investment Scheme

9.40   We have compared and contrasted the CGT reliefs in *TCGA 1992, s 162* and *s 165*. Are there any other opportunities in the CGT legislation to defer realised gains? Yes, of course: at least two. There is a general relief for gifts in *s 260* but this only applies where there is a charge to inheritance tax. This does not seem to have any relevance to incorporation.

What about reinvestment relief under *TCGA 1992, Sch 5B* though? Do not confuse this 'new' relief with reinvestment relief under the former *s 164A–N*. The current relief is related to investments in EIS companies and is perhaps better referred to as deferral relief. Could we make use of this?

Why not? Indeed, as mentioned earlier, some refer to it as 'The Third Way'.

9.41   It has to be said that the EIS legislation, both for the income tax relief in *ICTA 1988, Part VII, Chapter III* and the CGT reliefs in *TCGA 1992, s 150A–C* and *Sch 5B* is extraordinarily complicated. It does not help that the income tax provisions are similar, but not identical, to the CGT provisions. There are pitfalls aplenty and anyone seeking to use these reliefs should exercise great care. Even if a qualifying investment is successfully made, there is plenty of scope for things to go wrong after the event due to a plethora of anti-avoidance rules. In the writer's experience, the Inland Revenue will operate the legislation in such a manner as to seek to deny relief rather than offering an unwary investor the benefit of the doubt. Detailed analysis of the EIS reliefs is beyond the scope of this work.

9.42   Looking solely at CGT deferral, where an investor:

- subscribes in cash for new ordinary shares which are fully paid up;
- in a qualifying company which carries on a qualifying trade; and
- the company uses the money received in a trade within specified time limits,

[*TCGA 1992, Sch 5B para 1(2)*],

then a capital gain realised by the investor may be reduced by the amount of the investment (or a smaller amount specified in a claim) [*TCGA 1992, Sch 5B para 2(1)*].

Additionally, the investment must be made within a period beginning twelve months before and ending three years after the realisation of the original gain on (generally) disposal of an asset [*TCGA 1992, Sch 5B para 1(3), (1)(b)*].

The shares must be issued for bona fide commercial purposes and not as part of arrangements the main purpose, or one of the main purposes, of which is the avoidance of tax [*TCGA 1992, Sch 5B para 1(2)(d)*].

Subscribe for shares – qualifying trading company? Sounds like an incorporation. Can we make use of it?

9.43   With care, possibly. The route must be:

- Form the company and issue a small number of shares for cash. It is preferable that the initial shareholder is not (one of) the proprietor(s) of the business to be incorporated. This is for complex technical reasons which might lead the share issue to be regarded as a bonus or rights issue and not a new subscription.

- The business proprietor then enters into an agreement to sell the assets of the business to the company for cash. The deal must be at market value realising a chargeable gain. It is preferable that the company borrows money to do this, rather than have the proceeds left outstanding on loan account.
- The business proprietor then uses all or part of the cash consideration to subscribe for new ordinary shares in the company and claims deferral relief under the provisions of *TCGA 1992, Sch 5B*. It is important that cash must change hands to avoid falling foul of the anti-avoidance provisions in *Sch 5B para 13*. Further, the second and third steps above must not be combined. The shares must be subscribed for in cash – linking the steps would mean an asset/share exchange and the relief would not be due.
- The amount subscribed must be sufficient to cover the gross gain (i.e. pre-taper relief) on disposal of the original business assets. However, should the deferred gain come back into charge a deduction of taper relief (by reference to the original disposal) is permitted.

9.44   It is not necessary that the company acquires all the assets of the unincorporated business. The company simply has to use the subscription monies in its trade. The business proprietor would appear to have the best of all worlds. He can:

- retain selected assets;
- defer all gains on assets transferred to the company; and
- get taper relief on those assets even if the company and/or business is sold within two years after incorporation.

9.45   As an added bonus, income tax relief at 20% may be available on the subscription for shares provided that the subscription does not exceed £150,000 and the investor is not connected with the company (very broadly, does not own more than 30% of the issued ordinary share capital or voting rights). Admittedly, this will rule out income tax relief in many cases, though it could be an advantage on incorporation of a business with at least four otherwise unconnected proprietors. There is no test of connection for CGT deferral, so that more than 30% of the shares can be held by a proprietor if this is the only relief desired.

9.46   The qualifying company must exist wholly for the purposes of carrying on a trade [*ICTA 1988, s 293*] and there are limitations on the nature of the trade [*ICTA 1988, s 297*]. All relevant conditions must be satisfied until the termination date, usually three years from the date of the investment or the commencement of trade in the company if later [*TCGA 1992, Sch 5B para 19(1)* and *ICTA 1988, s 312(1)*]. If the conditions fail, the deferred gain becomes chargeable immediately.

Otherwise, the deferred gain is only chargeable on a disposal of the shares.

9.47   This section must end with a huge health warning! This is not necessarily a tried and tested route and the Inspector of Taxes could argue that the rather circular series of transactions is part of a scheme for the avoidance of tax. There is an advance clearance procedure, largely for establishing the qualifying nature of the company, though one could try to seek comment on the actual investment. Oh – and the EIS legislation is complex – if you think you understand it, you probably don't.

Taper relief

9.48 Who wants a specific CGT relief for incorporation at all? Probably only larger businesses, especially those with land and buildings to transfer.

Many smaller businesses heading for incorporation at the present time will not have significant chargeable assets in their businesses. If they operate from home or leasehold premises, the only possible chargeable asset is likely to be goodwill.

9.49 And a 'mate down the pub' is quite likely to have told the proprietor not only about the income tax savings of incorporation but also 'you can get £30,000 out tax free'.

Example 9.49

The logic behind this story goes:

Value of goodwill in business	30,000
(Sold to company for proceeds outstanding on director's loan account)	
Business asset taper relief @ 75%	(22,500)
Chargeable gain	7,500
CGT annual exemption (to cover)	(7,500)
Taxable gain	£nil

As the company trades profitably, draw down on the loan account. Result £30,000 tax free.

And the flaws in this argument?

- You cannot just put a 'value' on goodwill at £30,000. The number of stories around suggesting this possibility are frankly alarming. It must be properly valued by reference to the results of the business (see **14.8** and Inland Revenue Capital Gains Manual para 68520 et seq).
- The goodwill may not be transferable at all. For many small businesses, it will largely be personal to the proprietor (see **14.7**).

It is true that many small businesses will not need the reliefs in either *s 162* or *s 165*. Taper relief is enough. But the automatic creation of a tax free 'goodwill payment' is no more than a myth.

Footnote

9.50   The examples in this chapter ignore:

- the possibility that, for long-standing businesses, the CGT base cost of the assets is probably their market value on 31 March 1982 and not the original cost;
- (except where specifically stated) the availability of indexation relief for assets held pre-6 April 1998.

Further, the salient features of taper relief as they might affect the incorporation of a business and the shares in a newly incorporated company are covered in **Chapter 18**.

Planning points

- Watch for deferred gains on a previous rollover claim. Incorporation will bring these back into charge (**9.4**).
- Ensure *s 162* incorporation is evidenced by contract (**9.13**).
- Note shares in *s 162* incorporation must be issued only to the transferor(s) of the business assets (**9.11**).
- Watch for residual gains in *s 162* incorporation where there are large inherent gains and the balance sheet value is depressed by creditors (**9.14**).
- Consider part proceeds in cash in *s 162* incorporation to facilitate tax free withdrawal of funds (**9.18**).
- *Section 165* incorporation can be used to create a loan account on which to draw tax free (**9.31, 9.32**).
- Be wary in attempting to use EIS deferral. It is not tried and tested and full of pitfalls (**9.40–9.47**).
- Do small businesses need incorporation relief at all? (**9.48**).

Chapter 10

Stamp Duty

Basics

10.1   Stamp duty is an archaic, perhaps even arcane, tax. Maybe this is because its fundamental principles are still enshrined in legislation which is more than 100 years old, namely the *Stamp Act 1891*. However, it should be borne in mind that fundamental changes are on the way (see **10.26**). As these are likely to improve the situation for incorporations where there is no land transfer involved, it may be worthwhile delaying until the new rules are effective if a large stamp duty liability is otherwise foreseen.

As it stands, stamp duty is not a tax levied on profits, income or gains. It is not even a tax on transactions. Stamp duty is charged on 'instruments', broadly defined as documents, transferring title to property. It is a tax on documents [*SA 1891, s 122(1)*]. Legal title to certain types of property (e.g. freehold or leasehold land, goodwill, shares, creditors, debtors etc.) can usually only be transferred with a written document. Other property may be transferred by delivery (e.g. goods, plant and machinery etc.). In these cases, care needs to be taken that the title to such goods is not transferred by written document (and therefore liable to stamp duty). Subject to certification, stamp duty is not due on genuine gifts. There is no general market value rule (see **10.6**).

10.2   Stamp duty is administered by the Commissioners of the Inland Revenue within a unit known as Inland Revenue (Stamp Taxes). Certain information is available from the Stamp Taxes section of the Inland Revenue website at www.inlandrevenue.gov.uk/so.

10.3   The tax is widely misunderstood and deserves especial care. Whilst incorporation of some businesses may be effected without a document, these are likely to be in a minority (and the transfer of land will always require a document). In most cases, there are powerful reasons why a formal document will be necessary (see **11.28–11.30**). The act of incorporation may therefore involve a payment of stamp duty. As rates have risen rapidly in the last few years, it deserves attention. Indeed, UK rates of stamp duty are still below those of comparable taxes in other EU countries and may be expected to rise further.

Rates of stamp duty

10.4   There are two main categories of duty:

- fixed duty of £5, payable on certain documents such as declarations of trust, conveyances or transfers other than on sale, duplicate instruments, surrenders not for a consideration [*FA 1999, s 112(2)*].
- ad valorem (proportionate to value) duties, primarily as follows:

Transfers of shares (whatever value) 0.5%

Conveyance or transfer on sale

Consideration	Current Rates
Less than £60,000	nil
£60,001 to £250,000	1%
£250,001 to £500,000	3%
Above £500,000	4%

[*FA 1999, Sch13 paras 3, 4*].

Under *Finance Act 2003, s 55*, with effect from 1 December 2003, the stamp duty zero rate band limit for non-residential property increases from £60,000 to £150,000.

From 10 April 2003, stamp duty will no longer be payable on certain non-residential property transactions in disadvantaged areas. Previously, there had been an exemption from duty on property transactions not exceeding £150,000 in such areas (this limit remains for residential properties). SP 1/2003 sets out detailed guidance on the relief.

Payment at a rate other than 4% depends on certification as to the amount of consideration (see **10.19**). There is a separate system of charging duty on the grant of a lease [*FA 1999, Sch 13 paras 10–15*] (see **10.24**).

In most instances, consideration is taken to be the figure specified in the document, though there is now an obvious exception in the case of land and buildings transferred to a connected company (see **10.13**). The fundamental principle is that, when the document is executed, the stamp duty is known. There is no adjustment should the actual amount paid prove to be greater or smaller. Should the document not specify an amount, then there are differing rules according to whether the consideration is ascertainable or unascertainable. A detailed analysis of these is beyond the scope of this work but it is worth noting that, where the consideration for land is unascertainable, it is taken to be the market value immediately before execution of the document [*FA 1994, s 242*].

10.5   Ad valorem rates apply to the whole consideration, which is why stamp duty is often referred to as a slab system tax. This can produce high marginal rates of tax if the consideration falls just above one of the cut off points.

Example 10.5

Jon purchases a house for	£240,000
Stamp duty payable @ 1% (subject to certification)	£2,400
Jon purchases a house for	£260,000
Stamp duty payable @ 3% (subject to certification)	£7,800
Additional consideration	£20,000
Additional stamp duty	£5,400
Effective marginal rate	27%

10.6   If the consideration is less than market value, in general stamp duty is only due on the actual consideration. There is a significant exception for land transferred to a connected company (see **10.13**). Care should be taken over what is the actual consideration. It may include, for example, the assumption of liabilities. So, if an asset subject to an outstanding loan is transferred to a company and the company undertakes to discharge the loan, the stampable consideration is the actual price paid plus the liability on the mortgage [*SA 1891, s 57*]. The consideration is inclusive of VAT even where the VAT may be recoverable.

Ad valorem stamp duty is rounded up to the nearest multiple of £5.

Why stamp a document?

10.7   Stamp duty is sometimes referred to as a voluntary tax. There is nothing in the legislation to force a document to be presented for stamping. A document is not invalid if it is not stamped. However, an unstamped document cannot be used as evidence in a civil court [*SA 1891, s 14(4)*]. It cannot be used before the Special or General Commissioners of the Inland Revenue. A company secretary, the registrar of companies and the Land Registry in particular will refuse to act upon an improperly stamped document. Sometimes there may be no immediate need for a stamped contract. This has led to the practice of leaving the matter resting in contract. If the contract is not completed, no stamp duty is due until it is completed. For the time being, this practice remains valid, unless the consideration exceeds £10m. In those circumstances, stamp duty is now payable on the exchange of contracts unless a transfer is presented for stamping within 90 days [*FA 2002, s 115*].

If there is never going to be a commercial need to complete the contract, which may be the case with incorporation of some small family businesses, then letting the transfer rest in contract indefinitely might be a reasonable strategy. Be wary though of factors that might change, for example, the sub-sale of land included in the original incorporation. Normally, there is a relief to prevent two successive charges to stamp duty. However, in *Peter Bone v IRC [1995] STC 921* a business was incorporated including land to be sold shortly afterwards by the company. The intention was that the land would not be transferred to the company, but the former business proprietors would transfer it direct by way of sub-sale to the third party purchaser. The arrangements were such as to give rise to a double charge to stamp duty. If such ruses are contemplated there is a case for clear specific advice.

Adjudication

10.8   Adjudication [*SA1891, s 12*] is a post transaction review process, whereby the Inland Revenue formally assesses the duty (if any). This is an internal process within the Stamp Office and will be either voluntary or, where required by the legislation, compulsory. It may also be the first part of an appeal procedure.

The normal practice is for an instrument to be presented to a Stamp Office where a marking clerk stamps it. If he or the person presenting the document disagrees with the amount of duty alleged, the document may be presented for adjudication.

Also, the taxpayer may request the Commissioners to express their opinion on any executed instrument to determine whether it is chargeable with any duty and, if so, the amount.

Note that, even if no duty is payable, a document may still need to be presented to the Stamp Office and stamped with the words 'Adjudged not chargeable with any stamp duty'. If duty is chargeable, the Commissioners assess the duty and the document will be stamped 'Adjudged duly stamped'.

In certain circumstances, instruments will not be duly stamped unless they have been adjudicated, e.g.:

- where exemption is claimed in relation to company reorganisations, transactions between associated companies, transfers or letting to a charity, conveyances and transfers in contemplation of a sale, or maintenance funds for historic buildings;
- where the consideration for sale is reduced to the value of the property conveyed in consideration of a debt;
- court orders under *CA 1985, s 427* (company reconstruction or amalgamation).

Administration

10.9   *FA 1999* changed the regime for interest charges on ad valorem duty and penalties for late stamping for documents executed after 1 October 1999. For documents executed in the UK, stamp duty is due within 30 days of execution. Generally this is the date of completion of the contract, not the date of exchange of contracts (contrast with capital gains tax: *TCGA 1992, s 28*). If documents are executed outside the UK, stamp duty is due 30 days after execution (unless the document does not relate to UK land) [*FA 2002, s114*]; this was previously within 30 days of the document being brought back into the UK [*SA 1891, s 15B*]. Interest will run from 30 days after execution of the document wherever executed [*SA 1891, s 15A*].

10.10   The maximum penalties for failure to stamp by the due date are:

- within one year – the lower of £300 and the duty payable;
- after one year – the greater of £300 and the duty payable.

[*SA 1891, s 15B*].

Penalties may be reduced if there are appropriate mitigating circumstances.

10.11   Interest is charged at the rate applicable under *TMA 1970, s 86*, i.e. the rate prevailing for overdue income tax and capital gains tax. The interest is rounded down to the nearest multiple of £5, is paid gross and is not an allowable deduction for tax purposes. Interest calculated at less than £25 is not payable.

Transfer of land to a company

10.12   There is no general market value rule in the stamp duty legislation. In most instances, a document will be stamped according to the actual consideration determined by the contract.

10.13   However, this rule does not apply where land and buildings are transferred to a company which is connected with the transferor. This will be the case with many incorporations where the business premises are introduced to the new company even by way of gift. Since 28 March 2000, duty on such transfers has been charged by reference to the market value of the land and buildings [*FA 2000, s 119*]. The rule for connection is found in *ICTA 1988, s 839*: a controlling holding will make the shareholder connected with the company (for example).

10.14   Where the incorporation is effected by the route afforded by *TCGA 1992, s 162*, market value has always been applied to the transfer. The shares issued in exchange for assets transferred into the company are consideration for those assets and the contract price is their market value. This means of incorporation has been perceived as expensive in stamp duty terms. Although there used to be a method of mitigating the stamp duty liability by 'swamping' the share capital, this is no longer effective [*FA 2000, s 118*].

10.15   On the other hand, where the incorporation relies on *TCGA 1992, s 165*, to mitigate any gains, the contract price may be determined between the parties. It was therefore perceived as a cheaper route from a stamp duty point of view. This is no longer the case where real property (i.e. land and buildings) is involved.

Example 10.15

Barry incorporates his newsagent business. The shop premises are transferred at a price of £200,000, the consideration being a credit balance on a director's loan account. The premises are actually worth £300,000.

Before *FA 2000*, stamp duty would be charged on the actual consideration:

£200,000 @ 1% (subject to certification)	£2,000
The *FA 2000* rules impose market value and the duty payable is now:	
£300,000 @ 3% (subject to certification)	£9,000

The duty payable has increased by a factor of 4.5. This route is no longer the cheap option for stamp duty.

10.16   While there may be some incorporations where the company has diverse shareholdings which will be outside the test in *ICTA 1988, s 839*, these are likely to be the exception rather than the rule.

Goodwill

10.17   The nature of goodwill is explored at **14.6–14.8** and examples in that chapter explore the possible difficulties of ignoring goodwill on incorporation. It is actually unusual to see goodwill appearing in the balance sheet of a sole trader or partnership business. Because of this, and the potential stamp duty liability, it is easy to see why it may not have been properly treated in the past.

The potential liability to stamp duty was actually a disincentive to achieving a proper valuation of goodwill on incorporation. Indeed, the issue was often 'overlooked'.

This problem has now gone away. Goodwill is no longer an asset liable to stamp duty in respect of instruments executed on or after 23 April 2002 [*FA 2002, s 116*].

Incorporation

10.18   At this point, it is perhaps instructive to look at a typical incorporation, best demonstrated by an example.

Example 10.18

Grant decides to incorporate his musical business. The balance sheet looks thus:

Freehold property		200,000
Goodwill		20,000
Stock		15,000
Book debts		25,000
Cash on deposit		10,000
Cash in current account		5,000
		275,000
Less: Secured creditors	10,000	
Trade creditors	5,000	(15,000)
		£260,000
Proprietor's capital account		£260,000

The whole business is transferred to a company in exchange for an issue of shares. What stamp duty is payable?

The total consideration is:

Market value	260,000
Plus: Liabilities assumed	15,000
	£275,000

How might the stamp duty payable of £7,650 (£255,000 @ 3%, subject to certification and taking out the goodwill) be mitigated? Stock can be transferred by delivery. Cash in a bank current account, by concession, does not attract duty. Provided the contract is correctly worded so that title does not pass by contract, these may be excluded.

Stampable consideration:		
Total (as above) less goodwill		255,000
Less: Cash in current account	5,000	
Stock	15,000	
		(20,000)
		£235,000
Stamp duty thereon at 1%		
(subject to certification)		£2,350

Where there is composite consideration, as in the above example, form Stamps 22 must be submitted to the Stamp Office giving details of the apportionment of the consideration between the assets subject to the contract.

10.19   Where the stampable consideration exceeds one of the break points of £60,000, £250,000 or £500,000 a Certificate of Value should be endorsed on the document so that duty is calculated at the lower percentage. Certification is a process whereby the document contains a statement to the effect that the consideration (including any other associated transactions) does not exceed the threshold for a higher rate of duty [*FA 1999, Sch 13 para 6*]. In the example above, the stampable proceeds of £255,000 would attract stamp duty at 3% but are reduced to £235,000 attracting duty at only 1%. Accordingly, in the example above, the document of transfer should contain a statement to the effect that the transaction does not exceed £250,000 and is not part of a series of transactions, of which the aggregate consideration exceeds that amount.

10.20   Where the consideration is an allotment of shares as above, form 88(2) submitted to the Registrar must be accompanied by a stamped transfer agreement.

10.21   The incorporation process afforded by *TCGA 1992, s 162*, is somewhat intractable as regards stamp duty but there may be occasions on which it is to be preferred. The solution then might lie in the use of an unlimited company. In principle, the position remains the same but with one important difference. An unlimited company is not required to file form 88(2) with Companies House showing the allotment of shares. The incorporation could therefore rest in contract. The company is subsequently re-registered as a limited company, but there is still no need to file form 88(2) on share allotment. The scheme relies on a fine technical distinction and should not be attempted without expert legal advice.

10.22   A better solution, and this is almost always to be favoured, is to incorporate via *TCGA 1992, s 165*, and keep the dutiable consideration to a minimum. This might include:

- the company acting as agent to collect debtors and pay creditors for the unincorporated business (rather than accepting transfer of them);
- retaining land and buildings in personal ownership, though other factors will affect this decision (see **14.1**);
- transferring other dutiable assets at undervalue.

Leases

10.23   Where property is, for any reason, retained outside the company then rent may be paid (see **15.47**). In most cases, this will be informal without the need for a lease.

10.24   If, however, a new lease is granted, stamp duty will be charged on both the premium payable, if any, and also on the average yearly rent payable at the special rates shown below.

Length of term of lease	Rates of stamp duty chargeable on average rent (incl. of VAT if appropriate)

1. Indefinite or not more than 7 years
  (a) Rent £5,000 or less
  (b) Rent more than £5,000
	nil
	1%

2. More than 7 but less than 35 years	2%
3. More than 35 but less than 100 years	12%
4. More than 100 years	24%

There are special rules for furnished lettings.

Under *Finance Act 2003, s 56, Sch 5*, and with effect from 1 December 2003, the existing charge applying to leases will be replaced with a single 1% charge. This will be applied to the net present value of all rental payments due under the lease where this exceeds £60,000 for residential property or £150,000 for non-residential property.

10.25 It should also be noted that *FA 2002, s 121* has a similar effect for leases as does *s 119* when there is an actual transfer of the land and buildings. Where a lease is granted to a company and the lessor of the property is connected with it, there may be deemed to be payable a market value premium. Clearly care is necessary in arranging payments of rent in respect of property held outside the company; a formal lease may incur stamp duty.

Modernising stamp duty – consultative document

10.26 After the 2002 Budget announced substantial revisions to stamp duty, a lengthy consultation document was issued. Subsequently, following the November 2002 pre-Budget report, the Inland Revenue has published draft legislation for what has been called 'Modernised Stamp Duty' ('the new tax'). Press notices issued after the 2003 Budget suggest that implementation will take effect from 1 December 2003 and that it will be called 'stamp duty land tax'. The legislation is now contained in *Finance Act 2003*.

There will be a new self-contained statutory framework for the new tax, which will be very different from the existing stamp duty regime. Whilst stamp duty is a tax on documents, the new tax is a tax on transactions (and not on documents). There will be an administrative framework which requires taxpayers to submit returns, self assess, keep records and be prepared for a Revenue enquiry into returns submitted. Unlike the present one, there will be no adjudication procedure.

The administrative framework will be based on the self assessment regime for income tax and corporation tax.

The new tax will apply to all transactions in respect of interests in and rights over UK land and buildings and will be triggered by the payment of substantive consideration (whether on contract or at completion). This will include transactions in indirect holdings (so called special purpose vehicles) and the new tax will apply regardless of whether or not the transactions are effected inside or outside the UK.

The new tax will not apply to transfers of goodwill (which are already exempted from stamp duty with effect from 23 April 2002). Nor will it apply to transfers of debts. Shares and securities will continue to be subject to stamp duty reserve tax (SDRT) and to stamp duty as it currently applies.

The consideration for a transaction (upon which the new tax will be calculated) will include all consideration in money or money's worth (the definition for SDRT), which is rather wider in scope than currently.

Where the consideration is unascertainable, for example if part of the consideration payable is dependent on the happening of a future event, e.g. the grant of planning permission etc., the new tax regime will require a 'best estimate' to be made. The new tax payable, at least initially, will be based on this. Once the actual sums are paid, the original tax can be adjusted and either additional tax paid or a repayment of tax made. There will also be provision to pay tax by instalments in circumstances where final payment may not be received for more than 18 months.

The new rules make it clear that it is the 'purchaser' who is responsible for the return of notifiable transactions and the payment of any tax due, including new rules for interest and penalties for incorrect returns. This contrasts with the present position (which generally does not signify the chargeable person) where stamp duty is often thought of as a 'voluntary' tax albeit with interest and penalties for late payment.

The combined effect of the existing exemptions and the new proposals should ensure that stamp duty has much less of an impact on the process of incorporation, except where this involves transfer of land and buildings to the new company. The device of resting in contract will no longer be possible to defer the liability to stamp duty.

Planning points

- Remember, no document: no stamp duty. Transfer title to assets by delivery, not contract, where possible (**10.1**).
- Incorporation by the route afforded under *TCGA 1992, s 165* is more flexible than *s 162* (**10.21, 10.22**).
- Leave assets outside the company to reduce stamp duty (**10.22**) but do consider other tax effects.
- Bear in mind the impact of the new regime, to take effect at the end of 2003 (**10.26**).

Chapter 11

Legalities

Company formation

11.1   A distinction has to be drawn between a business and a company. There is often confusion between the two.

A business is an activity – the management of assets with a view to deriving profit. It may be carried on through one of several media, by various persons. These were reviewed in **Chapter 2** and a company is one of those persons. A company may carry on a business, but the two terms are not interchangeable.

11.2   The formation of a company may be termed incorporation (possibly correctly so). However, it is not the incorporation of a business. A newly created company is, in effect, an empty box. To avoid confusion, creation of a company is referred to here as 'formation'. Some further action is necessary to transfer the business (trade, profession or vocation) into the company and thereby incorporate it.

Companies can be either public (i.e. PLC) or private (i.e. Ltd). In this book we are concerned almost exclusively with private companies. The formation of PLCs requires specialist advice.

11.3   The first step then is to form the company. *CA 1985, s 10* requires the filing of documents and a fee (£20 as at April 2003) with the Registrar of Companies. There are three main registries in the UK, one each in England and Wales, Scotland and Northern Ireland, with several branches. Northern Ireland has its own companies legislation which is not considered in this book. Collectively these are referred to as Companies House.

11.4   The first document is a company Memorandum. The minimum requirements for this [*CA 1985, s 2*] are:

- the company name;
- the company domicile, i.e. where was it registered: England and Wales, Scotland or Northern Ireland;
- its objects and powers, the purpose for incorporation;
- a statement that the liability of the members is limited;
- the amount of the authorised share capital.

11.5   The next document required is the Articles of Association. These are the rules which govern the manner in which the directors and shareholders are to act. The default is Table A of the *Companies (Tables A–F) Regulations 1985 SI 1985/805* which is, in effect, a model set of Articles.

11.6   The third document is form 10, which is the application to form a company and includes:

- The company name. Note that there are certain restrictions on words which may be used in the name and it may not be the same as, or very similar to, the name of a company which is already in existence. Prior to the registration of a company, it is wise to check the index of names maintained by the Registrar of companies to ensure that the name required is not already in use.
- The names and addresses of the directors, together with their business occupation, nationality, date of birth and details of other directorships held. A company may have only one director, but he cannot also be the company secretary [*CA 1985, s 283(2)*].
- The name and address of the company secretary. *CA 1985, s 283(1)* requires every company to have a secretary.
- The full postal address of the registered office.

11.7   When the formalities are complete, Companies House will issue a Certificate of Incorporation. This specifies the name, date of incorporation and a unique number. Once the certificate has been issued, the company is formed. A private company may then immediately carry on business.

11.8   Until recently, in order to form a company, it has been usual to go to a company formation agent, who will take the necessary details and deal with the actual mechanics. Sometimes a ready made or 'off the shelf' company will be acquired. This is one which has already been formed, but which has carried on no activity whatsoever. In the latter case, it is then necessary to notify the details of the new directors, company secretary and registered office to Companies House. The name will be changed too (see **11.42**).

Companies can now be formed electronically and many accountants and solicitors have the necessary links with Companies House. The direct formation of a company, in this way, is quick, simple and relatively inexpensive.

11.9   There are usually multiple copies of the Memorandum and Articles of Association. Some or all of the following may want a copy:

- auditor or accountant;
- solicitor;
- bank;
- the Inland Revenue;
- company secretary;
- each director;
- each shareholder.

11.10   As previously indicated, the company when first formed is to all intents and purposes an empty box. It may not carry on business for some time after formation. However, before it can start trading, it will want to deal with certain administrative matters. Most important of these is probably the opening of a bank account. Accordingly, a board meeting should be held and minutes prepared.

11.11 The company should maintain a minute book, containing the minutes of all meetings of members and board meetings which have been held. [*CA 1985, s 382*]. In addition, it is required to maintain the following registers:

- register of directors [*CA 1985, s 2 88*];
- register of secretaries [*CA 1985, s 290*];
- register of shareholders [*CA 1985, s 352*];
- register of directors' interests in shares [*CA 1985, s 325*];
- register of charges (mortgages) [*CA 1985, s 407*].

All of these registers are open to public inspection. The upkeep and custody of them is often placed in the hands of a solicitor or accountant.

11.12 The company must prominently and legibly display its name in a conspicuous position at the registered office and any place from which it carries on business [*CA 1985, s 348*].

Issue of shares

11.13 Whilst a company may have a large authorised share capital, usually £1,000 on a standard incorporation, at first formation generally only two shares are issued.

11.14 As part of the incorporation of the business, more shares may need to be issued. This may be by means of a subscription for cash or an issue in exchange for assets transferred to the company. The manner of issue of the shares and to whom they are issued is dependent on the nature of the incorporation. Often this is governed by the manner of incorporation, especially the capital gains tax effects. These are explored in detail in **Chapter 9**.

11.15 Normally, there are two or more shareholders. However, it is possible to have a company with only one shareholder, though there are additional rules to be met and, if that member is also the sole director, the Articles of Association need special provisions.

11.16 The number of shares to be issued is often a subject for some conjecture. Whilst the shares will have a nominal value, typically £1, this in no way reflects their true value, especially when the business has been transferred in. When the incorporation is by way of transfer of a business to the company in exchange for an issue of shares to the owner, a substantial share premium may be involved. This is because the value of the business and assets acquired by the company exceeds the nominal value of the shares issued. It is important to keep a sense of proportion. Many proprietors will not wish to issue vast numbers of shares, thereby locking much of the value of the business into share capital. Equally, a company with only two shares at an enormous premium can be intractable.

Many small private companies do operate on minimal share capital, often only the originally issued £2, sometimes increased to £100. A rather larger number increases flexibility in later tax planning manoeuvres.

11.17 Often all the shares will be ordinary shares which have full rights to dividends, voting at meetings and entitlement to capital on a winding up of the company. This does not have to be the case and the company may issue preference shares which have a fixed right to dividends and no vote. There is a current fashion for splitting the ordinary shares into different segments, denoted A, B, C etc. This is to go along with the present situation which favours dividends as against salary as a means of remuneration. Whether having lettered shares is a good or bad thing in a small private company is addressed in **Chapter 16**.

11.18 Last but not least, the company must ensure that the shares are issued. This may seem obvious but it is amazing how often it is overlooked. Shares are not issued when the intending shareholder subscribes for them, nor even when he pays for them. They are issued when the name of the member is entered in the share register by the company secretary *National Westminster Bank Ltd v IRC [1994] STC 580*. At the same time, a share certificate is given to the member.

11.19 Details of allotments of shares must be provided to Companies House within one month on form 88(2).

Shareholders' agreement

11.20 As indicated above, the operation of a company is usually governed by its Articles of Association. If a company has been formed using standard Articles, or bought off the shelf, the Articles will usually be taken directly from Table A. Within the confines of the *Companies Act* this will give a fairly flexible manner of operation.

Many small private companies are built around a family hierarchy or a close personal relationship formerly subsisting as a partnership. There need to be mechanisms in place to deal with succession and the resolution of possible inter-party disputes. To a certain extent, these may be covered by tightening the terms of the Articles. However, the Articles only give rights to the shareholder in his capacity as such.

Therefore, it is common to have a side agreement, known as a shareholders' agreement. This is a private arrangement for dealing with matters concerning disposal of shares, governance of the company, rights of minorities etc. It is a private document (the Articles are open to public inspection) and only binding if all parties specifically agree to it.

Amendment of the Articles and creation of a shareholders' agreement is a complex technical matter and should only be undertaken with the advice of a lawyer.

Meetings

11.21   The company is required to hold its first annual general meeting (AGM) within 18 months after formation. Thereafter, it must hold an AGM in every calendar year, with no more than 15 months elapsed since the last [*CA 1985, s 366*]. The AGM gives the shareholders at least one opportunity in the year to meet and discuss or question the operation of the company's business. Alternatively, a private company may, by elective resolution, dispense with holding AGMs.

11.22   An extraordinary general meeting is any meeting of the shareholders other than the AGM. An EGM may be called from time to time to deal with matters requiring a decision of the shareholders.

11.23   Day-to-day management of the company is delegated by the shareholders to the directors. In many small private companies, the shareholders and directors are the same, or there will be significant overlap between the two. This fact is not often recognised by the individuals who are acting in both capacities. So long as everything is proceeding smoothly, this probably does not matter. There may be important distinctions when problems arise.

The directors may meet as often as they wish to discuss matters of general policy and day to day management of the company.

11.24   The procedures for convening and running meetings are beyond the scope of this book. A record of proceedings is to be maintained (the minute book) [*CA 1985, s 382*].

Document of transfer

11.25   A company has been formed and is ready to do business. The sole trader or partnership has a pre-existing business and wishes to incorporate it. That business will include a number of assets and, if the company is to carry it on in succession to the individuals, the assets must be transferred to it. This transfer could be effected by way of gift, though a sale, whether for full value or otherwise, is more likely. The proceeds of sale may be shares, loan stock, unsecured loans or cash. The whole arrangement is a formal transaction and there ought to be evidence that it has actually taken place.

11.26   To demonstrate the need for such evidence, an example will be helpful. The following may cause some amusement, but it is actually based on a real set of circumstances.

Fred Smith (FS) visits a tax adviser (TA) concerning the incorporation of his business. Imagine the following conversation taking place.

FS: I've incorporated my business and I've just been told that I can get a tax free payment for goodwill. Is that right?

TA: Possibly. When did the incorporation happen?

FS: Hmm. Just over a year ago I think.

TA: I see. And how was the business incorporated?

FS: Pardon.

TA: How did you get the business into the company?

FS: Well, my accountant got a company off the shelf, we opened a bank account and now the company does what I always used to do.

TA: And what's that?

FS: I am an independent financial adviser.

TA: Don't you mean that the company is an independent financial adviser? As a director, you will be a representative of the company. You have been appointed as a director?

FS: Yes, I suppose so. My accountant said he would deal with all the paperwork.

TA: Now, about this goodwill. What is the nature of it?

FS: Pardon.

TA: The goodwill. What exactly is it? I admit it's a difficult concept. It's the intangible right attaching to a business which might make a purchaser want to pay more for it than the value of the assets used. I assume you have a client list.

FS: Oh, yes. That's where I get the business from. I know people; they know me and referrals get me new work.

TA: So they are now the company's clients.

FS: I don't know. I hadn't thought of it like that. The clients know me, not the company.

TA: So what you are saying is that the client list (if that is the goodwill) has not actually been transferred.

FS: I don't know. I suppose it must have been. I'll have to ask my accountant.

TA: Is there no document of transfer? Since you cannot actually see or feel goodwill, you need some evidence that you have transferred it.

FS: I don't think so.

TA: How much did the company pay for it?

FS: I don't know. I don't suppose it did – it wouldn't have had any money. It was brand new remember.

TA: Have you got the final accounts of your sole trader business?

FS: No. My accountant said he would do them soon.

TA: It's no good asking for the opening balance sheet of the company then?

FS: The what?

TA: And how much do you think the goodwill of the business is worth?

FS: About £30,000.

TA: Who valued it?

FS: No one. My friend at the golf club said it would be about that much. Apparently, it always is when you incorporate a small business.

TA: What have you done with the other assets of the business? How are you dealing with things like motoring expenses?

FS: Look – we are getting off the point. What about my tax free goodwill payment?

TA: I suggest you ask your accountant.

FS: You can't help then. My accountant said he didn't understand.

TA: I cannot imagine he did. I suggest you ask if he has a good professional indemnity policy too. You see, I could have helped before the company started, but it's rather too late now.

It is hoped that the foregoing story will have provided a little amusement. Having made it to **Chapter 11**, readers at least deserve some light relief and will hopefully recognise some of the problems inherent in the interchange. It does have a considerable element of truth and it centres on a serious message.

11.27 With one main exception, referred to in **11.28** below, and a few others (see **11.31**), you may not actually need a formal document in order to incorporate a business. The author is well aware of many small business incorporations which seem to have proceeded without any documentation and where the companies now trade satisfactorily. However, in most instances, some form of documentation is to be advised. The nature and extent of it will vary according to the size and type of business, as well as the number and relationship of the proprietors.

In **Chapter 10** (see **10.1**), it was indicated that stamp duty is a tax on documents. If there is no document, there is no need to pay any stamp duty. This is perfectly true, at least for the time being. However, it is likely that this tax will respond to the electronic age by becoming a tax on transactions, whether there is a document or not.

In any case, not having a document of transfer is likely to prove a false economy in some instances.

11.28 Where the incorporation proceeds by a share issue under *TCGA 1992, s 162* (see **9.10–9.11**), the whole assets of the business are transferred to the company in exchange for an issue of shares. Market value prevails on everything because the shares are consideration and the transaction is between connected parties. There may be cash or quasi cash proceeds as well in the form of loan stock or a credit balance on a director's account. The requirements of *s 162* are very specific. In these circumstances, a formal contract (incorporation deed or call it what you will) is vital. If nothing else, the issue of shares must be reported to Companies House on form 88(2). The Registrar will not register this unless it is accompanied by a stamped contract.

11.29 Additionally, it will serve to demonstrate the assets transferred, place values upon them and show that the company is acquiring title to them. The valuation issue is important where some residual gain arises after the application of *TCGA 1992, s 162*.

The Inspector of Taxes will be an interested party to this and it is open to him to challenge any apportionment of the proceeds. However, this will be far more difficult for him if there is clear consistent evidence of a realistic apportion-ment, rather than a global valuation placed on the totality of the business.

11.30   Demonstration of title is important. Suppose the company wishes to sell assets some time after the incorporation, or even the whole company is to be sold. The purchaser will wish to know that the company has good title to the assets purporting to be held within it. How is this to be possible, especially for any intangible items, unless there has been a formal contract of sale from the sole trader or partnership to the company.

Which leads us on to Fred Smith's problem. He wanted a payment for his goodwill. Whether this should be tax free or not is another issue (see **9.49**). His problem was whether it had been transferred to the company at all. By its very nature, it is intangible. You cannot see it, feel it or pick it up and carry it around. So, how can you demonstrate that it has been transferred from one trading entity to another (the sole trader to the company) without a formal contract?

11.31   The author is not a lawyer touting for business but, in many instances, a formal document of transfer is an essential requirement:

* all incorporations under *TCGA 1992, s 162*;
* transfers of intangible assets;
* transfers of any significant capital assets (land and buildings will, in any case, require a conveyance);
* where it is necessary to demonstrate good title to assets in the company, e.g. where onward sale is anticipated.

11.32   That is not to say that a formal contract is always required though. Consider a very small business, without significant capital assets and where no property is involved. There might only be stock and some plant and machinery to transfer. The company agrees to collect debtors and settle creditors as agent for the unincorporated business. The assets involved can be transferred by delivery. For optimum effect, a specified payment might be made. A simple sales invoice should be adequate to formalise the transaction.

Accounting for the incorporation transaction

11.33   It is a mandatory requirement that the accounts of a company show a true and fair view. Where the incorporation is tax driven, many of the assets may have been transferred at less than market value. This is especially the case where use is made of the relief in *TCGA 1992, s 165* (see **9.25–9.32**). This does not remove the need for the assets to be shown on the company's opening balance sheet at fair value.

A revaluation of the assets may therefore be required but what does this mean in practice? Most incorporations, certainly those under *TCGA 1992, s 165*, will be acquisitions and therefore (Financial Reporting Standard) FRS7 'Fair values in acquisition accounting' will apply.

All identifiable assets and liabilities should be restated at fair value in accordance with FRS7. (Note that goodwill is not an identifiable asset and the company's accounts will not show it at market value). In practice, this will usually be the same as the market value which is needed for the CGT computation. All consideration payable should be stated at fair value. The difference between the two is positive or negative goodwill.

The revaluation will not, therefore, give rise to a revaluation reserve. In effect the revaluation occurs before the assets enter the company, not afterwards.

Positive and negative goodwill must then be accounted for under FRS10. A detailed consideration of this is beyond the scope of this work.

Company returns and notifications

Annual return

11.34   Every company is required to submit an annual return with a fee (£15 as at April 2003) [*CA 1985, s 363*]. The annual return contains information as to the share capital, shareholders and officers of the company. It must be submitted within 28 days of the return date which is determined by the date of formation of the company or the anniversary of the last filed return. Most annual returns are now made on form 363s which is computer generated by Companies House and the company secretary is asked to confirm the information already held on the registers.

Accounts

11.35   The company is required to maintain accounting records to enable it to comply with obligations concerning the financial statements [*CA 1985, s 221*].

11.36   The company must prepare statutory accounts in the format dictated by *CA 1985, Sch 4, 8* (depending on the size of the company). The accounts must be prepared in accordance with UK accounting standards issued by the Accounting Standards Board. The requirement to show a true and fair view is of paramount importance, even where an audit is not required. The accounts must be lodged at Companies House within ten months of the accounting reference date (seven months for public companies). The penalty for failure to do this by a private company ranges from £100 where the accounts are up to 3 months late to £1,000 where they are more than twelve months late.

11.37   One fear of small business proprietors is that incorporation leads to accounts becoming publicly available. Whilst this is the case, small and medium companies may deliver abbreviated accounts. Small companies do not need to include a profit and loss account, directors' report or cash flow statement. The balance sheet may be simplified and only a few main notes to the accounts are required to be submitted. The only concession available to a medium-sized company is the exclusion from disclosure of turnover and cost of sales.

For this purpose, a small company is generally one satisfying at least two of the following:

- turnover not exceeding £2.8m;
- balance sheet total not exceeding £1.4m;
- number of employees not exceeding 50.

A medium size company must generally satisfy at least two of the following:

- turnover not exceeding £11.2m;
- balance sheet total not exceeding £5.6m;
- number of employees not exceeding 250.

The above criteria must be examined carefully for other issues which are beyond the scope of this work.

11.38 The default accounting reference date is 12 months from the end of the month in which the company was formed. The company may change this to something more convenient, but not so as to have an accounting period exceeding 18 months. The change must be notified on form 225. The notice may be given during the accounting period or after it ends, so long as the date for delivery of the accounts has not passed [*CA 1985, s 225*].

11.39 It is worth noting that failure to deliver the annual return or accounts is actually a criminal offence. On conviction, a director could end up with a criminal record and a fine of up to £5,000 for each offence. Persistent failure can lead to a director being disqualified from acting in this capacity. If the registrar believes that the company is no longer trading, he may strike it off the register; the assets of the company then become the property of the Crown.

Audit

11.40 Under *CA 1985, s 384*, every company, except certain small companies and dormant companies, is required to appoint an auditor. The auditor is required to make a report to the company members on all annual accounts of the company.

11.41 Certain categories of small company are totally exempt from independent audit procedures. For this purpose, a small company is one:

- whose turnover is not greater than £1m;

- whose balance sheet total is not more than £1.4m;
- is not a public company, banking or insurance company, parent company or subsidiary undertaking (in general circumstances), an authorised person under the *Financial Services Act 1986* or otherwise subject to a statute based regulatory regime.

Following recommendation of the Company Law Review, it is widely anticipated that the turnover limit may soon increase, possibly to £4.8m. The Chancellor of the Exchequer seemed to add impetus to the possibility of such a change with an announcement in the 2003 Budget.

Other returns and notifications

11.42   A company may change its name. This is frequently the case where a shelf company has been purchased with an inoffensive temporary name or, possibly on a later company reconstruction. The change requires a special resolution of members, a copy of which is to be filed at Companies House within 15 days [*CA 1985, s 380(4)(a)*]. A fee (£10 as at April 2003) is payable.

11.43   A change of registered office must be notified on form 287. The change is not effective until the notification has been filed with the Registrar [*CA 1985, s 287*].

11.44   A change of company secretary must be notified on form 288a within 14 days of the change [*CA 1985, s 288(2)*].

11.45   Appointments of new directors must be notified on form 288a within 14 days of the change [*CA 1985, s 288*]. Any change in the details of existing directors, for example a new address, must be similarly notified.

11.46   The company may amend its Articles of Association by special resolution. The new Articles and a copy of the special resolution must be lodged at Companies House [*CA 1985, ss 18, 380*].

11.47   Various resolutions passed pursuant to *CA 1985, s 380* must be lodged at Companies House. The general time limit is 15 days from the passing of the resolution.

Resolutions

11.48   The *Companies Act* requires that various decisions of the company be made by members passing resolutions in a general meeting. There are broadly four types of resolution: Ordinary, Extraordinary, Special and Elective (this last type is not available to a public company).

Detailed consideration of these is beyond the scope of this book. However, it is worth noting that elective resolutions may be passed to dispense with requirements to hold an AGM in certain circumstances, to dispense with the requirement to lay accounts and reports before the company in a general meeting and certain other administrative points. A signed copy of an elective resolution must be delivered to Companies House within 15 days [*CA 1985, s 380(4)(bb)*].

Elsewhere (for example **11.69**) it is noted that a final dividend must be approved by the members of the company at the AGM. In the absence of an AGM, resolutions must be circulated amongst the members for approval.

Corporation tax returns

See also **2.66–2.69**.

Corporation tax self assessment

11.49   For accounting periods ending after 1 July 1999, a system of corporation tax self assessment (CTSA) has been in force. The primary legislation may be found in *FA 1998, Sch 18*.

The system is not dissimilar to that which has applied for income tax since 1996/97. The change was not so radical for companies which had previously had a system of Pay and File which had elements of self assessment though the Inspector of Taxes still issued a formal assessment and demand for tax.

11.50   Under CTSA, the company must compute its own profits, calculate the tax liability, render a return to the Inland Revenue and pay the tax without the need for the issue of an assessment. Normally the Inspector will request submission of a return. In the absence of such a request, the company must still notify the Inland Revenue if it has chargeable profits [*Sch 18 para 2*]. The request for a first return will assume an accounting period ended 12 months after the date of company formation unless the accounting reference date has been changed and notified to the Inspector of Taxes. A return on form CT600 is required to be submitted within 12 months of the accounting period end. This includes not only a computation of the company profits and the tax due but also:

- notification of the tax due where loans have been made to participators (see **16.16**);
- claims for group relief;

and other items specific to certain types of company.

11.51   Those familiar with income tax self assessment will know that the return usually stands alone. In contrast the CTSA return must be accompanied by accounts and other information as may be necessary.

11.52 A system of process now, check later, prevails. If there are no obvious errors, the return will be accepted at face value. However, in order to police the system, the Inspector of Taxes may enquire into the return. Notice of an enquiry is to be given within twelve months after the filing date [*Sch 18 para 24*].

Once the time limit for an enquiry has passed, or an enquiry has been opened and completed, the company has some degree of finality. In the absence of a discovery by the Inland Revenue, the return cannot then be challenged.

11.53 CTSA imposes a further administration requirement. The company must maintain such records as may be needed to enable it to submit a complete return. Those records must be preserved for six years from the end of the accounting period for which the return is required. Failure to keep records may incur a penalty of up to £3,000 [*Sch 18, 21, 23*]. The *Companies Act* also imposes a record-keeping requirement. The Inland Revenue has confirmed [*Tax Bulletin October 1998*] that a company which satisfies the requirements of *CA 1985, s 221*, will meet the necessary requirement for CTSA.

11.54 Payment of corporation tax is covered at **2.70–2.74**.

Income tax

11.55 Until abolition of advance corporation tax (ACT) on 5 April 1999, companies regularly paying dividends found themselves in an ancillary programme of tax payments.

These days this system only applies to payments of income tax. A company may be required to deduct income tax on:

- payment of interest to a non-UK resident company;
- payment of interest to an individual. This might include payments to its own directors (see **15.44**). The rate of tax to be deducted is the lower rate, i.e. 20%;
- payment of other annual payments, e.g. royalties. In this instance tax is deducted at the basic rate of 22%.

From 1 April 2001, a company does not need to deduct income tax when paying interest to another UK company.

Having deducted income tax, the company must account for it quarterly to the Inland Revenue on form CT61(Z) [*ICTA 1988, Sch 16*].

Employer returns

11.56 It is highly unlikely that any company will not be involved in the operation of PAYE. All but the very smallest businesses will have employees to whom wages or salaries will be paid. Therefore many small sole traders will be familiar with PAYE.

11.57   It is true that some very small sole traders, or husband and wife partnerships, may be just that and consequently will not be involved with payment of wages. On incorporation though, the proprietors adopt a new role. The company is now the principal and 'employs' them as directors. They may not necessarily be employees unless a contract, whether written or implied, treats them as such. They will be office holders under the *Companies Act*. Any remuneration paid to them, in either capacity, will fall within the ambit of PAYE.

11.58   Virtually every company must therefore register with the Inland Revenue and operate PAYE in accordance with the *Income Tax (Employments) Regulations 1993 SI 1993/744*. Very broadly, this means that, on every occasion of payment of wages or salaries, an appropriate amount of income tax and national insurance contributions must be computed and deducted.

11.59   On or before the 19th of the month following deduction, the relevant income tax and NIC must be paid to the Inland Revenue. Where the amounts are very small (£1,500 or less per month), payment may be made quarterly.

11.60   At the end of the tax year, the company must make a return on form P35 by 19 May. This details all employees, the gross payments made and amounts deducted. Failure to render the return will incur a penalty of £100 per group of 50 employees (or less) per month [*TMA 1970, s 98A*]. The company must also provide to the employee a certificate on form P60 by 31 May following the end of the tax year, providing the individual with pay and tax details.

11.61   Throughout this book, it is suggested that one of the advantages of incorporation is the flexibility for the proprietors to take payments from the company by way of dividend rather than salary. Nevertheless, it is advocated that a small salary should always be paid, in order to preserve the benefit position (see **5.23**).

This might be at such a level as to ensure that no deductions of tax or NIC are necessary. However, a PAYE scheme must still be opened and the relevant annual returns submitted in order to ensure that the earnings are recorded for benefit (primarily retirement pension) purposes.

Benefits in kind

11.62   The rules for taxation of benefits in kind and expense payments under *ITEPA 2003 Part 3; ICTA 1988, Part V Chapter II*, apply to all directors and employees earning £8,500 per annum or more. Given that an adult worker paid the national minimum wage of £4.20 per hour and working 40 hours per week will earn £8,736 in 2003/04, this means virtually everyone working for a company.

11.63   The employer company must provide a return on form P11D detailing such expenses and benefits to the Inland Revenue by 6 July following the end of the tax year [*Income Tax (Employments) Regulations 1993 SI 1993/744 Reg 46*]. The details contained in the form P11D, though not necessarily a copy of the form, must be supplied to the employee by the same date. The penalty for late submission of P11Ds is a maximum of £300 per form [*TMA 1970, s 98*]. It should also be noted that the penalty for fraudulent or negligent submission of an incorrect P11D is a maximum of £3,000 per form. The author has never seen penalties approaching anything like these theoretical maxima levied.

11.64   Actual submission of the returns is not the real administrative burden on the company. The greater obligation is maintaining accounting records sufficient to identify and quantify the amounts to be included on the returns. It is quite possible that some items returned could be matched by employee expense claims under *ICTA 1988, s 198*. In this circumstance, the company may short circuit the process by seeking a dispensation from the Inspector of Taxes. Amounts agreed to have no tax consequences may then be omitted. It is often thought that the Inland Revenue will not grant a dispensation to a director-only company. In the autumn of 2002 however, it confirmed that it would providing that certain conditions are met, primarily independent vouching [*Working Together 10, September 2002*].

11.65   Additionally, form P11D(b), which is the covering schedule including forms P11D, serves an additional function as the return for class 1A NIC. It cannot therefore be omitted.

Valid dividends

11.66   To take real tax advantage of incorporation, it is necessary to be flexible over the business proprietors' remuneration packages. It is likely that significant amounts will be extracted by way of dividends. These suffer lower effective rates of tax and there is no NIC liability. **Chapter 4** explores in some detail the impact of this at varying levels of corporate profit and in different personal circumstances.

11.67   Thus, it is necessary to pay careful attention to payment of dividends. Payment of a dividend is usually governed by a company's Articles of Association. In the absence of anything to the contrary, this will be in accordance with *Companies (Table A–F) Regulations 1985 SI 1985/805, Regs 102–108*. A final dividend must be recommended by the directors and approved by the company members in a general meeting. The directors may pay interim dividends if they are justified by the level of the company's distributable profit.

11.68   Firstly, note that a company may not pay a dividend at all unless it has distributable reserves [*CA 1985, s 263*]. This is not necessarily profits of the current accounting period; it may include retained profits of an earlier accounting period. The ability to pay a dividend may therefore be inhibited where the company (perhaps temporarily) is in a loss-making situation. Salary on the other hand can always be paid, assuming that funding permits. In recommending a dividend, the directors must also have regards to the company's cash requirements and solvency, as well as the position of each shareholder. Remuneration policy involving significant dividends therefore tends to assume a consistently profitable company.

11.69   A final dividend will normally be approved in the AGM at which the annual accounts are also approved. The company's ability to pay a final dividend will not be in question. It has been suggested that, in family or owner managed companies, very small salaries and substantial dividends are taken. Assuming that the proprietors need cash for day-to-day living expenses, such a procedure would appear to dictate payment of regular interim dividends. The alternative of taking loans to provide temporary funding is not permitted by the *Companies Act* and may have adverse tax consequences (see **Chapter 16**).

11.70   Typical timing for interim dividends may be quarterly, though there is an increasing fashion for monthly payments. This instantly places strain on the management accounting of the company. For an interim dividend to be validly paid requires distributable reserves just as much as a final dividend. The company's financial records must be adequate to demonstrate that this is the case. There may also be inherent underlying problems in the company cash flow – what if it is a seasonal trade with irregular receipts. Dividends may be precluded at times.

11.71   The ICAEW has recently issued a Guidance Note TECH 7/03 on determining realised profits for distribution. This follows from the draft in TECH 25/00 which was long (25 pages), and complex and has been nearly three years in gestation.

At the time that a dividend is declared, the directors should be able to take a reasonable judgement as to profits, losses, assets and liabilities, provisions, share capital and reserves. The note goes on to say that reliable management accounts will satisfy this requirement.

It may be that when the accounts are prepared, the interim dividends paid are found to be excessive. If, at the time of payment, the directors had reasonable grounds to assume there were distributable reserves then they do not need to be repaid. The position can be rectified if the company has adequate reserves in the following period.

Interim dividends may be affected by the introduction of a new accounting standard if it leads to items being recognised as liabilities or provisions in the accounts for that year. Here, directors must take into account the effect on the expected level of profit at the end of the year when they are determining the lawfulness of the interim dividend.

11.72   An alternative view, where the company is established and trading profitably, might be to declare and approve a large final dividend for a closed accounting period. The recommended payment though is in instalments throughout the next accounting period giving the shareholders the required cashflow without the need to worry about interim dividends.

11.73   Having established the availability of reserves, the appropriate procedure must be followed. For an interim dividend *Regulation 103* of *Table A* gives directors the power to pay if it is justified by profit. A final dividend must be approved by the members. Thus the following steps are necessary:

- Establish the distributable reserves.
- Determine the total amount to be distributed.
- Calculate the dividend per share.
- For an interim dividend, hold a board meeting and prepare minutes approving payment.
- For a final dividend, prepare AGM or EGM documents recommending a dividend. At the general meeting, the members must approve the dividend recommended by the directors. Prepare minutes.
- Make payment to the shareholders and prepare dividend vouchers. The vouchers should specify the net amount payable and the attributable tax credit.
- If elective resolutions were passed, a directors' written resolution should be prepared to validate the dividend payment.

11.74   The need for valid dividends is vital. The Inland Revenue may challenge dividends not properly declared and paid in accordance with company law formalities. Payment of a dividend in excess of distributable reserves will be illegal. A company can require the recipient to repay such a dividend. Repayment of the dividend is unlikely in the family or owner managed company circumstances, giving the Inspector of Taxes an opportunity to argue that an illegally paid dividend is a loan to the shareholders and subject to tax under *ICTA 1988, s 419*, (see **16.31**).

There is an extreme possibility that the Inland Revenue might seek to reclassify an illegal dividend as salary. The author acknowledges that this is unlikely, but it is theoretically possible and not without precedent (see **16.75**).

11.75   The real problem with dividends is that they are paid equally to all shareholders without preference to participation in the business. The proprietors might want some differential effect. Perceived ways to deal with this and the potential problems are covered in **Chapter 16**.

Planning points

- Ensure that there is a formal document of transfer in all relevant instances (**11.31**).
- Ensure that dividends are validly declared (**11.73**).

Other Considerations

12.1 Taxes of various types figure highly on the issues to be considered during the actual process of incorporation. There are also 'Companies Act' formalities and other legalities to attend to.

Alongside this, there are many practicalities which should be fairly obvious, but are often overlooked. This chapter endeavours to draw most of these together. So far as possible it is complete. Apologies are given if anything significant is missing. The list of people to tell is hopefully comprehensive though it is felt that someone will point out an omission of some type from this.

Oh, and a tax does appear here too. That is VAT. This is not because it is an afterthought (though the author admits to not practising in this area) but because, if you do things correctly, it should be a non-event.

Banking

12.2 It is difficult to know what to say on this point, other than that the company is a separate entity and will require a bank account.

The professional press frequently carries reports of difficulties in opening bank accounts for (small) companies. Comments include delays of up to three months in satisfying the formalities. One cannot help but think that the parties involved are not making every effort to help themselves.

The bank will usually require to see the Certificate of Incorporation of the company and a copy of the minutes appointing the bank and the officers who are to be the signatories to the account. Ever more stringent money laundering regulations will require those signatories to provide acceptable evidence of their identity to the bank. Many ask for a list of all shareholders with addresses.

Having got through this minefield, what will the banking costs be? Many report that bank charges for a new company are significantly higher than those for the previous unincorporated business. This may be a function of the charging structure which treats corporate enterprises as 'large' and able to pay greater amounts. In the small business environment is it a reflection that the proprietor was enjoying the benefits of a personal account, yet passing business transactions through it?

The author has encountered a contrary effect, with at least one report of banking costs going down. The logic to this was that the company account was for a new business and it was entitled to free or discounted charges for an initial period (even though the former sole trader did business with the same branch of the same bank).

There must be some financial reward for the first bank to cut through the red tape and apply a clear consistent policy which is transparently obvious to its customers.

Insurance

12.3   This is another area where it is difficult to know what to say. Any businessman can easily take the view that he is keeping the insurance industry alive.

Depending on the nature and size of the business, not to mention the proprietor's attitude to risk, some or all of the following general insurances might be required:

- motor;
- property and contents;
- public liability;
- employer's liability;
- loss of profits;
- permanent health etc.

More specialised businesses may require cover for professional indemnity. Dare one even mention cover against the risk of a tax investigation?

Depending on the movement of risk, liability and property on incorporation, the proprietor should make the necessary arrangements for renewal or replacement of insurance cover. This could be where the trouble starts. Insurance companies, like bankers, seem to see companies as a higher risk.

The author has seen a report of an 11-fold increase in general insurance premiums alleged to be just due to incorporation. This seems unlikely but one might need to be prepared for higher, if more realistic, insurance costs.

Insurance may show an unfortunate side effect of the rush to incorporate. Where cover is effected for loss of earnings due to ill health, this will almost certainly be limited to salary, not dividends. If the proprietor falls ill, insured replacement income could be very low if the remuneration regime is small salary/large dividend.

Mortgages

12.4   Most of us want to buy houses in which to live. Many of us change our homes quite frequently. Few of us have the cash to do it with. We need to borrow on mortgage.

The mortgage lender will want to see evidence of earnings as a basis for the amount of the loan. For the ordinary employee, that is easy. Produce last year's P60, perhaps backed up by a letter from the employer. For the self employed, it is not too bad either. Demonstrate the earnings of the business by providing accounts or copies of the self employment pages of the self assessment tax return.

What about the proprietor of the newly incorporated business though? Produce a P60 showing a salary of £4,615 and the lender is unlikely to be too impressed. Payment of dividends is at the whim of the proprietor (and the availability of distributable reserves in the company); indeed timing, just as much as the nature of payments, is part of the tax planning opportunity of using a company. And how many times have we said, the company's assets are not the proprietor's assets? Even the 100% shareholder of a one-man company cannot spend the company's money (not without adverse tax consequences at least).

Accordingly, many commentators report the desire to move house and obtain a new mortgage as a potential downside of incorporation, especially for very small businesses. However, it does seem to be more a theoretical problem than a real one. At least, so far, it has not been encountered much in practice.

Lenders do seem to afford more flexibility. For a very new company they will look at previous Schedule D earnings of a business. They will look at salary and dividends combined from the company and even (rightly or wrongly) look at the retained earnings of the company. If yours does not, try someone else.

The National Minimum Wage

12.5   Since 1 April 1999, all businesses have been obliged to pay at least the National Minimum Wage (NMW) to their workers. This caused a brief flurry of panic amongst the advisers of small private companies. Were directors entitled to be paid the NMW? If so, could such payment be enforced?

Was, for example, a loss-making company obliged to pay a salary to its directors and make the situation worse? Apart from that, the flow of small incorporations was, at that stage, already well underway. Remuneration planning often advocated the payment of small salaries in favour of dividends. Would such a policy fall foul of NMW legislation?

The rate of NMW for an adult worker aged 21 or over was increased in October 2002 to £4.20 per hour (and, it is intended, should be increased to £4.50 in October 2003). For a 40-hour week, this equates to £8,736 per annum (and many proprietors of small businesses will claim to work well in excess of 40 hours per week). Elsewhere in this book, payment of a salary at or just below the personal allowance of £4,615 p.a. is advocated. Is this a problem? It should be noted that neither dividends nor most benefits in kind count as remuneration for NMW purposes.

12.6 The uncertainty prevailed for rather more than a year. During this time, the Tax Faculty of the Institute of Chartered Accountants in England and Wales had discussions with the Department of Trade and Industry, which department is responsible for NMW policy, and legislation, and the Inland Revenue, which is responsible for enforcement. As a result, guidance on NMW for directors was prepared by the Tax Faculty and initially published by the Institute of Chartered Accountants as *Tax Guide* 7/00. The same text appeared in the Inland Revenue *Tax Bulletin* of December 2000.

The *National Minimum Wage Act 1998* adopts a simple principle. All individuals who are 'workers' are covered by the NMW legislation; individuals who are not workers are not covered. *NMWA, s 54* defines a worker as someone working under a contract of employment (an employee), or someone working under some other form of contract (called a worker's contract) under which he agrees to perform work personally for someone else, but is not self employed.

12.7 Individuals who are directors properly appointed under the Companies Act and who assume the rights and obligations of a director are office holders but not necessarily workers. For a director to also be a worker under *NMWA 1998* there has to be an extra legal arrangement between the two parties, which involves obligations on both sides. It follows that if a person is a director, but does not have an explicit employment contract, then he is highly unlikely to be subject to the NMW legislation, even when he carries out a wide variety of activities for the company. Such activities can be done in his capacity as an office holder (director) rather than as a worker. If a director has an explicit employment contract, he will be within NMW in respect of earnings under that contract, as he and the company will then have chosen to create a worker/employer relationship alongside the director/company one.

Informal enquiries of the Inland Revenue seem to suggest that it will not take enforcement proceedings without a complaint being lodged. And what company director is likely to complain that his own company is not paying NMW to him?

12.8 In family companies, the position of non director family members ought to be explored. In certain circumstances, family members of the proprietor of a business are excluded from payment of NMW. A company is not a member of the family. This exception therefore falls by the wayside. An employee of a company will always be a worker and entitled to NMW. A formal written contract is unlikely in close family arrangements, but this does not mean that no contract exists. An implied contract will usually prevail and family members, e.g. adult children, working in the business must be paid NMW.

Especial care is required where the family member who is an employee later becomes a director. First, it must be ensured that he is correctly appointed. This requires a board resolution and a return to Companies House. However, this does not necessarily conclude the matter. On appointment, the employment contract must be terminated. Otherwise, this will persist alongside the office of director and payment of NMW must continue. Of course, if 'director' is merely a glamorous title and the Companies Act procedures have not been followed, then he is not an office holder and, again, NMW must continue.

12.9 In summary then, if the director is solely an officer of the company appointed under the Companies Act, he is not a worker within the meaning of *NMWA 1998* and there is no need for payment of NMW, however extensive the duties. This leaves total flexibility for the remuneration package. On the contrary, if a contract of employment (whether expressed or implied) is in place for some other reason, then NMW must be paid to the director like any other worker. The scope for planning remuneration is accordingly restricted.

Professional bodies

12.10 Everything that has been said so far, assumes that there is a totally free choice as regards the medium of operation. Especially as regards some professions, this may not always be the case.

A complete analysis will not be attempted here for fear, if nothing else, that something might be missed. However, when considering incorporation, it would be wise to be wary at least with:

- accountants;
- lawyers;
- doctors;
- dentists;
- surveyors;
- architects; and
- veterinary surgeons.

Some of these are specifically barred from operating through the medium of a limited company, e.g. dentists, see *Dentists Act 1984, s 42*. Others may do so, at least in theory, but practical problems could defeat the process.

This may perhaps be best illustrated by the position of doctors and dentists.

12.11 The British Dental Association advises that dentists are not allowed to offer their services via a limited liability body. This is in line with the legislation cited at **12.10** and seems to encompass both NHS and private work. Before anyone points out that there are dental companies in existence, there is a curious exception. Such companies are an historical relic from the days before the formation of the National Health Service and are allowed to continue in operation provided that very stringent rules are met. At least for the time being, no new companies offering dental services may be created.

12.12 On the other hand, there seems to be no specific bar to incorporation of a doctors' practice. However, most general practitioners will practice wholly or partly through the National Health Service. The contracts for so doing are personal to the individual. So practical considerations may rule the day for ordinary doctors. This may change shortly, as new general practitioner contracts are expected to come into force during 2003 and these will be in favour of the practice rather than the individual.

So far as can be established, a general practitioner providing wholly private services could incorporate his practice. Equally, this seems to be the case for medical consultants (surgeons etc.). The Medical Protection Society has certainly confirmed that it is able to provide membership benefits to individuals providing their services through some other employer organisation (which is taken to include a company). A reply to a reader's query in *Medical Group News* of the Institute of Chartered Accountants in England and Wales, December 2002 said that 'There is nothing preventing medical practitioners from converting their practice to a limited company under the Medical Act'.

12.13   Do not switch off though and think that certain professionals can never take advantage of the benefits of incorporation. In the author's experience, many doctors (especially) and dentists (to a lesser extent) will derive income from non-NHS activities. This may include professional writing, lecturing, insurance reports etc. and, in some instances, the amounts are very substantial. There is no reason why the peripheral activities should not be carried on through the corporate medium. As this type of income is generally the top slice (with NHS activities providing the staple diet) the potential savings can be great as we will be looking at amounts otherwise taxed at the higher rate when earned (now with 1% NIC too). The ability to take dividends instead (some of which might, with care, be spread round family members) should provide a great advantage.

But, we needn't stop there.

Service companies

12.14   Just because the professional principal(s) cannot incorporate, does not mean that no part of the practice can though. Enter the service company. Some years ago, these used to be quite fashionable then, for perhaps inexplicable reasons, their use dwindled. Maybe the time is right for a revival in their fortunes.

All but the very smallest of professional practices will have non-professional staff, need to own assets etc. Why not collect all of these into the convenient shell of a company. Its trade is to provide accommodation, office services and any other ancillary matters to the main partnership. It can contract with all necessary suppliers, engage staff etc. It then sells the services on to the professionals with a suitable mark up on its costs. That mark up would need to be commercially established to ensure a deduction in the tax computations of the professional principals (who may still operate as sole practitioners or through the medium of a partnership). Dependent on the extent and nature of the services provided, figures in the range of 5%–15% seem acceptable.

12.15 What is then achieved is a movement of the top slice of professional income away from the immediate impact of high personal tax rates (and NIC) to the corporate medium with the usual benefits. The principals of the practice will usually be the shareholders of the service company and can take dividends etc. as desired.

12.16 It has to be said that there is a further advantage in the service company where major assets, such as property, are involved. The company acts as convenient wrapper for the assets. As principals come and go from the practice, it may be a lot simpler to deal with share acquisition and disposal, rather than proportionate shares of all assets held directly by a partnership.

The corporate partner

12.17 The author spent many years thinking that such things existed only in the minds of examiners who prepare tax examinations. He never encountered one in practice and then, in the last ten years, they seem to be everywhere.

The function still seems a bit uncertain. Is it the company for the business that doesn't really want to incorporate? It could have a role similar to the service company, but often does not; its sole business is to trade in partnership with individuals. It is true that it might take a large profit share. The service company takes a fixed mark up on costs; the corporate partner can take as big a share as the partners may agree amongst themselves (and the partnership deed permits).

In essence, therefore, a slice of the profits gets into the corporate sphere, but not all. So there is some measure of corporate advantage but not the totality of it. Think of it as an alternative for the business proprietor who does not want to go the whole hog.

Relief for interest paid

12.18 Incorporation of a business may cause changes in the way in which the proprietor can obtain tax relief for interest on any borrowing.

12.19 A sole trader may have fixed loans for the purchase of assets used in his business. He may have a bank overdraft to provide working capital. He may settle some business expenses by use of a credit card. In all cases he may incur interest. So long as that interest is expended wholly and exclusively for the purposes of the business and does not fall foul of the restrictions in *ICTA 1988, s 74*, then it is deductible in arriving at the trading profit for tax purposes.

12.20 The position of a partner is similar. In addition, though, he may have purchased an interest in the partnership. This in itself may have entailed borrowing. Other borrowings may have been incurred in order to contribute money to the partnership which, in turn, is used in the trade, profession or vocation of the partnership. Interest paid on a loan (but not an overdraft) incurred for this purpose is eligible for relief under *ICTA 1988, s 362*. Where this is the case, the interest is a deduction from total income under *s 353* and not a deduction in arriving at the profit of the business.

Relief under *s 362* may be restricted where the borrower has recovered capital from the partnership [*ICTA 1988, s 363*]. Stated simply, the capital account of the partner in a business must remain at a minimum of the same level as it was when the borrowing was first incurred. If it drops below this level, i.e. the partner has taken funds from the partnership either directly or constructively (see *s 363(2)*), then he will be deemed to have reduced the loan. The interest relief given is then proportionately reduced.

It is strongly recommended that separate capital and current accounts are maintained with a partnership. If, as is commonly the case, the two are merged the true position is clouded by the credit of profit to, and drawings from, the accounts. It then becomes all too easy to inadvertently overdraw the capital element and jeopardise the interest relief. Where a composite account does exist, the analysis to be performed each year to quantify the status of the account was considered in *Silk v Fletcher [1999] STC (SCD) 220*. It is not simply the cash movements, but items such as depreciation, debtors and creditors, which have to be considered. How many people will consider doing this as a matter of course? The Inland Revenue *Inspectors Manual* at *para 3854* comments that, unless there are separate capital and current accounts, drawings will be matched with profits 'as far as possible'.

12.21 Switch to the corporate medium and we then have two distinct entities to consider. First there is the trading position of the company. This is broadly similar to the position of the sole trader. Interest incurred wholly and exclusively for trading purposes is generally deductible in arriving at the taxable profit.

12.22 Do not forget though that a company will fall into the loan relationships legislation of *FA 1996, Part IV, Chapter II*. A loan relationship exists wherever a company stands as creditor or debtor to a money debt and that debt arises from a transaction for the lending of money [*FA 1996, s 81*]. Most financing arrangements are therefore caught and this legislation places particular constraints on accounting for debits and credits, as well as the timing of relief, especially where the parties to the loan relationship are connected. A company is at an advantage to a sole trader or partnership where a loan is incurred for non-trade purposes. Interest on such loans may be set against profits generally under *FA 1996, s 83*. A non-corporate entity would not get any relief at all.

12.23 Then there is the position of the shareholder. He may have borrowed money to purchase shares in the company or for onward lending to the company for use in its trade. This parallels the circumstances of a partner but will be new territory for a former sole trader. Relief is available this time under *ICTA 1988, s 360*, provided that:

- The company is a close company.
- The company is not a close investment holding company i.e. broadly it exists wholly or mainly for the purposes of a trade or one of several other specified purposes.
- The individual has a material interest in the company (broadly he owns 5% or more of the ordinary share capital) or he owns ordinary shares and works for the greater part of his time in the management or conduct of the business of the company (the Inland Revenue interprets the latter condition fairly tightly – see *RI 62*).
- The interest does not exceed a normal commercial rate.

As with partners, the relief is given against total income under *ICTA 1988, s 353*. Care is obviously necessary to ensure that tax relief can be obtained. Remuneration by way of minimal salary and large dividends could prove to be ineffective in these circumstances. There will be little or no tax on the salary to be relieved and the notional tax credit on the dividends is not repayable. This seems to dictate a larger salary (on which perhaps there would still be no tax because of the interest relief) with attendant NIC liabilities.

Again, relief may be restricted where capital is recovered from the company. A nasty trap awaits should the shares be gifted.

Example 12.23

Clare borrows £50,000 and subscribes for £1 shares in a new trading company. The interest paid qualifies for relief at her marginal rate of tax. Some time later, the shares have risen in value to £10 each and she decides to put 5,000 of them into trust. The deemed consideration is equal to the market value of the shares gifted and she is deemed to have recovered capital of this amount. In this case, that is £50,000. She will, therefore, get no relief on the loan outstanding even though she still owns 45,000 of the shares. When considering a gift of shares to a trust, check first whether they were acquired with the benefit of a loan and, if so, the effect on interest paid.

12.24   Relief is not available under *ICTA 1988, ss 353, 360* where the loan has been used to subscribe for shares in a company and a claim has been made under the Enterprise Investment Scheme provisions. This includes both income tax relief under *ICTA 1988, s 289A*, and capital gains tax deferral under *TCGA 1992, Sch 5B*.

12.25   On the face of it, where a partnership business is incorporated and the company makes a payment to the former partners for their shares in the assets of the business, this constitutes recovery of capital in respect of any borrowing they may have had to purchase their interests in the business in the first place. However, under *ESC A43*, the Inland Revenue will not deny relief in these circumstances if a new loan taken out by the individual at the time of incorporation would itself have qualified for relief. After the incorporation, the rules for recovery of capital will continue to apply in the normal way.

12.26 Additionally, the former sole trader might have had a loan to purchase a major capital asset of the business, especially property. If the asset is retained outside the company on incorporation, then the interest may be unrelievable unless rent is paid (see **15.49**).

12.27 For the sake of completeness, it should be added that an employee (director) may claim relief for interest incurred on a loan to purchase an asset used in employment. The asset must be eligible for capital allowances in the hands of the individual [*ICTA 1988, s 359*]. The interest must be paid within three years of the end of the year of assessment in which the loan was taken out. The obvious candidate for this relief was the motor car. However, this is now excluded from capital allowances in the hands of the employee by *FA 2001, s 59*, with effect from 6 April 2002. This provision is now unlikely to be of much use.

Who to tell

12.28 Everyone you can think of really who might have contact with the business. The more important ones will include the following, though readers may think of others particular to certain businesses:

1. Bankers.
2. Insurance companies.
3. Pension provider – if the unincorporated business has employees there may be a stakeholder pension scheme. This must be transferred to the company.
4. Accountants – though it is to be hoped that they will have been involved with the process of incorporation and are therefore well aware.
5. Solicitors – ditto.
6. Employees – where a business is transferred to a company, the successor company will be required to observe all terms and conditions of employment which apply to the employees of the business prior to the transfer [*Transfer of Undertakings (Protection of Employment) Regulations 1981 SI 1981/1794*].
7. Customers – depending on the type of business, it may be necessary to enter into new contractual arrangements, issue new terms of business or amend letters of engagement.
8. Suppliers.
9. The Land Registry where the title to business premises has been transferred.
10. Landlord of any rented premises.
11. Utility companies – gas, water, electric, telephone etc. to ensure continuing supply to the correct person post-incorporation.

12. Rating authorities.
13. Hire purchase, lease or finance companies in respect of any assets transferred to the company.
14. The Inland Revenue – to advise cessation of the unincorporated business, notify existence of the new company, amend or create appropriate PAYE schemes, IRNICO to amend arrangements for payment of NIC.
15. HM Customs & Excise – to transfer VAT registration or arrange new registration for the company and deregister the unincorporated business.
16. The Driver and Vehicle Licensing Authority – to amend vehicle registrations.
17. Amend telephone directory entries.
18. Amend trade directory entries.

12.29   In addition, arrangements will be needed to get new supplies of letterheads and invoices.

It should be noted that these must contain details of the company number, where registered (e.g. England and Wales) and the registered office address. It is not a specific requirement to include the names of the directors but they are often shown.

You might also need new business cards.

And, if you live in the electronic age, do not forget to change the website.

Value Added Tax

12.30   Most businesses will be registered for VAT. The threshold as at April 2003 is £56,000 (either taxable supplies in the last twelve months or there are reasonable grounds for believing that they will exceed that amount in the next 30 days). Admittedly, some very small businesses following the current fashion for incorporation may not be registered, nor will any specialist business making wholly exempt supplies. For practical purposes, let's assume all businesses are registered.

12.31   The disposal of the assets of a business is to be treated as a supply made in the course or furtherance of that business. Accordingly, VAT will be chargeable on the sale of such items as stock, plant and machinery, fixtures and fittings [*VATA 1994, Sch 4 para 5*]. HM Customs & Excise also regard a sale of goodwill as a taxable supply [*C&E Press Notice No.790, 10 December 1982*].

12.32   However, the general rule is that no taxable supply is made and VAT should not be charged where the assets of a business are transferred to another person, e.g. a successor company, in connection with the transfer of all or part of the business as a going concern.

12.33 *Other Considerations*

Therefore, the transfer of a business as a going concern is neither a supply of goods nor a supply of services for VAT purposes. This applies where the assets are to be used by the transferee in carrying on the same kind of business as that carried on by the transferor; and where the transferee is a taxable person, or immediately becomes one as a result of the transfer. If only part of the business is transferred as a going concern, the same rule applies where that part is capable of separate operation [*VAT (Special Provisions) Order 1995 SI 1995/ 1268, art 5*].

12.33   The transfer of a going concern (TOGC) rule is mandatory provided all the following conditions are met:

- The effect of the transfer must be to put the new owner in possession of a business which can be operated as such.
- The business, or part business, must be a going concern at the time of the transfer.
- The assets being transferred must be intended for use by the new owner in carrying on the same kind of business. They can include stock, machinery, goodwill, premises and fixtures and fittings.
- The new owner must be registered for VAT or, at the time of the transfer, become liable to be registered or be accepted for voluntary registration.
- There must be no significant break in the normal trading pattern before, or immediately after, the transfer.
- If only part of the business is being transferred, that part must be able to operate alone. It does not necessarily have to operate alone in the hands of the new owner. All that is required is that it has the capability to do so.
- There must not be a series of immediately consecutive transfers of the business.

[*C&E Notice 700/9*].

12.34   There is an exception to the TOGC rules. This is where the assets being transferred include land and buildings which are potentially taxable, i.e. on which the transferor has exercised the option to tax, or there is a sale of the freehold of a new or incomplete building liable to VAT at the standard rate, and the successor company has not notified Customs & Excise of an election to waive exemption in respect of the property concerned. The transferor must then charge standard rate VAT in respect of the supply of the property.

12.35   When the ownership of a business is transferred to a different legal entity, it is possible for the transferee to take over the transferor's original VAT registration number provided:

- registration of the original business is cancelled from the date of the transfer; and
- the new business is not already registered, but is liable or entitled to be registered.

The process is effected by completion of form VAT68.

[*VAT Regulations 1995, SI 1995/2518, art 6*].

Due notice should be given to Customs & Excise so that registration of the company can be effected before it needs to start trading.

It is to be noted that transferring a VAT registration number from one business to another transfers the responsibility for any debits and credits both before and after the transfer to the new owner. The decision to transfer a VAT number must be taken in the light of any adverse history or potential liability which may be assumed by the company.

The records of the original business must be transferred to the successor company [*VATA 1994, s 49*].

12.36 Alternatively, if it is decided to break the link with the old business, the company may apply for fresh registration. The former business proprietor must deregister immediately after the transfer. It is not necessary for the transfer of all the assets of a business to take place for it to be a TOGC. However, what is transferred should be sufficient to enable continued operation of the same business as was carried on by the transferor.

12.37 One problem may arise if the business premises are not transferred to the company. The reasons for this are explored at **14.1** and payment of rent is addressed at **14.23** and **15.47–15.49**. The problem concerns VAT which was recovered in respect of the property's original purchase or in respect of subsequent refurbishment. In this case, all or part of the VAT reclaimed may be repayable to Customs & Excise. This might be avoided if the option to tax is made on the property and VAT is charged on the rents paid by the company.

If the option to tax is made, the former business proprietor will need to retain the existing VAT registration. Transfer to the company is not possible and the company should register separately.

If the option to tax is not made, the repayment of input VAT on the property costs will depend on the amounts involved, the timing of incorporation and whether the property falls within the capital goods scheme.

12.38 Although incorporation of the business does not involve a supply for VAT purposes, this does not prevent the recovery of input tax on any related expenses. If the transferee company acquires assets by way of a TOGC and the assets are used exclusively to make taxable supplies, the VAT incurred on the costs of acquiring those assets should be attributed to those taxable supplies and can be recovered in full. In the case of the transferor, since the sale of the business as a going concern is not a supply, the input tax incurred on the costs of sale cannot be attributed to any supply by the transferor. These costs are therefore treated as an overhead expense but, when there is a direct and immediate link with the transferred part of the business, the input tax can be attributed to that part and be apportioned, if necessary, by the transferor's agreed partial exemption method [*C&E Business Brief 8/2001, 2 July 2001*].

12.39   It is crucial for all businesses to establish whether there is a TOGC or not. There is no safe option – if VAT is charged on a transaction which turns out to be a TOGC, both parties will have misstated their VAT liabilities where, at worst, Customs & Excise can both require the vendor to account for the amount he has incorrectly treated as output tax and deny input tax recovery to the purchaser. If VAT is not charged, but Customs & Excise decide there is no TOGC, the transferor will have a VAT liability which it may be impossible to recover from the transferee.

Uniform business rate

12.40   Another tax pops in at the tail end.

If there are specific business premises, then payment of uniform business rate is a fact of life. However, it may sneak up on a few people unawares.

Many smaller businesses, particularly in the service sector, IT consultants etc., will operate from home. The office could be a purpose built study or, more typically, the spare bedroom. It could well be equipped with desk, phone, computer, filing cabinets etc.

It is reported [*John Newth – Tax Journal 19 August 2002*] that the Valuation Office Agency has begun an initiative to reclassify a room in the home, used solely for business, as subject to business rates and not council tax. This attitude is now reflected by commentary on the Valuation Office Agency website www.voa.gov.uk. This, at least, is the theory. Whether local councils actually have the resources to apply business rates to anyone running a business from home is another matter.

One would fear that any such argument has to carry more weight if the occupier of the room is actually a company, rather than the house owner wearing 'another hat' as a self employed individual. A plate at the door indicating a company registered office may tip the balance of argument. Indeed, having the registered office at home is almost certainly inviting an enquiry from the local Council as to what business activities are carried on there.

One defence to the attack might be to ensure that no one room is specifically set aside for business purposes. With the paraphernalia of modern business, this could be difficult.

Planning points

- Consider carefully whether directors' service contracts are needed as this may inhibit remuneration planning (**12.9**).
- Consider restrictions imposed by professional bodies (**12.10**).
- Where total incorporation is not possible, consider a service company (**12.14–12.16**).
- When incorporating, tell everyone you can think of (**12.28**).
- Check that incorporation is a TOGC for VAT (**12.39**).
- Where business premises are retained outside the company, watch for VAT problems (**12.37**).
- Consider whether to transfer the existing VAT registration number to the company (**12.35**).

Chapter 13

Inheritance Tax

Transfers and reliefs

13.1 Inheritance tax (IHT) is a tax on chargeable transfers. That is to say, when an individual's total estate is reduced by a gratuitous transfer (whether by lifetime gift or bequest on death), IHT is charged on the value transferred [*IHTA 1984, s 1*], subject to a number of exemptions and reliefs. Transfers of value may also be made by trustees or, indeed, close companies. In the latter case, they are apportioned through to the participators.

Incorporation is a commercial transaction. There should be no gratuitous intent to it. In theory therefore there is no charge to IHT or it should be excluded by *IHTA 1984, s 10*.

One might think that this is the end of the story and this might be the shortest chapter in the book. On the other hand, there may be instances where transfers of value do arise, or there is a reduction in the value of an individual's estate.

13.2 Where there is a gratuitous reduction in an individual's estate, most lifetime transfers are potentially exempt transfers (PET). Providing there is no death within seven years, no actual liability should arise. Note that, should a close company make a transfer of value and this is apportioned to the participators, this is not a PET and IHT is immediately chargeable.

13.3 The charge to IHT may be reduced by several reliefs, the most significant of which in relation to business assets are business property relief (BPR) and agricultural property relief (APR). Incorporation of a business may have side effects on the availability or rate of these reliefs. These changes will be explored.

Valuation

13.4 This book cannot possibly cover the scope of business valuation, especially private company shares which is an art in itself. However, if IHT is charged on the reduction of an individual's estate, one ought to consider whether incorporation might bring this about.

13.5 In English law at least (the position is slightly different in Scotland), a partner is treated as though he owned a proportionate share in all the assets of the business. The valuation of the partner's business interests should be on that basis. It is unusual to apply any significant discount. A 25% minority partner in a partnership might thus have a partnership interest valued at something approaching 25% of the total business.

13.6   On incorporation, the partner becomes a 25% minority shareholder in a private company. He no longer owns the underlying assets – the company does. The votes on his shares are insufficient to enable him (alone) to influence the decisions of the members in general meeting on any aspect of the company business. That shareholding must therefore be given a hefty discount to the net asset value of the company to reflect the absence of control, lack of marketability etc. One might expect a discount of perhaps 60% at this level of holding.

It must be concluded that the act of incorporation has apparently reduced the value of his estate. In these circumstances, it ought to be possible to satisfy the Capital Taxes Office (where necessary) that, whilst there is a reduction in the value of the estate, there has been no transfer of value. This is because the incorporation was a bona fide commercial transfer, with no gratuitous intent, following *IHTA 1984, s 10.*

Gifts

13.7   Possibly without the parties realising it, some incorporations may involve an element of gift. The transactions leading to and from incorporation really are not the place to undertake estate planning. This ought to be a separate issue, though the time of incorporation may be a valid point at which to consider such matters, possibly because the shares in the new company are of relatively modest value. This should be a separate exercise though and not confused with the incorporation process.

13.8   Whilst the interests of the shareholders in the newly formed company will, in most instances, be identical to the interests of the proprietors in the unincorporated business, this is not exclusively the case. Some sole traders may have non-working spouses. The income tax personal allowances, lower rate and basic rate bands of one partner could be wasted. To a certain extent employment of the spouse in the business could alleviate the problem.

However, incorporation may be viewed as a solution to equalising the situation. A company will be formed with the spouses as equal shareholders. When the business is transferred into the company on incorporation, the former business proprietor will, on the face of it, lose half the value of the business, with a corresponding increase in the spouse's estate. So long as we are dealing with husband and wife (both of whom are domiciled in the UK), this may be no problem. Transfers between spouses are exempt [*IHTA 1984, s 18*].

13.9   The business proprietor may be tempted to be more creative though, by setting up a company which has some shares owned by (adult) children. The intention is to let them have dividend income to utilise their basic rate bands for income tax purposes (see **16.62**). This might be perceived, for example, as a relatively efficient way of funding university education. In this instance though, the transfer of value on incorporation is only partially exempt.

To the extent that anyone other than the original business proprietor or spouse takes shares, the real problem is that the transfer of value made in such circumstances is not a PET. It is a chargeable transfer. The recipient of the gift is a company, not an individual, even though the effect of it is to increase the estates of the children. That this is a correct construction of *IHTA 1984, s 3A(2)(b)* is confirmed by the Inland Revenue *CTO Advanced Instruction Manual at paras C44* and *C31*. In most instances the transfer of value in such circumstances will be relatively small. However, the proprietor needs to be aware of the erosion to his IHT nil rate band.

IHT may not be the only inhibitor to such proposals. Depending on the structure adopted, the route of achieving it, and the nature of the business one might also need to be wary of the settlements legislation (for further details see **16.69**).

Business Property Relief

13.10   Every business proprietor must be aware of this relief and the impact that incorporation might have on it. The rate could be halved and the assets encompassed by it restricted.

The relief is given in respect of relevant business property which, ignoring quoted companies and trust interests, amounts to:

*   a business or interest in a business;
*   securities of a company which, either alone or together with other securities or unquoted shares, give the transferor control of the company immediately before the transfer;
*   any unquoted shares in a company;
*   any land or building, machinery or plant used wholly or mainly for the purposes of a business carried on by a company controlled by the transferor, or by a partnership of which he is a partner.

[*IHTA 1984, s 105(1)*].

13.11   On the face of it, any business or any shares in an unquoted company qualify. Thus a limitation is imposed so that it is, in effect, only trading businesses whether corporate or unincorporated which qualify. This follows from *IHTA 1984, s 105(3)* which excludes:

*   a business or interest in a business which consists wholly or mainly of dealing in securities, stocks or shares, land or buildings, or making or holding investments;

- shares in a company whose business consists wholly or mainly of one of the foregoing.

For convenience, such businesses are referred to in the remainder of this chapter as 'investment businesses'.

Qualifying business

13.12 This leaves a basic definition that BPR applies to businesses and shares in unquoted companies, but not where the business is mainly an investment business. There is no further explanation and one must rely on case law. Business is actually nowhere defined in the Taxes Acts. The author ventures to suggest his own definition for capital gains tax purposes at **9.1**. Further case law and hearsay evidence is cited at **20.5–20.7**.

It seems to require some sort of positive activity and a view to a profit. For IHT, it specifically includes a profession or vocation [*IHTA 1984, s 103(3)*] – this subsection is otherwise a bit superfluous in pointing out that a business includes a business. Case law revolves largely around property letting activities which, whilst accepted to be a business, are considered to be wholly or mainly making or holding investments, see for example *Burkingyoung's Executor v IRC [1995] STC (SCD) 29*. Several attempts have been made to demonstrate that caravan parks qualify. Most have failed – see for example *Hall (Hall's Executors) v IRC [1997] STC (SCD) 126* though, in a case where the rents were unusually low and other activities significant, success was achieved – see *Furness v IRC [1999] STC (SCD) 232*.

13.13 The Inland Revenue accepts that furnished holiday lettings are a qualifying business where the lettings are short-term and the owner is substantially involved with the holidaymaker in terms of activities on and from the premises [*Capital Taxes Office Advanced Instruction Manual L99.3*]. A building or property dealing business can qualify where land and property is held as stock.

13.14 This apart, one is left to make up one's own mind and will conclude in most cases that a qualifying business is broadly equivalent to a trade, profession or vocation.

Sole trader

13.15 Provided that the business of the sole trader is not excluded by the investment activity test, the whole of the value should qualify for BPR in the event of death or chargeable transfer for IHT purposes. This may be subject to the comments on excluded property (see **13.34–13.35**) below.

The rate of relief is 100% [*IHTA 1984, s 104(1)(a)*].

Partner

13.16   As regards the business itself, a partner is in broadly the same position as a sole trader.

100% BPR should be available in respect of a chargeable transfer of the business interest. As *IHTA 1984, s 105(1)(a)* refers only to an interest in a business, the extent of participation is irrelevant. Thus, a partner with a 5% share in a business (say) can obtain exactly the same relief pro rata to value as a partner with a 90% share.

13.17   At this point, it is worth exploring a little further what is a qualifying business. The actual nature of relevant business property was discussed at **13.10** above.

13.18   *IHTA 1984, s 105(3)* excludes a business which consists 'wholly or mainly' of [investment activities]. Standing this on its head, a business with mainly trading activities should qualify for BPR. Like so many other commonly used terms in the Taxes Acts, 'mainly' is not defined and usually taken to have its ordinary dictionary definition of more than half.

For most businesses, the answer would be obvious. There is only one activity and either it qualifies or it does not. There will be some though with more than one activity. For example a building firm, which normally builds and sells houses, decides to retain one or two and let them. The building trade qualifies for BPR; the property letting does not. The activities of the firm may be considered in the round. It has only one business, part of which qualifies and part of which does not. If the totality of the activities amounts to a business, then the different activities should be viewed as part of a whole. If the letting is less than half of the total, then the whole business qualifies for relief (even though part of it taken in isolation would not). This much used to be stated in Inland Revenue *Shares Valuation Manual 15.5* (though the entire manual was withdrawn from public consumption late in 2002. In this respect see **13.27** below). Note that this is an all or nothing test. Either the composite business qualifies, or it does not. There is no partial relief.

13.19   The next question is how to measure whether a business consists mainly of investments or not. This aspect was explored in *Farmer (Farmer's Executors) v IRC [1999] STC (SCD) 321*. The business was essentially a farm, though it had diversified and had ancillary income, chiefly from the letting of redundant farm buildings. The Special Commissioner decided that it was necessary to look at the business in the round and consider all relevant factors, including turnover, profit, capital employed and time spent by the employees. In this context, it was obvious that the business consisted mainly of farming. It was not sufficient to look at one factor (profit) as the Capital Taxes Office had sought to do.

13.20   A partner may also own assets personally, but which are used in the business. The broader aspects of this situation are explained in more detail in

Chapter 14. So far as BPR is concerned, the individual can obtain relief in respect of a chargeable transfer, provided that the asset in question was land or buildings, machinery or plant used wholly or mainly for the purpose of the partnership business, and he is a partner.

There is no relief for the asset held outside the partnership, unless the partnership interest itself is relevant business property. Again, there is no minimum participation limit in the partnership. So a partner can get BPR in respect of property let to a partnership of which he is only a small minority partner.

The rate of relief is 50% [*IHTA 1984, s 104(1)(b)*].

13.21   A loan account with a partnership does not qualify for BPR. In *Beckman v IRC [2000] STC (SCD) 59*, a woman and her daughter carried on business in partnership. The mother retired from the business, which continued with the daughter as a sole trader, but retained an interest in the business through her loan account. The Special Commissioner found that, following retirement from the business, the mother's rights were simply those of an ordinary creditor and no BPR was due, in respect of her loan to the business at the time she died.

Company shareholder

13.22   Again with the rider that the business of the company is not mainly excluded investment activities, all shares in unquoted companies qualify for BPR when there is a chargeable transfer for IHT. BPR is available both to working and passive shareholders. It is not necessary for the shareholder to be a director of the company.

There is no minimum size of holding, nor any specification as to the type of share. Therefore, preference shares qualify just as much as fully participating ordinaries.

Securities in an unquoted company may also qualify, but only if either alone, or along with other securities or unquoted shares, they gave the transferor control of the company.

The rate of relief is 100% [*IHTA 1984, s 104(1)(a)*].

13.23   Where any property would be relevant business property, but is subject to a binding contract for sale at the time of a chargeable transfer, then BPR is not available [*IHTA 1984, s 113*]. Beware therefore company Articles or shareholder agreements that impose buy and sell arrangements on the members of the company. They may be designed to protect continuing family ownership of a business, but could mean that no IHT relief is available on the death of a shareholder. What is to be preferred is a double option agreement, under which the surviving shareholders have an option to buy and the deceased's executors have an option to sell. This does not amount to a binding contract and should avoid the problem.

13.24 As with a partnership, a business proprietor who is a shareholder may retain property outside the company. This may qualify for BPR if all of the following conditions are satisfied:

- it is used for the purposes of a business carried on by the company;
- the shares held by the transferor of the asset are themselves relevant business property;
- the transferor controlled the company.

[*IHTA 1984, s 105(1)(d) & (5)*],

The rate of relief is 50% [*IHTA 1984, s 104(1)(b)*].

13.25 As far as the main business interest is concerned, incorporation should have no effect on the availability of BPR should the proprietor die or wish to transfer all or part of the business. A sole trader gets 100% relief on all assets of a qualifying business, as does a partner. A shareholder in a qualifying trading company also gets 100% relief.

13.26 For assets used but not retained within the business vehicle, the situation may worsen. A sole trader would get 100% BPR if the asset comprised part of the business. A partner would get 50% relief irrespective of the extent of his participation in the business. A shareholder gets 50% relief only if he controls the company. For further commentary on this aspect, see **14.33–14.35**.

13.27 Where the company has a composite business of qualifying and non-qualifying activities, the shares still qualify unless the total consists mainly of investment activities. Indeed, the now defunct Inland Revenue *Shares Valuation Manual 15.5* envisaged this situation in relation to a company by saying:

> 'In the case of a hybrid company where the business of a company may include several activities including some which, in themselves, would not qualify as relevant business property (e.g. property investment) provided that the company as a whole qualifies for relief the property investment activities are still part of the business and will not be an excepted asset.'

The new *Shares Valuation Manual* issued in February 2003 adopts the same principle at *para 27660* though it is less explicit in its commentary.

13.28 As with partnerships (see **13.21**), a loan to a company does not qualify for BPR. Whilst it has been suggested at various points throughout this work that the incorporation transactions may lead to a positive balance on a director's loan account, this should not be left in place indefinitely. It gives a means of drawing cash from the company without further tax charge but, if it is still in place when the shareholder dies or wishes to make a chargeable transfer of shares, the value is excluded (see **13.35**) from BPR. The solution may be, if the funds are required in the company and inheritance tax is a concern, to capitalise the loan for more shares. The freedom to draw down is then, of course, lost.

Replacement property

13.29 The availability of BPR depends on the holding of a certain type of business asset. Additionally, it must be held for a minimum period of two years [*IHTA 1984, s 106*].

13.30 Where IHT becomes payable on a failed PET, BPR is only available to reduce the tax payable if the conditions for BPR are satisfied, both at the time of the original gift and at the time of death [*IHTA 1984, s 113A(3)*].

13.31 This does not necessarily mean that the same relevant business property must be held throughout. The two year minimum holding period need not be satisfied by the same relevant business property nor, indeed, does the relevant business property on a failed PET have to be the same asset as that which was originally gifted.

It is possible to carry forward the qualifying conditions into replacement property. So, where one item of qualifying business property is replaced by another, the conditions for BPR remain satisfied. There may even be a gap in ownership. The two-year minimum holding period is satisfied if both assets are held for a total of two years within five years before the transfer of value [*IHTA 1984, s 107*].

13.32 Thus, incorporation will involve a switch from a business held personally (qualifying under *s 105(1)(a)*) to shares in a trading company (qualifying under *s 105(1)(bb)*). All other conditions being satisfied, one replaces the other and the availability of BPR continues throughout. There is no need to establish a new minimum holding period for the shares.

Excluded property

13.33 We have seen that a composite business may qualify for BPR, even if some activities taken in isolation would fail the tests, so long as the total business is not mainly one of holding investments. If that 'mainly' threshold is exceeded, none of the business qualifies.

13.34 Especially with a company (perhaps less so with a partnership) the activities may incorporate something which does not amount to a business at all, e.g. the passive holding of a share portfolio. Also, there may be assets or funds within the business that are not used wholly or mainly for its purposes. If this situation has prevailed for at least two years prior to the date of transfer, and they are not then required for the future use of the business, these are excepted assets. To the extent that the value of the shares or business reflect these assets, BPR is restricted [*IHTA 1984, s 112(2)*].

In *Barclays Bank Trust Co Ltd v IRC [1998] STC (SCD) 125*, the deceased held shares in a family company. Included in the company's assets was cash of £450,000. The Special Commissioner found that only £150,000 might reasonably be needed for the business and £300,000 fell to be excepted from the value attracting BPR.

This latter point should be taken as a warning to business proprietors tempted to use a company as a moneybox to retain accumulated profits. Such action may limit the availability of BPR on the shares.

13.35   Where adjustment falls to be made on account of excluded property, this is achieved by the simple expedient of reducing the total value of the company shares by the proportion which the value of excluded assets bears to the total assets of the company.

13.36   The excepted assets rule should not be confused with the existence of non-qualifying business activities. The latter are considered in the context of whether the business of the company is wholly or mainly investment.

Composite example

13.37   Roger owns 35% of the shares in his family company. These are valued at £400,000. His wife, Brenda, owns 20%. The company's net assets of £1.5m include surplus cash of £500,000. Roger also owns the business premises worth £250,000 which he lets to the company.

If he were to die, what should be included in his estate for business assets and what BPR is due?

Share value	£400,000
Less: Value of excepted assets:	
$£400,000 \times \dfrac{500,000}{1,500,000}$	(133,333)
	266,667
BPR @ 100%	(266,667)
	nil
Property value	250,000
BPR @ 50%	(125,000)
(adding Brenda's shares as related property,	
Roger controls the company)	
	125,000
Add: Share value due to excepted assets	133,333
Chargeable transfer	£258,333

Agricultural Property Relief

13.38   The other principal relief from IHT is far more limited in application, but reflects the nation's rural heritage. This is for agricultural property and the manner in which it is given is rather different to BPR. Because of this, incorporation is possibly less likely to have an impact on its availability.

Agricultural property and the relief

13.39   Agricultural property means agricultural land or pasture and includes any building which is occupied with the agricultural land or pasture and also includes cottages, farm buildings and farmhouses, as are of a character appropriate to the property [*IHTA 1984, s 115(2)*]. It is beyond the scope of this book to examine what may or may not be included in this definition.

The amount of the relief is 100% if either:

*   the transferor's interest in the property carries the right to vacant possession or the right to obtain it within the next 12 months. (By virtue of *ESC F17* this may, in practice, be extended to 24 months);
*   the property is let on a tenancy beginning on or after 1 September 1995.

[*IHTA 1984, s 116(2)*].

There is an additional category for certain holdings in place since 1981. Otherwise, the relief is 50%.

13.40   In addition, for the relief to be available, the agricultural property must not only be owned but occupied by the transferor for a period of two years [*IHTA 1984, s 117(a)*]. For this purpose, occupation by a company controlled by the transferor is treated as occupation by the transferor personally [*IHTA 1984, s 119(1)*].

Failing personal occupation, Agricultural Property Relief (APR) is available where the land has been occupied by any other person for the purposes of agriculture for seven years.

Thus, where dealing with a relatively new holding of land, incorporation may influence the availability of APR if the owner of the land does not control the company.

Agricultural value

13.41   APR is only available in respect of the agricultural value of agricultural property. That is to say the value which it would have if it were to be used perpetually for agriculture.

With farm diversification and the opportunity to sell off redundant buildings etc. for development, the actual value may be higher. This development or hope value does not attract APR.

13.42 Much agricultural property will also satisfy the conditions for BPR. Where, on the face of it, both reliefs are available then APR takes precedence [*IHTA 1984, s 114(1)*]. This does not prevent a claim for BPR on the excess over the agricultural value.

13.43

Example 13.43

Stuart owns and farms 100 acres of agricultural land valued at £600,000. This includes a barn with planning permission for conversion to a house valued at £100,000 (its agricultural value is £5,000). Three acres of land is zoned for development adjacent to a village. It is considered to be worth £240,000 (agricultural value £7,500).

What reliefs would be available if there were a chargeable transfer?

Land value			£600,000
Less:	Development value of barn £100,000 – £5,000	95,000	
	Hope value of land £240,000 – £7,500	232,500	(327,500)
			272,500
APR @ 100%			(272,500)
			nil
Add:	Excess value due to development potential		327,500
			327,500
BPR @ 100%			(327,500)
			nil

Sole trader

13.44 A sole trader farmer who owns his own land should automatically satisfy the conditions of *IHTA 1984, s 116(2)(a)* and 100% APR is available.

Partner

13.45 If the land is owned and occupied by the partnership, it will again satisfy the conditions of *s 116(2)(a)* and 100% APR is available to each partner pro rata to his share of the property.

13.46 However, it is quite common that only one or two of the partners will own the land. If the land is formally let to the partnership on a tenancy created on or after 1 September 1995, the condition in *s 116(2)(c)* should be satisfied and 100% APR is available. If it is a long-standing partnership and the tenancy was created before 1 September 1995, then only 50% relief will be available. There may be less formal arrangements in place giving a short-term right to vacant possession (as in **13.39** above) in which case the rate would be 100%.

13.47 With close family relationships there may not be a tenancy at all and it is arguable that the land owner can gain vacant possession within 12 months (or 24 months under *ESC* F17) so that 100% relief is still available. This is a complex subject beyond the scope of this work.

Company shareholder

13.48 If, on incorporation, the land is placed within the company then the business proprietor ceases to own it. Rather, he has shares in the new company the value of which reflects the value of the land held therein. These shares are clearly not agricultural property in themselves but their value will reflect the underlying agricultural property.

13.49 If that is the case, then APR may be available on the share value to the extent that that value is attributable to the underlying agricultural land providing that the shares give the transferor control of the company [*IHTA 1984, s 122(1)*].

13.50 Assuming that this will be a trading company, it is more than likely that BPR will be available in respect of the shares as well. This will relieve the excess value of the shares over the agricultural value of the land holding. If the control test is not satisfied, then BPR should be available on the whole value. Loss of APR should therefore be no real disaster.

13.51 Turning to the situation where the land is held outside the company, on a new incorporation it is perhaps best to ensure that a formal tenancy is put in place. This would satisfy the conditions of *s 116(1)(c)* and, all other things being equal, 100% APR is maintained.

Property in or out

13.52 It has been demonstrated that the availability of APR and BPR may be adversely affected by incorporation of a business. To a certain extent, the loss of APR may be overcome by the availability of BPR.

However, it has to be admitted that BPR could be reduced where assets are held outside the newly formed company. IHT is not the only factor affecting the decision as to whether major assets should be transferred to the new company, or retained outside.

The next chapter explores the various issues involved.

Planning points

- The act of incorporation is not gratuitous and, of itself, should not lead to a chargeable transfer (**13.6**).
- Beware of inadvertent gifts where the new company shareholders are not the same as the unincorporated business proprietors (**13.9**).
- Composite businesses attract BPR on all assets even though a part viewed in isolation may not qualify (**13.18**).
- BPR on assets held outside the company may be restricted by incorporation (**13.26**).
- Consider capitalising loans in the company to avoid excepted asset problems (**13.28**).

Assets Held Outside the Company

14.1 Why would anyone want to keep assets outside the company? The neat and tidy minded would surely transfer all the assets of the former unincorporated business. Intractable though it might be in certain circumstances, this would permit the use of the CGT relief afforded by *TCGA 1992, s 162*. However, if the asset were a valuable building, there would be substantial stamp duty to pay and this might be avoided.

There are other reasons why assets might be left outside the company:

- Commonly, properties (land and buildings) used by a partnership are not owned by all the partners. In a family scenario, it is often the elders of the family who own the properties. They do not want incorporation of the business to disturb this arrangement. Inclusion of the properties in the company would mean the value is spread around everyone who is a shareholder.
- The rationale for incorporation might be to facilitate, or lessen the impact of taxation on, disposal of the business. In this event, certain assets might be retained by the proprietors and it therefore makes sense to leave them out of the company.
- As demonstrated below (see **14.23–14.27**), the retention of assets outside the company might provide a ready income stream, albeit taxable but at least free of NIC. Where the company might be a convenient route to passing the business down the generations, this also creates a sort of quasi pension fund.
- Keeping valuable assets outside the company might also be done in the hope of restricting claims by creditors of the company. The benefit of limited liability is, after all, a prime rationale of incorporation. However, especially in the small family company, this is unlikely to be a real benefit as personal guarantees may be required.

Thus, there are several reasons why it might be preferred to keep assets outside the company.

Despite the evidence for this, many readers will no doubt be surprised by the first main issue addressed here.

Goodwill

The man who forgot about goodwill

14.2 Why on earth does this appear here at all? Surely it is fundamental to the concept of incorporation. Indeed, many readers will have heard the story about the adviser who forgot goodwill. Maybe this is apocryphal, or has been embellished by the telling and retelling of the story.

The gist of it goes something like this.

14.3

Example 14.3

Matt transferred his successful printing business to a company, having been advised that there were no tax problems. Having looked at the closing balance sheet for the sole trader and the opening balance sheet for the company, the Inspector of Taxes asked for the capital gains tax computation. Matt's accountant was puzzled. The balance sheet looked something like this:

Sole trader closing balance sheet.

Capital account	
Opening balance	38,000
Profit for tax year	75,000
Less: Drawings	(60,000)
Closing balance	53,000
Represented by:	
Plant and machinery	27,000
Net current assets	26,000
Net assets	53,000
Opening company balance sheet:	
Share capital	1,000
Directors' loan account	52,000
	53,000
Plant and machinery	27,000
Net current assets	26,000
Net assets	53,000

Matt's accountant maintained that no chargeable assets were transferred. The Inspector asked about goodwill and the accountant replied that it was minimal and personal to Matt. The Inspector insisted that business contacts, reputation etc. were valuable, saleable and could be passed to the company. Grudgingly, the accountant accepted a valuation of £40,000 and promptly submitted an election under *TCGA 1992, s 165* as nothing was paid for goodwill. The Inspector rejected the election, citing the opening balance sheet of the company as evidence that the incorporation proceeded under *s 162*. He computed the gain thus:

Market value of goodwill at date of transfer	40,000
Less: Cost (business started from scratch after 31.3.1982)	(nil)
Gross gain	40,000
Net assets of company per balance sheet	53,000
Add: Goodwill	40,000
Value of company (A)	93,000
Assets received other than shares (B)	52,000
Gain assessable:	

$$40,000 \times \frac{52,000 \text{ (A)}}{93,000 \text{ (B)}} \qquad\qquad £22,365$$

See *TCGA 1992, s 162(4)*.

Business asset taper relief may have saved the accountant's pride and reputation in this circumstance, but what if the business were ten times the size? So what is the point of this story? Perhaps mindful of the potential risks of ignoring goodwill altogether, recent commentaries on incorporation often stress that it should not be forgotten.

The man who remembered goodwill (but still had a problem)

14.4 No one seems to tell the story of the man who tried to transfer the goodwill of a business to a company and failed. The basic concept is simple. Following the route to incorporation afforded by *TCGA 1992, s 165* (see **9.25–9.32**), the process goes:

- Sell the goodwill to the company either for full value or under value, leaving the proceeds outstanding on loan account.
- The first step is perceived to have created a capital gain which is reduced or extinguished by retirement relief, business asset taper relief etc. Indeed, for the last few years, this has been a popular way of 'banking' retirement relief before it was abolished on 5 April 2003. If the unincorporated business has been established for many years, the base cost of the goodwill can generally be taken as the value at 31 March 1982. Indexation relief will then be available up to 5 April 1998. Any unrelieved gain will then be held over under *s 165*.
- Once the company starts to make profits, the proprietor can draw down on the loan account (representing the proceeds of sale of goodwill) without incurring further tax liabilities.

14.5 In due course, the final tax computations and self assessment return for the unincorporated business are submitted to the Inspector of Taxes. Indeed, following best practice the adviser should follow the CG34 procedure and, shortly after the transaction took place, seek guidance on the valuations of the capital assets transferred to ensure that the computations submitted are accurate so that the correct tax (if any) may be paid on the due date.

It is at this point that the adviser may come in for a shock when a letter from Inland Revenue Shares Valuation lands on his doormat one morning. Typically, this will say that the Inspector of Taxes has sought guidance on the valuation of the goodwill transferred to the company and then drop the bombshell that, in their view, this is little or nothing.

What has been forgotten?

Nature of goodwill

14.6   At this point, maybe we should backtrack and think carefully about what goodwill really is. It is an issue often glossed over by professional commentaries, none of which seem to address its true nature, wherein lies the crux of the problem. On the other hand, the Inland Revenue manuals cover the major issues extensively (see *Capital Gains Manual* at *para 68000* et seq.). Readers who wish to steer clear of the potential pitfalls are strongly advised to refer to that commentary.

So, what is goodwill? You cannot see it, feel it, pick it up and carry it around, or let's be honest, even describe it. It is the intangible right attaching to the business which makes a potential purchaser want to pay more than the value of the assets used in the business. The courts have tried to define it, with varying success. Perhaps the leading commentary is that of Lord MacNaghten:

> 'What is goodwill? It is a thing very easy to describe, very difficult to define. It is the benefit and advantage of the good name, reputation and connection of a business. It is the attractive force which brings in custom. It is the one thing which distinguishes an old established business from a new business at its first start.'

IRC v Muller & Co Margarine Ltd [1901] AC 217.

Goodwill is a fungible asset. Students of the English language might point out that fungible is a noun, not an adjective. However, the Inland Revenue uses it in the descriptive form of goodwill at *Capital Gains Manual para 68055.*You can add to it, take away from it, but all along there is only one goodwill attached to a business. That is not to say that all goodwill is the same thing. It may grow or diminish as parts are acquired or disposed of but the parts cannot be identified separately.

14.7   Following case law, the Inland Revenue favours a kind of zoological classification, likening the behaviour of business customers to certain types of animal. Look at *Capital Gains Manual para 68011* and a degree of logic begins to become apparent.

Developing the theme, one can see that there are, in essence, three components to goodwill though they are not separable and, where the different types are present in one business, they become parts of an inseparable whole.

- First, there is personal goodwill. It is inherent in the technical skills, personal attributes etc. of the business proprietor. Customers come to the business because they want the attention of the individual. Commonly cited examples are the celebrity chef or well known photographer. The Inland Revenue takes the view that this type of goodwill cannot be sold. It is inseparable from the individual. In the field of incorporation, one might argue that the individual can be 'tied' to the company by means of a service contract. However, it is difficult to see how this amounts to a transfer of goodwill. The rewards offered under a service contract must represent payment for the continuing use of personal skills (which remain with the individual). Such a contract would also inhibit the tax planning opportunities afforded by trading in the corporate medium.
- The second category is inherent goodwill. This attaches, not to the skills of the individual proprietor, but rather to the location. Customers go to the business because of its location. It might be the case with a hotel; customers go to it because of its pleasant surroundings, ease of access etc. Equally, customers will go to a retail shop because of where it is, convenience factors etc. *Capital Gains Manual para 68456* lists many more examples. This type of goodwill can be transferred, but only with the premises. A business of this type could endeavour to change premises but might often find that some of its customer base (assuming continuation of a similar business there) remains at the old location.
- The third category is free goodwill. This is what we really want on incorporation of a business. It is not fixed with any particular attribute of the business. It is the measure of the business value over and above its net assets. It might include a transferable customer list, brand name, general reputation etc. The reason it is so easy to overlook is that, unless purchased in the first place, it rarely appears on the balance sheet of an unincorporated business.

14.8   At which point, we probably have sufficient knowledge to go back to the man who remembered the goodwill, but still had a problem. No doubt he valued the goodwill by reference to the 'super profit' of the business.

Example 14.8

Mike is the chef proprietor of a successful restaurant business. Last year, the gross profit was £200,000. The super profit might be established thus:

Gross profit	200,000
Less: Drawings (say)	(50,000)
Less: Interest on capital (say)	(20,000)
Super profit	£130,000

Goodwill valued at 1–2 times super profit
(say £125,000 – £250,000)

The author has seen multipliers as high as 10, but this is unrealistic in an incorporation. We are dealing with a connected party transaction and it is necessary to establish the true market value, hence the intervention of Inland Revenue Shares Valuation.

The problem? Most of the goodwill is personal (attaching to Mike and his reputed skills as a chef), or inherent (attaching to the location of his premises). Mike's adviser forgot this and merely included £200,000 (on a multiplier of 1½) in the CGT computation relating to incorporation of the business. After business asset taper relief and annual exemption, this gave a tax bill of just under £17,000, which Mike thought acceptable for the ability to draw £200,000 from the new company without further tax charge. So now the adviser is faced with explaining to Mike why the Inland Revenue will not agree.

Could he have done anything better?

As regards the personal goodwill, probably not. Mike does not want a service contract with the company. The advantage of taking a dividend and not a salary has been explained to him and he wants to exploit this. In any case, it is questionable whether a service contract would make any difference. It merely gives the company an opportunity to exploit Mike's goodwill: it does not effect a transfer.

As regards the goodwill inherent in the restaurant premises, perhaps. Mike had various personal reasons for not placing this in the company. The Inland Revenue seems to accept that some measure of inherent goodwill attaches to a lease [*Capital Gains Manual para 68031*], so Mike could have leased the premises to the company. This does not, however, transfer all of it.

Result

14.9   The Inland Revenue seems to take the view that much of the goodwill attaching to any small business derives from the skills, abilities and other personal attributes of the proprietor. In other words, the transfer of goodwill might be a nice idea, but in many instances the scope to do it may be severely limited. You may have to face the fact that the goodwill must be left outside the company.

14.10   And, how does the example of Mike end? His new company is paying him £200,000 and IR Shares Valuation maintains that the value of the free goodwill truly transferable is well below this. The majority of the goodwill remains outside the company. What then is the nature of the payment? At this stage the company has not traded and, in the absence of any borrowings, has no funds. Its payment is therefore, to all intents and purposes, an IOU represented by a credit balance on a loan account. Possibly this could have the character of:

- Schedule E remuneration – a sort of signing on payment for agreeing to provide his services to the company. This seems a distinct possibility and will have attendant PAYE and NIC liabilities.
- A distribution within *ICTA 1988, s 209* chargeable to income tax. This option seems unlikely as the company has not traded and has no reserves.

Nonetheless, some commentators seem to think that it is a possibility and it must be borne in mind that *ICTA 1988, s 209(4)* does deem an asset transferred to a company at overvalue as a distribution. The author has seen it suggested that the debt should be structured as a non-assignable personal loan to ensure that its value is nil and there can be no distribution. This seems to be going a little beyond reality, calling for excessive legal drafting beyond the demands of many small businesses.

- A loan to a participator under *ICTA 1988, s 419* leading to tax chargeable on the company (see **16.14**).

There is no easy resolution to the mess. One could endeavour to argue up the value transferred but this may be difficult. Some residual liability might have to be accepted, in which case accepting a liability under *ICTA 1988, s 419* may be preferable with later write off or repayment as the company trades profitably. Alternatively, the document of transfer could express the proceeds as being £x 'or such lesser amount as may be agreed with the Inland Revenue' though, on enquiry, this would seem to provoke a challenge.

Capital gains tax rollover relief

14.11   A general relief for replacement of business assets is afforded by *TCGA 1992, s 152*. A business, whether incorporated or not, may dispose of an asset used in its trade and realise a capital gain. The tax payable could cause cash flow difficulties if it is intended to apply the proceeds in the purchase of a new asset for use in the business.

Rollover relief can apply in such circumstances, the effect of which is to treat the original asset as disposed of for the consideration which gives neither a gain nor a loss. Correspondingly, the base cost of the replacement asset is depressed.

14.12

Example 14.12

Julie sells the shop from which she traded for £120,000. It originally cost £100,000. She immediately replaces it with another shop costing £150,000.

Disposal of first shop:	
Proceeds	£120,000
Less: Cost	100,000
Gross gain	20,000
Proceeds restricted to ensure no gain/no loss *s 152(1)(a)*	(20,000)
Net gain (indexation relief ignored)	nil

14.13 *Assets Held Outside the Company*

Acquisition of second shop

Cost	150,000
Reduction for rolled-over gain	
s 152(1)(b)	(20,000)
Base cost carried forward	£130,000

Note that this treatment results in loss of taper relief on the original gain. It is the gain before taper which is held over.

14.13   Where the full proceeds arising from the disposal of the first asset are reinvested, then the full gain is rolled over. In some circumstances, only part of the proceeds may be so used. In this instance, partial relief may be available under *TCGA 1992, s 153*. The mechanism of this is such as to treat the new expenditure as coming first from the base cost of the asset sold and only then the gain realised. Therefore no relief can be obtained until the amount reinvested exceeds the original base cost (plus indexation).

14.14   A formal claim is required in order to obtain rollover relief (either full or partial). In addition, the new expenditure must be incurred within twelve months before to three years after the first disposal. The Board of the Inland Revenue is empowered to extend these time limits under *TCGA 1992, s 152(3)*. The circumstances in which the Inland Revenue may allow extension of the time limit are set out in Revenue Interpretation *RI5*. In the author's experience, it will do so where there is clear evidence that attempts were being made within the original time limit to find a suitable replacement asset.

14.15   Also, *TCGA 1992, s 153A* caters for provisional application of the rollover relief provisions. Say the disposal of the old asset occurs in February 2003. An individual will be required to return the gain on his self assessment tax return for the year ended 5 April 2003 and pay the CGT due on 31 January 2004. There could nevertheless be an intention to acquire a replacement asset (at any time up to February 2006) so that no tax is actually due. He can therefore declare the intention to make a rollover claim in his tax return for the year ended 5 April 2003, deferring payment of the liability, to be replaced by a final claim made on acquisition of the new asset.

14.16   The relief only applies to certain classes of asset, set out in *TCGA 1992, s 155*. These include:

- land or buildings occupied (as well as used) for the purpose of the trade;
- fixed plant or machinery;
- ships, aircraft and hovercraft;
- satellites, space stations and spacecraft;
- goodwill;
- milk quota, potato quota, ewe and suckler cow premium quota, fish quota;
- certain rights and assets held by a member of Lloyd's.

Depreciating assets

14.17   Where the new assets acquired are depreciating assets, then *TCGA 1992, s 154* provides for a rather different treatment. A depreciating asset is defined in *s 154(7)* as one which:

'At that time is a wasting asset, as defined in s 44, or within the period of 10 years beginning at that time it would become a wasting asset.'

Broadly, a wasting asset is one with a predicable life not exceeding 50 years and Revenue interpretation *RI42* comments on the position of leasehold land where the lease has 60 years or less to run.

14.18   In this case, the gain is not applied in reducing the base cost of the second asset. It is merely calculated and deferred until the first of the events given by *s 154(2)*, namely:

- disposal of the second asset;
- cessation of use of the asset for the purposes of a trade carried on by the owner;
- expiration of a period of 10 years beginning with the acquisition of the second asset.

14.19   This, in itself presents a nasty trap on incorporation. Where a sole trader (or partnership) holding an asset with such a deferred gain, transfers his business to a company this would be a disposal and the gain is realised. This gain cannot be deferred under *TCGA 1992, s 162* or held over under *s 165* (see **9.3–9.5**).

Asset used by company

14.20   All of the above assumes that the trader (whether a company or otherwise) holds the asset in question. This chapter is primarily concerned with the effects of assets held outside the company.

This situation is catered for in the rollover provisions by *TCGA 1992, s 157* which extends the basic rollover provisions to the situation where:

- the person disposing of the old asset and acquiring the new asset is an individual; and
- the trade or trades in question are carried on, not by that individual, but by a company which both at the time of the disposal and the time of the acquisition is a company the voting rights in which are exercisable, as to not less than 5%, by him.

14.21   The wording 'a company the voting rights in which are exercisable, as to not less than 5%, by him' is a recent import on 6 April 2003 from *FA 1998, s 140(3)* replacing the previously used 'personal company' borrowed from the now demised retirement relief provisions. Clearly, an individual could have more than one company which satisfied this criterion, which begs the question must both the old and the new asset be used by the same company, or could one company use the old asset and a different company the new one? Or even, could an individual dispose of an asset used by him as a sole trader and replace it with an asset used in the trade of a family company?

The preferred construction appears to be that the words 'trade or trades in question are carried on by a company' in *TCGA 1992, s 157(b)* actually identify the company which must be the same company on both side of the equation. Certainly this is the view taken by the Inland Revenue (see *Capital Gains Manual para 61251*). Thus, in these circumstances, where an individual disposes of an asset used by a company, in order to achieve rollover relief the new asset must be used by the same company.

14.22 Of course, the company may pay rent for the use of an asset held by the shareholder. That may be under a formal lease or otherwise and could be a full market rent or something less. The rollover legislation is totally silent on this point and the Inland Revenue takes the view that it is not a determining factor (see *Capital Gains Manual para 61260*). So rollover relief is equally applicable whether the individual permits the company to use the asset free of charge, or whether a substantial rent is paid.

Rent

14.23 Whatever the personal considerations for keeping assets outside the company, one must next consider whether the company be allowed to use them informally, or whether a contractual entitlement with the payment of rent should be established. There could be a range of variation between these extremes.

Quite often we will be concerned in these circumstances with major valuable assets, such as land and buildings. The rationale for keeping them out of the company may be ownership by different family members to the shares in the company; for example, father owns the business premises, but his sons also participate (and are shareholders) in the company. It then makes sense to secure the company's position.

This can have added advantages for the property owner, though one has to have regard to the effect on other significant tax reliefs.

The degree of formality of the arrangement is one for personal decision in the context of the overall business structure. Sometimes a proper lease may be constructed, containing the usual duties of landlord and tenant and requiring payment of a market rent with regular review. In a close family situation, an informal agreement with the amount to be agreed from time to time might be satisfactory.

Effect on property owner

14.24   Payment of rent may be seen as another relatively tax efficient means of extracting profit from the company.

14.25   So far as the company is concerned, the rent should be an allowable trading deduction.

14.26   So far as the property owner is concerned, the receipt is of investment income to be included in his self assessment tax return, with tax payable on 31 January following the end of the tax year concerned. This cash flow advantage will only be a one-off when the arrangement starts, as later years will probably require a payment on account.

14.27   The balance of tax liability may not be significant as between the company and the individual. Indeed it may actually be disadvantageous if, as with many small business arrangements, the company pays corporation tax at 19% and the individual pays income tax at 40%. Nevertheless, if the proprietor needs cash to spend, in most circumstances this must be accepted. The great advantage lies with NIC. The rent is not earnings for this purpose, so neither primary nor secondary Class 1 contributions are due. Given that, on payment of a salary, these could amount to a total of up to 23.8%, it can be seen that there is a huge gain in taking rent rather than additional salary.

Effect on tax reliefs

14.28   The tax advantages of paying rent are fine, providing that they do not have a deleterious effect on other tax reliefs. The prime concerns would obviously be:

- inheritance tax: BPR and APR (both of which are considered in the section immediately following);
- capital gains tax: rollover relief, taper relief, holdover relief for business assets, Enterprise Investment Scheme.

We have already seen (**14.22**) that payment of rent is not a factor in determining the availability of CGT rollover relief.

14.29   For the purposes of taper relief, 'business assets' include any asset used for the trade of a qualifying company [*TCGA 1992, Sch A1 para 5(2)(b)*]. By a strange lacuna following the revisions to taper relief in *FA 2000*, the owner of an asset no longer needs a minimum shareholding in a company for it to be a qualifying company. It simply has to be (in many instances) a trading company and unlisted [*TCGA 1992, Sch A1 para 6(a), (b)(i)*]. So the payment of rent should not affect taper relief.

14.30   Should the asset owner be minded to make a gift of it, this could well realise a capital gain. Such a gain can be held over under *TCGA 1992, s 165* so long as the asset is used in a trade carried on by a company. The asset owner must have voting rights which are exercisable as to not less than 5% [*s 165(2)(a)(ii)*] with the definition of personal company substituted by *FA 1998, s 140(4)*. Provided then that the asset owner has 5% or more of the ordinary share capital, this should not be a problem. As with rollover relief, payment of rent does not seem a material factor.

14.31 If the company was created in such a fashion as to give the shareholder EIS income tax relief under *ICTA 1988 Part VII Chapter III* or deferral relief under *TCGA 1992, s 150C* and *Sch 5B*, a degree of care may be required. Both reliefs can fail where the investor receives value from the company. If he is also the owner of the asset outside the company, then the arrangements must be structured very carefully so as to ensure that they are seen to be on strictly commercial lines. Payment of an excessive rent could prejudice the EIS reliefs. (For EIS reliefs generally, see **6.8–6.16**).

Inheritance tax

14.32 The general principles of the main IHT reliefs (BPR and APR) are explored in detail in **Chapter 13**.

We are concerned here solely with assets held outside the company.

Business Property Relief

14.33 Relevant business property includes, under *IHTA 1984, s 105(1)(d)*:

> 'Any land or building, machinery or plant ... used wholly or mainly for the purposes of a business carried on by a company of which the transferor then had control'.

For this purpose, 'control' has the meaning given in *IHTA 1984, s 269*, so that in effect he controls powers of voting on all questions affecting the company so as to yield a majority of votes being capable of being exercised on them (and, for this purpose, any shares which are related property may be included). Whilst the decision in *Walding v IRC [1996] STC 13* gives some guidance on the meaning of voting control, this can be a problem. Companies with a straight 50:50 split as between shareholders are not uncommon.

The author recalls a situation where a trading company was owned as to 50% exactly by each of two brothers who also owned land occupied by the company 50:50. There was no shareholder agreement or other documentation. He was forced to conclude that, in the event of the death of either brother, no BPR at all would be due in respect of the land.

Additionally, to obtain relief by *s 105(1)(d)*, the transferor's interest in the shares (which give control) must also be relevant business property [*IHTA 1984, s 105(6)*].

14.34 It should be noted that the amount of relief available in these circumstances is only 50%. Therefore incorporation can worsen the situation. An asset used in a sole trader business should attract 100% BPR as part of the business. An asset used in a partnership business should attract 50% BPR, whatever the extent of the owner's participation in the partnership. Where the business is incorporated and the asset is held outside the company, then BPR is only available at 50% and only then if the owner has:

- a controlling interest in the company; and
- the shares themselves are relevant business property.

It follows that, where the company's trading property is held by the (senior) proprietor, there is a strong incentive for him to retain a controlling shareholding which may in due course inhibit tax planning manoeuvres aimed at passing the business down the generations.

14.35 Take extreme care if a perceived solution is to later transfer the property to the company. This might be by way of a gift from the owner to the company. Whilst a chargeable gain might be realised, this could probably be relieved by a holdover claim under *TCGA 1992, s 165*. However, a gift to the company is a chargeable transfer but not a PET [*IHTA 1984, s 3A*]. Assuming that his interest in the company is less than 100% (if it were at that level the problem would not have arisen) this leads to some actual IHT being payable or, at least, erosion of the nil rate band.

14.36 After which problems, it is pleasing to report that payment of rent by the company for use of the asset does not appear to affect BPR.

Agricultural Property Relief

14.37 After the possible difficulties with BPR, it comes almost as a pleasure to report that APR seems to have been designed with the investor in mind.

If the asset in question held outside the company is agricultural land then APR at 100% is available in accordance with *IHTA 1984, s 116* if the owner's interest:

- carries the right to vacant possession with 12 months; or
- has existed since before 10 March 1981 and certain other conditions are satisfied; or
- is in property let on a tenancy beginning on or after 1 September 1995.

A newly incorporated business will almost certainly have been set up to fall in the latter category. The size of the landowner's interest in the company is immaterial.

Failing all else, APR is still available for let land at 50% and the size of the owner's interest in the company is immaterial.

Planning points

- Do not forget goodwill (**14.3**).
- On incorporation, establish the true nature of goodwill to ensure it is transferable (**14.7**).
- Gains on personal assets used by a company can only be rolled over into a new asset used by the same company (**14.21**).
- Payment of rent for personal assets used by the company may be a cost effective way of extracting profits (**14.24–14.26**).
- Holding assets outside the company may restrict BPR (**14.34**).

Chapter 15

Other Forms of Remuneration

The company car

15.1   Is this the most emotive topic in the whole world of taxation? Everyone seems to have a view on it and every view seems to differ. For every employee who wants to give up his company car because he 'cannot afford the tax', there is another employee desperate to get one.

It is yet another area where there is no right answer or, at least, no single answer will suit everybody. There are just too many variables to factor into the equation to even suggest a useful rule of thumb. One may need to consider at least:

- the value of the car;
- the total running costs;
- the age of the car (depreciation is the biggest single cost of running a new car and will drop sharply even when the car is as little as one or two years old);
- the total mileage travelled;
- the balance between business and private mileage.

The author is aware of business incorporations which have foundered solely on the issue of personal car costs for the proprietor. Biased or even totally prejudiced opinions seem to hold sway rather than a rational analysis of the facts in any case.

It does not help that we will be comparing the Schedule D rules for the unincorporated business with the employment income rules for the company director. They are totally dissimilar and, it has to be said for the employment income side of things, totally arbitrary.

Also, many businessmen seem to have an overly optimistic view of how few private miles they travel. Whilst things have moved on from a few years ago, some of the private use add backs in Schedule D income tax computations do seem to leave something to be desired. Is there a reluctance, where a small private use adjustment has been accepted, to disturb the status quo?

15.2   It is simple to establish the cost of private motoring for a sole trader. Simply apportion the total running costs between business and private miles. The business proportion is deductible in the Schedule D income tax computation; the private proportion is not. Consider the following:

15.3   *Other Forms of Remuneration*

Example 15.2

Arthur is an independent financial adviser. He runs a Ford Mondeo 1.8 LX. He does about 15,000 miles a year of which 5,000 are private. Total running costs are about £7,500. His marginal tax rate is 22%.

His private motoring costs him:

$$\frac{5,000}{15,000} \times £7,500 = £2,500$$

The business proportion is an allowable cost of the business.

Employment income benefits

15.3   To make a meaningful comparison, maybe we should briefly recap the current system.

Since 6 April 2002, employment income scale benefits, for private use of an employer provided car, have been based solely on the original list price of the car and its emissions measured in grams per kilometre (g/km) of carbon dioxide (CO_2) [*ITEPA 2003, Part 3 Chapter 6; ICTA 1988, Sch 6* as substituted by *FA 2000, s 59, Sch 11*]. For 2002/03, where the figure was 165 g/km or less, the benefit was 15% of list price. Where it was more than 265 g/km the benefit was 35%. Between the two it was graduated in steps of 1% additional tax charge for each additional 5g/km of CO_2, rounding down actual figures of CO_2 to the nearest amount divisible by five [*ITEPA 2003, ss 134–136, 139; ICTA 1988 Sch 6 paras 3–4*].

There are no longer age or mileage related discounts.

Diesel engines emit less CO_2 than comparable petrol engines but are perceived to be 'dirty' in other ways so suffer a 3% surcharge, unless they meet 'Euro IV' standards of cleanliness, but not so as to exceed the 35% scale charge maximum [*ITEPA 2003, s 141; ICTA 1988 Sch 6 para 5D*]. The first Euro IV compliant diesel cars are becoming available for sale in the UK in summer 2003.

The starting point of 165 g/km is to be reduced in the second and third years of the scheme. So for 2003/04 the scale runs from 155–255 g/km and for 2004/05 from 145–245 g/km [*ITEPA 2003, s 139; ICTA 1988 Sch 6 para 4*]. *Finance Act 2003, s 138* reduces the starting point to 140 g/km in 2005/06.

There are special rules for cars registered before 1 January 1998 and for cars registered since that date for which there are no published emission figures [*ITEPA 2003, ss 140, 142; ICTA 1988 Sch 6 para 5C, 5F*].

15.4   Examples of scale benefits applying in 2003/04:

Car	Original list price	Emissions	Scale benefit
Small hatchback	£9,000	170g/km	18% = £1,620
Medium range hatchback	£16,000	200g/km	24% = £3,840
Large executive saloon	£40,000	290g/km	35% = £14,000

Note that the scale benefit is an arbitrary measure of income derived from the use of the car. The actual cost to the employee is the tax paid on that amount. Assuming a marginal tax rate on the first two of 22% and on the third of 40%, the actual payment required is:

£356, £845 and £5,600 respectively.

15.5   Let's go back to the original example of Arthur and assume that he incorporates his business. The car is transferred to the company so his private use benefit in kind is as follows (in this and subsequent examples the scale rates are for 2003/04):

Example 15.5

The facts are as in Example 15.2 above. The original list price of the Ford Mondeo was £15,000. The CO_2 emissions are 187g/km.

Arthur's private motoring now costs him:

Scale benefit £15,000 × 21%	£3,150
Tax due @ 22%	£693

15.6   The other side of the coin is, of course, that the company can deduct all the running costs in arriving at its profit. Arthur's business use/private use proportion is irrelevant since the full costs to the company are deductible either as a general cost of earning its profits or in providing employee remuneration. One can assume that the tax relief is comparable as between the sole trader and the company if it is a small company, since the tax rates of 22% (personal) and 19% (company) are similar.

Use of own car

15.7   Also since 6 April 2002, a statutory scheme of approved mileage allowance payments (AMAP) has been in place, where an employee uses his own car for the purposes of his employer's business. The prescribed rates are:

15.8   *Other Forms of Remuneration*

First 10,000 miles per annum   40p
Thereafter   25p

and that is it [*ITEPA 2003, ss 229–236; ICTA 1988, s 197AD–AG, Sch 12AA*].
Well, actually, the employer could pay a higher rate of mileage allowance but
the excess over the AMAP is liable to income tax and NIC (except that, for
NIC purposes, the prescribed rate has thus far ignored the 10,000 mile upper
limit, i.e. it is 40p per mile regardless of the level of mileage).

There is no longer the alternative, as there was with the pre-6 April 2002 fixed
profit car scheme, of maintaining a detailed record of all costs, business
mileages etc. and claiming an exact percentage of total costs.

The new scheme can hardly be described as generous, especially as quite a few
superminis have published mileage costs above 40p, let alone any larger cars.

The dissimilarity with the Schedule D rules must also be noted. A sole trader
(or partner) can deduct the business proportion of all costs. Why should there
be total discrimination between the two systems? Why did no-one howl with
anguish when the new employment income scheme was announced? It seems
that no-one did; that's the scheme and we must live with it.

15.8   Back to Arthur again. If he incorporated his business, but retained the
car outside the company, the result would be as follows:

Example 15.8

The facts are as in Example 15.2 above.

Arthur's business motoring now costs him:

$$\frac{10,000}{15,000} \times £7,500 =$$ £5,000

Less: approved mileage allowance payments
10,000 × 40p   (4,000)
                                                                          1,000

Arthur's private motoring costs him:

$$\frac{5,000}{15,000} \times £7,500 =$$ 2,500

Total unrelieved motoring costs   3,500
Dividend paid by company to give same total outlay   (2,669)*
Net outlay by Arthur   £831

Total running costs of car   £7,500
Less: AMAP payments   (4,000)

Additional profit in company   3,500
Less: Corporation tax @ 23.75% (say)   (831)
Dividend payment   2,669*

202

The company's expenditure is now only £4,000 on AMAP, rather than the full £7,500 running costs of the car. It has therefore been assumed that, given the close association of the company and its proprietor, it will distribute its 'excess' profit by way of dividend. This subsidises Arthur's cost.

15.9   There is really not much to choose between having the car in the company or outside the company. But note that both have a substantially lower cost to Arthur than his original sole trader position.

More examples

15.10   It is perhaps instructive to repeat the exercise for a different car. Arthur might represent a typical small business owner. What about a proprietor of a rather more substantial business who wishes to reward himself with a larger executive car? The following examples repeat the steps above for a car of significantly higher cost:

15.11

Example 15.11

David is a chartered certified accountant. He drives a BMW 535i. He does about 12,000 miles a year of which 6,000 are private. Total running costs are about £12,000. His marginal tax rate is 40%.

His private motoring costs him:

$$\frac{6,000}{12,000} \times £12,000 = \qquad \underline{£6,000}$$

The business proportion is an allowable cost of the business.

15.12

Example 15.12

The facts are as in Example 15.11 above. The original list price of the BMW was £37,000. The CO_2 emissions are 283 g/km.

David's private motoring now costs him:

Scale benefit £37,000 × 35%	£12,950
Tax due @ 40%	£5,180

The full cost of running the car is an allowable cost to the company.

15.13

Example 15.13

The facts are as in Example 15.11 above.

David's business motoring now costs him:

$\dfrac{6,000}{12,000} \times £12,000 =$	£6,000
Less: approved mileage allowance payments	
$6,000 \times 40p$	(2,400)
	3,600
David's private motoring costs him:	
$\dfrac{6,000}{12,000} \times £12,000 =$	6,000
Total unrelieved motoring costs	9,600
Dividend paid by company to give same total outlay £7,776* less tax @ 25%	(5,832)
Net outlay	£3,768
Total running costs of car	£12,000
Less: AMAP payments	(2,400)
Additional profit in company	9,600
Less: Corporation tax @ 19% (say)	(1,824)
Dividend payment	7,776*

15.14   As a sole trader, David has a very substantial outlay for his private motoring. If he incorporates and takes the car into the company, he has a large tax liability on employment income approaching the unincorporated cost. The curious thing is that, notwithstanding the low AMAP receipts, leaving the car out of the company is the best deal, providing that the company is prepared to meet the same total outlay by paying dividends.

Valid comparisons?

15.15   It is inevitable that some readers will question the validity of the comparisons. What these do is to look at the proprietor's net outlay in each scenario. With everything else constant, this should be valid. In Arthur's case that is so, because the tax relief on the business car costs is reasonably consistent. So Arthur should be better off by incorporating.

Likewise, we have compared David's net cost in each scenario. The possible inexactitude to this is that, as a sole trader, he gets tax relief on the business proportion of the costs at 40%. Using a company, the tax relief is quite probably only at 19%, so the business's net cost of running the car is higher.

This probably means that the company car is the worst option. It is curious but the funded private car seems the best.

It is accepted that there may be many more ways of looking at the problem. That is not the objective here. There are plenty of software products on the market which purport to compare a company car with a personally owned car. Most of these are geared to the large company employee with a simple choice. They tend not to factor in the other side of the equation, i.e. the closely controlled company where the employee is the proprietor.

15.16   The real conclusion is that the company car rules should not be a disincentive to incorporation.

A subsidy?

15.17   Do not forget the *FA 2002* rules for enhanced capital allowances on low emission cars (see **8.14**). Buy an appropriate car costing £15,000 and 100% first year allowances are due. Buy any other car costing £15,000 and it takes around nine years to write off 90% of the cost. This is a huge cash flow difference. It may not help the luxury executive car driver, but users of more modest vehicles should bear it in mind.

Cars for all the family

15.18   If the business proprietor wishes to provide cars for other members of the family, who may not even work for the business, the new rules are a godsend. Under the old rules, a second car was always taxed at 35% of original list price. This is no longer the case; CO_2 emissions rule. So a modestly sized car for wife, son, daughter etc. probably gets taxed at 15% of original list price and the business gets full tax relief on all the costs. And, with the right choice, there is a 100% first year allowance too.

Private fuel

15.19   Suppose our typical business proprietor incorporates and puts his car into the company. Should the company pay for the fuel? The answer is almost certainly an emphatic no.

From 6 April 2003, previous tables of scale charges for the provision of private fuel in a company car have been abandoned. Now the emissions percentage is applied to a fixed base figure. For 2003/04, that figure is £14,400 [*ITEPA 2003, ss 149–152; ICTA 1988, s 158 as substituted by FA 2002, s 34*]. So, if we go back to the previous examples:

15.20   *Other Forms of Remuneration*

15.20

Example 15.20

Arthur: Emissions percentage 21% (see Example 15.5)

Fuel scale charge £14,400 × 21%	£3,024
Income tax due @ 22%	£665
With petrol @ 77p/litre this equates to	863 litres
But he only does 5,000 private miles requiring	630 litres

So he is better off paying for his own private fuel.

15.21

Example 15.21

David: Emissions percentage 35% (see Example 15.12)

Fuel scale charge £14,400 × 35%	£5,040
Income tax due @ 40%	£2,016
With petrol @ 77p/litre this equates to	2,618 litres
But he only does 6,000 private miles requiring	1,140 litres

So he is much better off paying for his own private fuel.

15.22   Company payment of private fuel is therefore only beneficial where private mileage is very high, which no business proprietor seems to want to admit to.

15.23   The preferred alternative should be for the individual to meet all fuel costs and seek reimbursement of business mileage from the company. In January 2002, the Inland Revenue published non statutory guideline rates for this purpose.

Company Cars – Advisory Fuel Rates

Engine Size	**Petrol**	**Diesel**	**LPG**
1400cc or less	10p	9p	6p
1401–2000cc	12p	9p	7p
Over 2000cc	14p	12p	9p

The figures are based on a range of typical company cars and fuel costs of 77p per litre for petrol, 78p per litre for diesel and 39p per litre for LPG (liquefied petroleum gas). The table will be revised should fuel prices vary substantially from these figures. Reimbursement at the appropriate mileage rate for the car according to the table will incur no income tax or NIC. Higher figures will be accepted if it can be demonstrated that the actual costs vary substantially from the guidelines. More detail can be found on the Inland Revenue website www.inlandrevenue.gov.uk under advisory fuel rates for company cars.

Tax favoured benefits in kind

15.24 So far, proprietorial remuneration has been considered as a straight choice between salary and dividends. There is extensive analysis in **Chapter 4**. It is this fundamental choice which provides the real tax incentive for incorporation. But they are not the only ways of extracting profit from a company. The next most popular has to be the benefit in kind (BIK).

Until 6 April 2000, when Class 1A NIC was imposed as an employer only charge on virtually all benefits in kind (see **5.12–5.18**), there was an advantage in taking benefits. Now, there is little practical difference. With the new employee Class 1 NIC charge above the upper earnings limit, benefits are marginally more attractive in the case of a high earning employee.

Earlier in this chapter there was a fairly extensive analysis of the provision of a company car. It is impossible to conclude whether this is a good or bad thing. It is partially dependent on the nature of the vehicle and its use; seemingly just as important is personal opinion. However, there are BIKs which still do enjoy tax advantages.

15.25 Further, the availability of new tax credits, the working tax credit and the child tax credit, may not be the first issue to spring to the mind of the business proprietor. In most cases, income is likely to be too high to permit a claim to working tax credit but, where there are children in the family, the family element of child tax credit is not tapered away until income exceeds £50,000 p.a. In calculating income for this purpose, most BIKs are excluded. On the margin, more benefits and less cash could be advantageous.

Let's now consider the more important of the benefits. Remember that all these advantages can only be enjoyed by incorporating. In the Schedule D environment, use of all the assets set out below would be taxable by reference to a proportion of cost.

The company van

15.26 No, do not get heart failure. This is not a suggestion that the business proprietor should become 'white van man' and spend all his days hogging the outside lane of the M25 two feet from the bumper of the car in front. But, if you can live with a 'van', then it has to be said that there is a huge tax advantage.

The benefits code charge for a van is:

Under four years old at the end of the year	£500
Over four years old	£350

[*ITEPA 2003, ss 155–165; ICTA 1988, s 159AA, Sch 6A*].

That's it. No more, not even a fuel scale charge.

15.27   So, what is a 'van'? We are not concerned about the Ford Transit, Renault Kangoo et al. Those really are vans and the proprietors of many a small business will use them. On incorporation, no contest. They really ought to go into the company which gets full tax relief on all running and capital costs. The user (business proprietor) pays tax of £200 maximum (£500 at 40%). Now that cannot be bad.

15.28   However, will the more image conscious proprietor switch from a car to a traditional van? Unlikely. What can we do? Look carefully at what is a van for this purpose. Combining and paraphrasing the old and new definitions it amounts to:

A mechanically propelled road vehicle which is a goods vehicle of a construction primarily suited for the conveyance of goods or burden of any description.

[*ITEPA 2003, s 115; ICTA 1988, s 168(5A)*].

Enter the dual purpose vehicle, especially the double cab pickup. What the Americans might call a 'sports utility'.

Yes, they can carry a load but, with four seats, air conditioning, central locking, CD player and even leather seats, can it be said that they are primarily constructed for the carriage of goods? No, not really. Surely they are equally suited for goods or passengers (you could almost think of them as cars where the boot space has no lid). Where does that leave us – car or van? For a long time this was an insoluble problem. For a more detailed analysis, the reader's attention is drawn to the author's article *'W(h)ither the Company Van'* in *Taxation* of 7 February 2002.

However, times move on. In the Budget of 2002, the Chancellor announced a review of the taxation treatment of company vans. And then, suddenly, without announcement, the Inland Revenue placed an entry on its website. This is to the effect that double cab pickups which meet the Customs & Excise definition of a commercial vehicle (basically, having a payload of one tonne or more) will be accepted as being vans. Be careful – some do, some don't.

The 2003 Budget progressed matters by announcing a formal consultation on the tax treatment of employer provided vans. Given that this encompasses environmental issues, one can see an emission-based regime looming, though this cannot be before 2004/05.

Mobile telephones

15.29   Much as the author is reluctant to mention that bane of modern life, the mobile phone, this has to be the ultimate employee perk. No tax at all. The provision of a mobile phone is exempt from an employment income tax charge [*ITEPA 2003, s 319; ICTA 1988, s 155AA*]. There seems no logic to this (there was an earlier brief flirtation with a fixed scale charge of £200), but there it is.

In the present context, perhaps the new company director should throw away his personal landline telephone and switch exclusively to mobiles for all the family. The company pays all the costs and gets a full tax deduction; he pays no tax. He also tries not to worry about his family getting microwaved brains!

Incidentally, make sure that it is a contract mobile phone. If it is the type which requires prepaid top up cards, then the BIK will not be exempt. The cards will fall into the voucher rules of *ITEPA 2003, s 87; ICTA 1988, s 141.*

VAT may be irrecoverable if the phone is provided to a family member and there is no business use.

Computer equipment

15.30   A computer provided by the company for an employee's personal use is a tax free benefit where the scale charge (usually 20% of the capital cost plus running expenses such as a service contract) would otherwise be less than £500 [*ITEPA 2003, s 320; ICTA 1988, s 156A*]. Where the figure is higher, £500 is deducted from the otherwise taxable benefit (i.e. it is not an all or nothing charge). This equally applies where the provision is to a member of the employee's household and it must be a loan of the equipment. Actual transfer is not exempt.

Computer equipment includes printers, scanners, modems, disks and other peripheral devices designed to be used by being connected to or inserted in a computer, as well as the provision of a right to use computer software. This begs the question of a digital camera. Where computer equipment is concerned for capital allowances (see **8.12**) digital cameras are excluded. This is because they do not need to be connected to a computer in order to be used. It must be assumed that the same logic applies here.

For the relief to apply, the computers must be available to employees (not necessarily all employees) and directors on the same terms. Where there are employees, the provision to a director cannot be on advantageous terms. This begs the question of the very small company where the directors are the only employees. In *Taxation 12 October 2000, page 49*, Graham Sillett took the view that:

> '... this requirement [the combined effect of the former *ICTA 1988, s 156A(2)(a)* and *(b)*] is satisfied provided the equipment is made

available to all directors and on the same terms. The relief also applies where there is a sole director/employee (i.e. a one man company) or a husband and wife are the sole directors/employees.'

The attitude of the Inland Revenue seems favourable. In *para 21700 of the Schedule E Manual*, which concerns this relief and particularly the exclusion of arrangements which favour directors over other employees, it concludes:

'Note that in the case of one man companies, or other companies which have directors but no non director employees, there is no group of employees with which to compare the provision to directors. So for such companies exemption cannot be denied.'

What else?

15.31 First a reminder. Class 1A NIC applies to most taxable BIKs. If there is no tax, there is no NIC.

15.32 Don't forget pensions. Many business proprietors, whether unincorporated or not, will use a personal pension policy to provide for retirement. Issues relevant to incorporation are addressed at **4.31–4.42**.

15.33 However, incorporation opens up a new world of opportunity for pension provision through corporate schemes, whether they be fully insured or self administered (see **6.43–6.48**).

15.34 Loans and closely controlled companies are not happy bedfellows. Where carefully administered, there may be a modest advantage (see **16.23–16.26**, **16.46**).

15.35 The company bicycle seems slow to catch on, though its provision is exempt from income tax [*ITEPA 2003, s 244; ICTA 1988, s 197AC*]. Perhaps it is the requirement that it must be used mainly for qualifying journeys which are between home and the place of work, or between one workplace and another. As with computers (see **15.30**), the provision must be to employees generally. Safety equipment is included.

Of course, if the business proprietor is not motivated by the thought of the company provision of a multi-geared, titanium-framed, mountain bike (costing several thousand pounds) for his commuting, then he could always use his own bike for business journeys. The AMAP [*ITEPA 2003, ss 229–236; ICTA 1988, Sch 12AA*] extends to cycles at the very generous rate of 20p per mile. Now there must be a good tax free profit in that.

15.36 The provision of car parking facilities at or near the place of work is exempt from income tax [*ITEPA 2003, s 237; ICTA 1988, s 155(1A)*]. If the company operates from town centre offices and there is need to use a public car park, clearly the company should pay.

15.37 Modest expenditure on a Christmas party or similar function is not taxed [*ITEPA 2003, s 264* previously *ESC A70*]. 'Modest' was £75 per head (not per employee) up to 2002/03 though the 2003 Budget has doubled the limit to £150. The event must be open to staff generally. But, back to the micro company, there does not seem to be any bar on a directors only (plus spouses) event.

15.38 There are numerous other tax free benefits, though these are not listed here because they seem to be of little practical relevance to the process of incorporation.

15.39 However, this section just has to end with an item totally impractical but so surreal that it cannot be overlooked for its comedy value. Enter the cyclists' breakfast.

The Treasury has the power to exempt certain minor benefits by Statutory Instrument [*ITEPA 2003, s 210; ICTA 1988, s 155ZB*]. Those exemptions now include cyclists' breakfasts [*Income Tax (Exemption of Minor Benefits) Regulations 2002, SI 2002/205*].

Where the employer (our newly incorporated company?) sponsors a cycle to work scheme, then it may provide to participants a free breakfast without a charge to tax. This was limited to six occasions per year though the 2003 Budget removed this limit and such a benefit can now be supplied on any number of designated cycle to work days in the year. Breakfast doesn't just mean tea and toast, or even eggs and bacon. It is any qualifying meal provided in recognition of the employee using a cycle on the journey from home to work on a designated day. So, could the managing director sit in a chauffeur-driven Jaguar to within one mile of the office, then get his bike out of the boot of the car and painfully pedal the last bit? Arriving somewhat late, he then goes for a slap up five-course lunch with wine, liqueur, cigar etc. provided by the company. Is this breakfast?

The whole scheme seems to come straight from the annals of 'Yes Minister'. The author would dearly love to know who started it – surely someone somewhere must have had a scheme of this type in order to lobby for the relevant legislation.

The director's loan account

15.40 At various points throughout this book, suggestion has been made that, during the course of the incorporation, the company should pay the former business proprietor for certain items (e.g. stock at **7.22**, major capital assets at **9.32,** or plant and machinery at **8.27**).

At the outset, the company is unlikely to have significant amounts of cash, generally none at all. The proceeds of these transactions will therefore be left outstanding as credit balances on the loan accounts of the directors.

It has previously been pointed out, but is worthy of restatement, that the company is a completely separate entity to its shareholders and directors. The credit balance on the director's loan account is, in effect, the director's money. It is a debt due from the company which, for the time being, has been loaned back.

When the company trades profitably, the proprietor may wish to draw down on this loan. It is, after all, his money. The tax consequences of creating the loan will have been considered at the outset as part of the incorporation transaction. Drawing from the account will incur no further tax liability.

15.41   What about the interim period though? That is, until the company has generated sufficient reserves to make the repayment. Indeed, the proprietor may want the loan to persist longer than that – if the company needs working capital, such an arrangement might be cheaper than borrowing from a bank.

If the loan was made on arm's length terms, the lender would expect a commercial reward for the use of his money. This would be in the form of interest. Why then should the proprietor not charge the company for the use of his money? Why not indeed. It is surprising how many do not when it is a relatively efficient way of extracting cash.

Therefore, the proprietor could charge a commercial rate of interest on the loan. Often the author has seen application of the benefits code official rate of interest which is 5% for 2003/04. A rather higher figure might be more realistic though. A bank might charge something like 4% over the base rate and require security. It is suggested that a figure of this order might be more appropriate. Care should be taken not to go too high lest an Inspector of Taxes might argue that the interest is beyond a reasonable commercial rate and thereby deny relief in the company's corporation tax computation. The corollary to this is that the excess might be taxed in the recipient's hands as a distribution rather than interest.

15.42   The interest is, of course, a taxable receipt in the hands of the director, though no NIC is payable which makes the arrangement preferable to extra salary. In addition, where we are concerned with very small companies and modest amounts of remuneration, the interest will be taxed at the savings rate of 20% [*ICTA 1988, s 1A*] rather than the basic rate of 22%.

15.43   Care must be taken to ensure that the interest is actually paid, as this will be a loan relationship of the company. Accordingly, relief will be denied to the company for the period in which interest is accrued, unless it is paid within twelve months of the accounting period end [*FA 1996, Sch 9 para 2*].

15.44   On payment of interest to an individual, the company is required to deduct income tax [*ICTA 1988, s 348(2)*]. For this purpose the applicable rate is 20% [*ICTA 1988, ss 4(1), 350(1)*].

The company is required to account for any such tax deductions on a quarterly basis using form CT61.

15.45   A certificate showing the gross amount of interest paid and the tax deducted must be provided to the individual [*ICTA 1988, s 352*]. The tax deducted satisfies the full liability where the individual's total income does not exceed the upper limit of the basic rate band. If the individual is liable at the higher rate, he must account for the balance through the self assessment system.

15.46   It may also be possible to obtain some modest cash flow advantage by exploiting the loan relationship late payment rule. Interest on a loan account may be deducted on an accruals basis providing the interest is paid within twelve months. The recipient individual will be taxed on the interest when it is actually received. Therefore, if interest is paid close to the twelve month date, the company will get a deduction in the corporation tax accounting period of accrual, but the individual gets taxed much later.

Example 15.46

The company has an accounting date of 31 May. Interest of £10,000 is accrued in the accounts to 31 May 2003, but it is not paid until 30 April 2004. The company gets a deduction for the interest reducing its tax payable on 1 March 2004. The recipient includes the interest in his self assessment for 2004/05 and does not pay tax until 31 January 2006.

Rent

15.47   **Chapter 14** explores reasons why a business proprietor might want to keep major assets outside the company. Frequently, this will be property which is nevertheless used by the company.

If the company uses the property, why not make it pay rent? The logic is similar to the payment of interest on a director's loan account above (see **15.41**), but in this instance there are less constraints.

The rent should, of course, be at a reasonable commercial level so as to ensure a deduction in the company's corporation tax computation. On the other side, it will form part of the individual's Schedule A business computation. Deductibility and assessability are both on the accruals basis so there is no option for a timing advantage.

15.48   The rents will be chargeable to income tax at basic rate or higher rate but, again, there is no NIC. Once more, this is a cheaper option than extra salary.

Where the property concerned is the proprietor's house, the company may pay for the use of office accommodation. Under *Finance Act 2003, s 137* there should be no income tax liability where an employee regularly works at home and the employer contributes to the additional costs. The Budget announcement stated that this would be limited to an amount of £2 per week. This amount is tax free without the need for evidence of actual costs.

15.49 If the property attracts IBAs or ABAs, then the situation may actually demand payment of rent to avoid such allowances being stranded without relief (see **8.43, 8.52**).

15.50 There is also the possibility that the property owner will have borrowed funds to facilitate his purchase. This leaves him needing money in order to meet the interest payments. Rent is the obvious choice and the interest payments will be deductible in arriving at his Schedule A profit. Sometimes, the proprietor will not take rent but, rather, arrange for the company to meet the interest payments on his personal borrowings. Such interest is still a permitted deduction in the company's hands. It is also treated as a notional Schedule A receipt of the proprietor relieved by the interest payable – see *Inland Revenue Tax Bulletin, June 1997*.

Overall comparison

15.51 At this point, it might be instructive to compare the effects of profit extraction by the various methods (tax rates on dividends are the effective rates on the amount received).

Method of Extraction	Company	Individual	NIC
Salary	Deductible PAYE	Taxable 10/22/40%	Company 0/12.8%; Individual 0/11/1%
Dividend	Not deductible	Taxable 0/25%	No
BIK	Deductible	Taxable 10/22/40%	Company 12.8%
BIK (exempt)	Deductible	Tax-free	No
Loan interest	Deductible (if paid within 12 months)	Taxable 10/20/40%	No
Rent	Deductible	Taxable 10/22/40%	No

Planning points

- Think carefully about the destiny of the proprietor's car but do not let irrational prejudices lead to false conclusions (**15.1–15.16**).
- Modest cars for family members can be a valuable benefit (**15.18**).
- Company provided fuel is almost certainly a bad deal (**15.20–15.22**).
- Consider a van instead of a car (**15.26–15.28**).
- Select a range of tax favoured benefits to suit (**15.29–15.37**).
- Pay interest on director's loan account (**15.41–15.46**).
- Pay rent on company used personal property (**15.47–15.50**).

Chapter 16

The Close Company

16.1   Most family and owner managed private companies are closely controlled. The definition of a close company is given in *ICTA 1988, s 414*:

> 'For the purposes of the Tax Acts, a 'close company' is one which is under the control of five or fewer participators, or of participators who are directors . . .'

[*ICTA 1988, s 414(1)*]

16.2   Many people will equate the term participator with the word shareholder. This is not strictly correct. Participator is a rather wider term and includes:

- any person who possesses, or is entitled to acquire, share capital or voting rights in the company;
- any loan creditor of the company;
- any person who possesses, or is entitled to acquire a right to receive or participate in any distributions of the company;
- any person who is entitled to secure that income or assets of the company will be applied directly or indirectly for his benefit.

[*ICTA 1988, s 416(1)*]

16.3   Control may be by any number of directors who are participators; there is no limitation to five in this leg of the test.

16.4   To be a close company, control under the first leg of the test must be by five or fewer participators. In establishing control, though, one needs to look not only at the rights of each participator personally, but also the rights of:

- any other company he might control;
- his associates.

[*ICTA 1988, s 416(6)*].

'Associate' in turn includes:

- any relative (husband or wife, parent or remoter forebear, child or remoter issue, brother or sister, or partner);
- the trustees of certain settlements.

[*ICTA 1988, s 416(3), (4)*]

16.5 *The Close Company*

16.5   The above précis is a fairly drastic oversimplification and anyone envisaging problems with close companies should study the legislation in *ICTA 1988, Part XI, Chapter I* carefully. The complexities may be illustrated by the case of *R v IRC, ex p Newfields Developments Ltd [2001] STC 901* where companies were held to be associated by apparently disparate trustee shareholdings. What the legislation and case law does serve to demonstrate is that one needs to be very careful in establishing whether a company is close or not. There are many large private companies with apparently very diverse shareholdings which remain close. The author recalls, some years ago, spending three days with the company secretary poring over the share register of a very large private company, trying to establish whether the company was close. It is not a simple job. There were hundreds of names on the register and one cannot identify associates just by names (which may change). When looking at trustee holdings, it is necessary to know who was the settlor and who are the beneficiaries. It really is a daunting task.

16.6   It is almost worth assuming that all private companies are close, unless it can be proven otherwise. The only specific exceptions are:

* a company which is not resident in the UK;
* a company whose shares are dealt on a recognised stock exchange where not less than 35% of the voting power is held by the public;
* a company controlled by one or more other companies which are not close;
* certain other minor specified exceptions.

[ICTA 1988, ss 414(1), (5), 415]

16.7   Why all the concern about close companies anyway? As is pointed out elsewhere, a company is an entirely separate entity from its shareholders and directors. Despite this, there is a very strong interrelationship between many small trading companies and their proprietors. Because of this, for many years they have been perceived by the authorities as vehicles for avoidance. It is indeed true that the directors and shareholders (often the same individuals) are able to exercise total influence over the financial transactions of small companies. Therefore, specific legislation is in place to inhibit the worst excesses which might otherwise be possible.

Currently, there are two specific anti-avoidance provisions in place. These comprise:

* an extended definition of what comprises a distribution [*ICTA 1988, s 418*];
* a specific code to deal with loans to participators [*ICTA 1988, s 419 et seq*].

16.8   There has, in the past, been a system of close company apportionment to prevent avoidance of higher rates of personal tax by retaining profits within a company. The effect of this measure was to treat a certain level of retained profit in a close company as if it had been distributed and charge appropriate rates of income tax on it. This was repealed in 1989/90 but some commentators suggest that similar provisions may be reintroduced to counter what the

Government might perceive as a loss of tax due to the imbalance of dividends/salary payments (described throughout this work, and elsewhere), as a means of mitigating the total tax liability. Indeed, in some ways, the personal service company legislation in *ITEPA 2003, Part 2, Chapter 8; FA 2000, Sch 12*, could be viewed in this light, since its effect is to treat the company profit as if it were paid out by way of salary.

16.9   This may also be the time to explore other anti-avoidance legislation, and case law, in the Inspector of Taxes armoury which might be applied to limit excessive manipulation of the rules which might otherwise reduce overall tax liabilities. Chief amongst these provisions must be the settlements legislation in *ICTA 1988, part XV*.

Loans to participators

Companies Act position

16.10   The general rule is that a company is prohibited from making a loan to a director [*CA 1985, s 330(2)*]. There is a distinction between private companies and relevant companies. A relevant company is broadly a public company or an associate and the rules there are even more restrictive. It is assumed here that we are concerned primarily, if not exclusively, with private companies, so the position for relevant companies is not explored.

The rules on loans to directors extend to:

* connected persons, such as a spouse or minor children;
* a company in which the director is interested in at least 20% of the equity share capital;
* a company where he can control more than 20% of the voting rights.

16.11   There are limited exceptions to the basic rule that loans are forbidden under the *Companies Act*. Accordingly, the following are permitted:

* a loan not exceeding £5,000 [*CA 1985, s 334*].
* a loan for expenditure incurred, or to be incurred, by the director in the performance of his duties as an officer of the company [*CA 1985, s 337*]. Note that the expenditure must be approved by the members of the company in general meeting.
* a loan, where the ordinary business of the company includes the making of loans, and the terms are no more favourable than would be offered to an unconnected person. The company's ordinary business will not include the making of loans unless it is, for example, a bank – unlikely with a close company.

16.12   Where there is overdrawing on a director's loan account, the accounts of the company must contain a note showing the maximum level of the overdrawing.

16.13   For private companies (unlike public ones), loans to a director do not attract criminal sanctions. The civil remedy is for the company to require the borrower to return the amount loaned, though in practice this is unlikely to be used by a family company.

The tax charge

16.14   It would be excessively naïve to think that, because it is a breach of the Companies Act, directors do not take loans from their companies. On the contrary; such loans often arise. Indeed there is an attitude of mind with some family company proprietors that the company is an extension of their banking facility. There is, therefore, specific tax legislation to penalise the process.

This is to be found in *ICTA 1988, s 419*, and concerns participators rather than directors. However, in many close company situations, an individual is quite likely to be both director and participator. In any case, the tax charge applies equally where the loan is made to an associate of the participator. The definition of 'associate' is widely drawn and found in *ICTA 1988, s 417(3)* and *(4)*. It includes, but is not limited to, husband or wife, children or grandchildren, parents and brothers or sisters.

16.15   The nature of the impost is curious. It is charged as if it were corporation tax but it is not actually corporation tax and cannot be set against any other liabilities. Before the abolition of advance corporation tax (ACT) on 6 April 1999, it was charged at the ACT rate (indeed, often called notional ACT) but it was not ACT either. Now it is simply charged at a fixed rate of 25% of the net advance to the participator [*ICTA 1988, s 419(1)*]. Throughout this chapter, it will be simply referred to as 's 419 tax'.

16.16   Since the advent of corporation tax self assessment for accounting periods ended 1 July 1999 or later, a company must self assess the liability and include it on form CT600A [*FA 1988, Sch 18 paras 1, 8*]. Payment is due nine months after the end of the accounting period [*ICTA 1988, s 419(3)*]. Although described as corporation tax, the instalment procedures for large companies appear to have no relevance.

16.17   The s 419 tax charge can apply not only to a simple loan or advance of money to the participator but also in certain other circumstances. These include the incurring of a debt by the individual to the close company or the assignment of a third party debt to the company.

In the former case, a debt incurred by supply of goods or services by the company in the normal course of its trade may be ignored unless the credit given exceeds six months or is a greater period than afforded to an arm's length customer [*ICTA 1988, s 420(1)*].

16.18   There is also a minor exception for loans of less than £15,000 made to a borrower who works full time for the company and who does not have a material interest (broadly 5% of the ordinary share capital, including the interests of associates) [*ICTA 1988, s 420(2)*].

Repayment of the loan

16.19   The tax charge is, in effect, only a deposit with the Inland Revenue for so long as the loan remains outstanding. Relief is given under *ICTA 1988, s 419(4)* where the loan is repaid.

This means that, where the loan is repaid to the company before the due date for payment of the tax, no payment is actually required. Strictly a return should be made with a claim for relief to achieve this position; in this instance through form CT600. No interest charge arises in respect of the period for which the loan was outstanding.

16.20   Where the loan is repaid on or after the day on which the tax becomes due, then the tax is not repaid until nine months from the end of the accounting period in which the repayment is made [*ICTA 1988, s 419(4A)*]. In this circumstance, the claim is no longer appropriate to form CT600 and a free-standing claim under the provisions of *TMA 1970, Sch 1A*, should be made.

Example 16.20

Mark and Steven are directors and shareholders of M&S Agricultural Machinery Ltd. During the accounting period ended 31 December 2002 each of them borrowed £10,000 from the company.

(a)   On 25 September 2003, Mark repays his loan to the company. This is before the s 419 tax liability falls due and a claim for relief is made. No tax is payable.

(b)   On 5 October 2003, Steven repays his loan to the company. The tax liability is:

£10,000 @ 25% =   £2,500
payable on 1 October 2003.

Relief is claimed but the tax is not repayable until 1 October 2004.

The slight delay in repayment by Steven compared to Mark means that the company must deposit the tax liability with the Inland Revenue for a whole year.

16.21   There may be a temptation in some minds to 'bed and breakfast' the loan; that is to say, repay it shortly before the end of the accounting period. A supposedly fresh loan of a similar amount is then taken out a few days into the next accounting period. This is an artificial transaction and, on discovery by an Inspector of Taxes during an enquiry, likely to be set aside, see Inland

16.22   The Close Company

Revenue *Enquiry Manual para 8565*. For reasons of establishing the true liability to s 419 tax, an enquiry under CTSA into the return of a close company will often ask for a full analysis of movements on the director's loan account. The Inland Revenue takes the view that the charge is not restricted to complete accounting periods but can apply for the quarter in which the loan was advanced, though this point is rarely taken [*ICAEW TR806, August 1990*].

16.22   If partial repayment of a loan is made, the Inland Revenue will allow it to be offset against the outstanding balance in any order which the taxpayer specifies [*Inland Revenue Corporation Tax Manual para 6662*]. Care should be taken over this.

Example 16.22

Richard is a major shareholder in a small transport company. In the accounting period ended 31 December 2001 he borrowed £10,000 from the company. In the accounting period ended 31 December 2002 he borrowed a further £10,000 from the company. On 1 September 2003 he repays £10,000.

Option (a)

Repayment set against 2001 loan:

1 October 2002, tax due on 2001 loan £10,000 @ 25% =	£2,500
1 September 2003, 2001 loan repaid, relief claimed under s 419(4) & (4A)	
1 October 2003, tax due on 2002 loan £10,000 @ 25% =	£2,500
1 October 2004, tax repayable on 2001 loan =	£(2,500)

Option (b)

Repayment set against 2002 loan:

1 October 2002, tax due on 2001 loan £10,000 @ 25% =	£2,500
1 September 2003, 2002 loan repaid, relief claimed under s 419(4)	
1 October 2003, no tax due	

It will be seen that in repaying the later loan first there is a twelve month cash flow advantage.

In the absence of any specified manner of repaying the loans, the Inland Revenue will set the repayment against the earliest borrowings first.

Loan write off

16.23   Where a loan has been made by a company to a participator and the loan is subsequently written off, then any tax paid by the company may be repaid pursuant to a claim under *ICTA 1988, s 419(4)*. The loan must be formally waived. It is not sufficient for the company simply to agree not to collect the outstanding balance as the liability would then technically remain.

16.24   The individual is treated as if he had received a distribution of an amount equal to the original loan. This will be an addition to his income for the year of the write off and taxed as such [*ICTA 1988, s 421(1)*].

16.25   This may be a very useful tool. One disadvantage of dividends as a means of remuneration is that they must be paid proportionately to all shareholders in the company irrespective of their contribution to the success of the business. Where it is desired to direct a payment to one individual only, then consider making a loan to him and subsequently writing it off. He is left in the same position as if he had received a dividend but the other shareholders need not have received anything. The need for correct documentation, a formal deed of waiver, cannot be stressed too highly.

The individual may also obtain a modest cash flow advantage.

Example 16.25

Vectra Ltd makes a loan of £10,000 to Bill, its shareholder, on 1 April 2002 (within its accounting period ended 31 December 2002). The loan is written off on 10 April 2003. No s 419 tax is due as the loan was repaid before the due date. Bill is treated as if he received a dividend on 10 April 2003, to be included in his tax return for 2003/04. Any higher rate income tax is due on 31 January 2005 (if Vectra had simply declared and paid a dividend on 1 April 2002, Bill would pay the higher rate tax on 31 January 2003).

16.26   Note that the attentions of the Inland Revenue National Insurance Contributions Office (IRNICO) could muddy the waters. Following old Contributions Agency practice, it considers the write off of a loan to be earnings within *SSCBA 1992, ss 3, 6* [*Inland Revenue National Insurance Manual para 12020*].

Identify the loan

16.27   Note that *ICTA 1988, s 419* refers to:

> '. . . where a close company . . . makes any loan or advances any money to an individual who is a participator in the company . . .'

There is no reference to whether or not the participator has a net indebtedness to the company. So there can be a credit balance between the individual and the company but yet a s 419 tax liability still arises. See *ICAEW Tax Faculty Note TAX 11/93*.

16.28   Suppose the individual is both a shareholder and director of the company. He has contributed money to the company by way of a fixed capital account but various private expenses are charged to his director's current account which becomes overdrawn. The company has advanced money within the meaning of *s 419(1)* even though the true position is that the company owes money to the individual, not the other way round. This is a point taken by the Inland Revenue. The author recalls a situation where the 'elder statesman' of a family company had contributed almost £1m to the company by way of a fixed debenture. The company paid most of his personal living expenses, which exceeded the company profit, and his current account was regularly overdrawn. Tax had to be paid under *s 419* even though there was no real borrowing by the individual.

16.29   The legislation is almost couched in simplistic terms as though there might be a single transaction whereby the company advances money to the participator. It is rarely this easy. Often the situation arises because the company meets personal expenses of the shareholder (remember the company's assets are not the proprietor's assets?) which must be charged to his current account with the company. If there are inadequate funds in the account to meet the expenses, it will become overdrawn and this is when the spectre of *s 419* rears its head.

More often than not, for the practitioner who has to resolve such situations, it is first a question of finding the loan. It is not uncommon that a company director/shareholder will use a personal credit card to meet a whole range of expenses, both business and personal. The reason is frequently that a personal card is cheaper to operate than a company one. However, a company cheque is used to repay the credit card company. The company then has a composite payment, being a mixture of legitimate goods purchased for the company business, expenses incurred by the individual which might be relieved by a claim under *ITEPA 2003, s 336; ICTA 1988, s 198*, and wholly private items. It must be carefully analysed with 'drawings' charged to the director's account.

(Strictly PAYE/NIC issues should be considered at the same time. The company's settlement of the director's pecuniary liabilities is remuneration subject to tax and NIC. There may also be P11D consequences).

There is nothing inherently wrong with using a personal credit card to meet business expenses; after all, many ordinary employees will do it to meet expenses incurred in the duties of their employment. It is the manner of reimbursement that causes the problem. The cardholder should settle the balance and then seek reimbursement for business items from the company. It is not easy to convince the hard-pressed businessman of this – especially the former sole trader who is used to the 'sort it out at the year end' approach. Often the true position can only be established after the year end when the company accounts are completed, by careful analysis of all relevant payments. It is important that this is done before the 'nine month date' to give an opportunity to rectify the situation.

16.30   The purpose of the loan has no bearing on the matter either. It is not unusual for a company participator to be a member of a partnership too. Indeed, service companies for partnerships and corporate partners are described at **12.14–12.17**. If there are surplus funds in the company, these should not be used to finance the partnership. A loan to a partnership of which the company participator is a member is caught by *s 419* just as much as a direct loan to the participator. Further, contrary to some opinions, there is no relief from s 419 tax because there is a business purpose to the loan; a loan is a loan and that is it. Where there are genuine trading transactions between a company and a partnership (with common members), these should be on arm's length terms as regards the credit afforded by the company to the partnership or else a s 419 tax charge will arise [*Grant v Watton [1999] STC 330*].

Illegal dividends

16.31   The processes necessary to ensure that a dividend is validly declared and paid are explored at **11.66–11.74**. What is the position if a dividend is paid illegally, perhaps because the company has insufficient distributable reserves?

Strictly the payment by the company is then contrary to the *Companies Act* and therefore illegal. Where a shareholder knowingly receives such a dividend, it is repayable to the company. The nature of the payment in the interim must therefore be a loan. Seemingly it should attract a tax charge under *s 419*.

The author has not yet seen an Inspector of Taxes take this point, though it does seem a valid one. With the current growth in the number of small companies, it might be expected that Inspectors will look more closely at the process of dividend declaration and payment. If these do not stand up to scrutiny, then the conclusion seems fairly obvious. Section 419 tax could well be due.

Note that regular monthly drawings cannot be taken and simply classified at a later date as 'dividends'. If the statutory processes for declaration and payment are not followed, then the way may be open for the Revenue to argue that the payments are not dividends at all but, rather, loans.

Beneficial loans

16.32   Whilst there is a possibility of a loan or advance to an individual who is a participator, it is probably reasonable to assume that he will also be a director of a family or owner managed company. Either as an employee or office holder, he will be within the benefits code provisions of *ITEPA 2003, Part 3; ICTA 1988, Part V, Chapter II*. That includes a charge on beneficial loans [*ITEPA 2003, s 175; ICTA 1988, s 160*].

The s 419 tax in respect of loans or advances to directors/participators is a liability of the company and effectively a loan to the Inland Revenue for so long as the loan to the participator remains outstanding. *ITEPA 2003, s 175; ICTA 1988 s 160* charges income tax on the individual as if the loan were earnings (though there are limited exceptions) and it is an actual liability. Further, it is repeated in each tax year that the loan remains outstanding.

16.33   The basic charge is usually calculated by taking the average balance outstanding in the tax year and applying the official rate of interest [*ITEPA 2003, s 182; ICTA 1988, Sch 7 para 4*]. Where there is a frequent or regular fluctuation in the amount of the loan, it may be preferable to elect for the alternative basis, which is in effect a daily calculation [*ITEPA 2003, s 183; ICTA Sch 7 para 5*]. Note also that the Inland Revenue can elect for the alternative basis where it is to its advantage.

16.34   The official rate of interest is defined in *ITEPA 2003, s 181; ICTA 1988, s 160(5)* and *FA 1989, s 178* and set for 2003/04 at 5% [*Taxes (Interest Rate) Regulations SI 1989/1297* and *IRPR 12 December 2002*].

16.35   If the borrower pays any actual interest to the company, then the amount of the tax charge is reduced by that payment. The charge will not be reduced if the interest payable thereon is merely accrued but not paid. At least, the Inland Revenue takes this view though at least one commentator suggests that, on a strict construction of the legislation, it might be possible to argue for an accruals basis.

16.36   A loan which is less than £5,000 is ignored for these provisions [*ITEPA 2003, s 180; ICTA 1988, s 161(1)*]. This is an absolute maximum; larger loans cannot be reduced by this threshold.

Clearing the loan

16.37   Obey the mantra 'the company's money is not the proprietor's money' and you cannot go far wrong. Whilst there will be certain company shareholders/directors who cannot or will not understand this, they are hopefully in the minority. Loans to participators are not that uncommon though. It is suspected that many do it inadvertently. The proprietors will previously have run unincorporated businesses and, without meaning to be derogatory, they are not terribly financially astute. With an unincorporated business, they are used to the concept that the business profit is theirs. If there is money in the bank, they will spend it. Any necessary adjustments are dealt with by the accountant at the end of the year.

The true meaning of running a company is perhaps not adequately explained to them. The proprietor sees money in the company bank account and spends it on matters personal to himself or his family. He does not fully appreciate that withdrawal of funds from the company requires particular mechanisms and has attendant tax liabilities. So his loan account with the company becomes overdrawn. The situation needs to be rectified.

16.38   Two common solutions are:

- payment of a salary or bonus;
- declaration and payment of a dividend,

the net payment of which is credited to the loan account in order to clear the overdrawn balance.

It is demonstrated elsewhere in this book (especially **Chapter 4**) that, given the present tax regime, a dividend is likely to be the preferred route of taking money from a company, as the overall tax liability is lower. Is it therefore totally optional how the overdrawn loan account is cleared? Is there a completely free choice?

Unfortunately, the answer is probably no. Backtrack swiftly and reconsider how the loan became overdrawn in the first place. Maybe there was a specific cash advance to the proprietor, but this is more likely to be the exception than the rule. There could be:

- payment by the company of the individual's personal expenses;
- payment by the company (of a debt incurred by the company) to provide goods or facilities for the individual;
- drawings in anticipation of a salary or dividend.

16.39   There is no specific legislation that says such advances are not advances of salary (see *ICAEW Memoranda TAX 21/92* and *TAX 5/94*). Where the company meets a pecuniary liability of a director, that is remuneration. Tax should be deducted under PAYE and NIC accounted for at that point. Where the company makes a payment of its own liability, one should stop and consider whether charging the expense to the director's account is the correct thing to do with it at all. Benefit in kind implications may arise. Only the last item – drawings – is open to possible doubt and different interpretation.

Anecdotal evidence suggests that some Inspectors of Taxes are insisting that overdrawn loan accounts must be cleared by a salary or bonus, especially if that is the route which has been adopted in the past and particularly where items leading to the overdrawing have the characteristics of remuneration anyway. (Remember, not only new companies are faced with this choice but also some established companies may be switching from payment of salaries to dividends in order to get the tax benefits.)

There is some support in law for this line of approach. If a director has no specific contract of employment, he will perform his duties for the company as office holder under the *Companies Act*. That being the case, remuneration is normally voted at the company's annual general meeting. However, that does not have to be the point at which tax and NIC are due.

16.40   For PAYE purposes, tax falls due on the individual's receipt of the relevant remuneration. The time of receipt may be summarised as the earliest of the following:

- when payment is made of, or on account of, the emoluments;
- when a person becomes entitled to a payment of, or on account of, the emoluments;
- when sums on account of the emoluments are credited to the director's current or loan account by the company;
- where the amount of emoluments for a period is determined before the period ends and the office holder or employee is a director, the time when the period ends;
- where the amount of the emoluments for a period is not known until the amount is determined after the period has ended and the office holder or employee is a director, the time when the amount is determined.

[*ITEPA 2003, s 686; ICTA 1988, s 203A*].

16.41   For NIC purposes, *Social Security (Contributions) Regulations SI 2001/1004, Reg 22*, has similar deeming provisions. Whether the director draws cash, equivalent to salary, or uses a company cheque to settle a personal bill, the company must consider whether the debiting of the transaction to the director's account constitutes a payment of earnings or deemed earnings. It follows that where a director's account goes into credit following the AGM, subsequent drawings against the credit balance are irrelevant for contributions purposes.

Thus, income tax and NIC are very probably due on amounts debited to the loan account which have the character of earnings. This could well be the time of overdrawing and not the time of clearance. Especially as regards NIC, careful analysis of movements on the account is necessary to establish the correct position.

Really it is the possibility of a NIC liability which is the driver to this attitude. The Inland Revenue will resist possible reclassification of earnings as dividends because of the loss of NIC. The official view on the correct procedures can be found at Inland Revenue *National Insurance Manual paras 12014–12020*.

If the withdrawal from the loan account, leading to or enhancing the overdrawn balance, can be demonstrated to be on account of a dividend then no NIC is due.

16.42   That is not necessarily the end of the story. If a mixture of salary and dividends is credited to the loan account, then the Inspector will still treat drawings as if they were salary.

There appears to be a solution, though the author admits never to having seen this used in practice. Perhaps it is to come with the increasing vogue for dividends. That is to have two loan accounts. Loan account 1 (the salary account) is credited with after tax salary and bonus and director's expenses should be recorded against this one only. Loan account 2 is credited only with dividends and the proprietor is free to draw on a credit balance. Perhaps this is a vain hope; if the parties got in this mess because the proprietor could not do things properly in the first place, what hope is there for a convoluted arrangement like this?

16.43 Do note that credits to the loan account must be of after tax bonuses. The company must account for tax at the proper time, which is the earliest date on which payment is regarded as made (see **16.40** above). It is not sufficient to reserve amounts of PAYE and NIC due – they must actually be paid, see *R v IRC ex p McVeigh [1996] STC 91*.

16.44 Note carefully that all of this became necessary because of s 419 tax. This is due where the loan was outstanding nine months after the end of the accounting period in which it arose. Payment of a salary or dividend to clear the overdrawn balance must be made before this date. The Inland Revenue will accept book entries within the company's accounting records as satisfying loan repayment [Inland Revenue *Company Taxation Manual para 6662*]. Repayment only takes place when the book entry is made. Any temptation to predate such an entry must be resisted.

16.45 Despite this, note that where clearance is by way of dividend, entitlement to an interim dividend only arises when it is paid (in cash). In this instance, the company should pay a dividend cheque to the individual who then reintroduces an equivalent amount to credit the loan account. A final dividend, by contrast, is approved by the shareholders in general meeting; once this has been done, a book entry may be sufficient for credit to the loan account.

Additional distributions

16.46 The definition of distributions generally is given by *ICTA 1988, s 209*, and is considerably wider than a simple dividend. The scope is widened even further for close companies.

16.47 *ICTA 1988, s 418* treats the provision for a participator (or his associate) of living accommodation, entertainment, domestic or other services and any other benefits as if they were a distribution. The consequence is that such expenses are not deductible in the company's corporation tax computation and the individual is treated as receiving a dividend liable to higher rate income tax (on the grossed up amount) if appropriate.

16.48 Benefits already chargeable to income tax under the benefits code (the participator may be a director too) are excluded as is living accommodation provided by reason of employment if it would be exempt under *ITEPA 2003, Part 5, Chapter 3; ICTA 1988, s 145*, and pensions or similar items.

16.49 The measure of the distribution is the amount to be calculated under the rules of *ITEPA 2003, Part 3; ICTA 1988, Part V, Chapter II* if the benefit, expense etc. were to be provided to an employee. Note that the Inland Revenue considers this rule to catch money benefits as well as benefits in kind [Inland Revenue *Company Taxation Manual para 6616*].

It can also be applied to excessive amounts of pensions, annual payments, rents etc. which are disallowed as an expense to the company on the grounds that they are not wholly and exclusively for the purposes of the trade [*Company Taxation Manual para 6617*].

Shareholding structures

16.50   Many owner managed and family companies will only have one class of shares, fully participating ordinaries within the meaning of *ICTA 1988, s 832*. This favours simplicity and was historically satisfactory. The payment of dividends is increasingly becoming a priority in paying remuneration for a company. The tax advantages are potentially high but this is not the only factor in the equation. Other considerations are addressed at **4.10–4.20**.

High on the list of drawbacks must be the so-called 'blunderbuss' effect of a dividend payment. Declare a dividend and the payment hits all the shareholders. They all get the same amount (proportionate to their shareholding) irrespective of their contribution to the business. A bonus on the other hand is very closely focused and specific to one individual (but has tax and NIC disadvantages). What we want is the tax treatment of a dividend with the more exact direction of a bonus.

Dividend waivers

16.51   Just because a dividend is declared does not necessarily mean that particular shareholders have to accept it. Some could waive their entitlement.

16.52   To be effective, the waiver must be in the form of a deed and should be executed and delivered to the company prior to the shareholder becoming entitled to the dividend, thereby avoiding any liability to tax due on the declared dividend. The dividend waiver must not be executed for any form of other consideration and cannot be backdated; i.e. the date on the deed must be the date it is signed and witnessed. Backdating a deed is forgery (a criminal offence). The waiver must be executed before the date the shareholder becomes entitled to the dividend. A waiver can be effective for all future dividends, for any future period of time, or for specific dividends.

16.53   There must be sufficient distributable reserves available to pay the dividend, without the need for a waiver. If a waiver is made because there are insufficient profits, in order to increase the other shareholders' dividends, then it is likely to be concluded that the waiver was intended.

16.54   It is also necessary to ensure that the dividend waived does not remain the income of the waiving shareholder under the settlement provisions in *ICTA 1988, ss 660A–660G*. Where the waiver is executed to enable another shareholder to receive an increased dividend, this would be regarded as income arising under a settlement within *s 660A(1)*. The settlor would remain fully taxable on the amount of the dividend waived.

Proprietorial companies will commonly involve minority holdings for spouses, with the intention of placing enough income in the hands of the spouse to absorb his/her personal allowances and perhaps the basic rate band. Therefore the husband may waive his dividends in order that those to the wife are increased. It is likely, in this case, that the settlements legislation will apply and the dividend will remain taxable on the husband.

16.55   Not all dividend waivers are, however, vulnerable to challenge. The presence of the following factors indicate that the settlements legislation is likely to apply:

- the level of retained profits is insufficient to allow the same rate of dividend to be paid on all issued share capital;
- there has been a succession of waivers over several years where the total dividends payable in the absence of the waivers would exceed accumulated profits;
- there is other evidence which suggests that the same rate would not have been paid on all issued shares in the absence of the waiver;
- the non-waiving shareholders are persons whom the waiving shareholder can reasonably be regarded as wishing to benefit by the waiver;
- the non-waiving shareholder will pay less tax on the dividend than the waiving shareholder.

16.56   The dividend waiver should not be used as a regular tax planning tool. The Inland Revenue perceive it as a means of avoidance and there are standing instructions for Inspectors to submit cases involving dividend waivers, in combination with certain other factors in family companies, to the Financial Intermediaries and Claims Office [Inland Revenue *Company Taxation Manual para 1527*].

16.57   It is also worth noting that the waiver of a dividend might constitute a transfer of value for inheritance tax purposes. However, this is not the case where the waiver is made within twelve months of the declaration of the dividend [*IHTA 1984, s 15*]. This is an argument against long-term waivers.

16.58   So a dividend waiver might provide an occasional solution. It is not a long-term fix and relies on certain shareholders to 'do the right thing'.

For further reading, see '*Dividend Rights and Wrongs*' by Peter Vaines, *Taxation* 11 November 1999.

One must not forget the impact of tax credits (working tax credit and child tax credit – both payable from 6 April 2003). In particular, the *Tax Credits (Definition and Calculation of Income) Regulations SI 2002/2006, Reg 15* says that if a claimant has deprived himself of income for the purpose of securing entitlement to, or increasing the amount of, a tax credit, he is treated as having that income. At the time of writing, tax credits are brand new and working practices have yet to be established. If the person waiving the dividend is also a claimant of tax credits he should be aware that, for this purpose, he may still be treated as having the dividend foregone. Could this have an effect in real life though? The tax credit claim form has nowhere to make an entry for notional income even if one was disposed to. A subsequent attack would require close liaison between the Revenue at local district level and the Tax Credits Office, as well as a mutual understanding of the respective pieces of legislation.

Preference shares

16.59 One of the prime objectives is to derive income from the company in the most tax-efficient manner. Ordinary shares give full participation in the company in the way of voting rights and rights to the underlying capital. Preference shares, on the other hand, give a fixed right to dividend, usually no vote and limited access to the capital base. This might sound ideal.

There is no doubt that preference shares do serve a useful purpose in larger companies with arm's length ownership and financing arrangements. However, it is suggested that they should be used sparingly and with due caution in the closely controlled company.

It is the right to income without capital which causes the problem. Immediately thoughts, especially those of the Inland Revenue, turn again to the settlement legislation in *ICTA 1988, ss 660A–660G*.

In *Young v Pearce and Young v Scrutton [1996] STC 743*, two male shareholders of a company arranged for non-voting preference shares to be issued at par to their respective wives. The object was to get income to the spouses to make use of the income tax basic rate bands. The arrangement was held to be a settlement and the dividends on the preference shares were taxed on the husbands.

It seems that the same arguments could be applied wherever shares with a fixed right to income are transferred to family members, such as spouses, children etc., with the intention of exploiting otherwise unused tax capacity.

Lettered shares

16.60 There is a relatively recent and increasing fashion for splitting the ordinary share capital of a company into lettered sub-divisions, i.e. A, B, C, D etc. In all material respects, the shares are otherwise similar.

Clearly the objective is to be able to pay differential rates of dividend. Thus the A shares could get £1 (per share) while the B shares only get 50p and the Cs get 75p.

16.61 On an arm's length basis this would appear to be a valuable tool. The larger company may issue shares to valued employees (which action in itself may have tax consequences). Each employee gets a different sub-class of share and there is therefore the capacity to pay different rates of dividend, thus more specifically rewarding the individual's true performance while still achieving the tax and NIC advantages.

16.62 Can the same be true in a closely controlled family company? If the founding father owns A ordinary shares, can B, C, D etc. be given to his wife, children etc? There would seem to be comparatively little doubt if there were a single class of ordinary shares. Transferring these is a valid method of passing on the business, inheritance tax planning etc. and there would seem to be no question of the settlements legislation biting (except where minor children are involved; see for example *Butler v Wildin [1989] STC 22*). This is not just a means of passing on income. Full voting rights and the underlying capital go with the ordinaries. Contrast the comments regarding the settlements legislation at **16.69**.

16.63 Surely the same logic must apply to lettered shares. If they are merely a sub-division of the ordinary share capital, they will get a vote, rights to capital etc. It is only the amount of the dividend which could change. Whilst one might be a bit wary of interim dividends which can be paid at the instance of directors who might be the 'top sub-division' shareholders, final dividends are probably acceptable. The final dividend must be approved by a majority of shareholders in a general meeting which would include all the lettered sub-divisions. There should, then, be no argument that the A shareholders are dictating the dividends payable to B, C, D etc. The author is inclined to the view that this arrangement works though, as it is a relatively new concept, it remains to be seen whether an alternative challenge appears from the Inland Revenue.

16.64 One additional point to watch is that the dividends really do go to the shareholder: For example, husband holds A ordinary shares in a company; wife holds B ordinary shares. Dividends are declared so as to favour the B class. That dividend must be paid to the wife to a bank account in her name. She must be free to spend the proceeds as she wishes. If both dividends were to go to a joint bank account, from which general living expenses were met, the argument that there is a settlement might begin to reappear since the income would not clearly have been paid to her.

Share issue on incorporation

16.65 With the very small business, one thought behind incorporation is the ability to transfer income to a non-working spouse where the business is operated by the other spouse. Some care is necessary to ensure that the correct structure is in place. Incorporation through the route afforded by *TCGA 1992, s 162*, would be precluded because of the precise conditions regarding share issue (see **9.11**).

16.66   How then will the spouse get the shares? Care must be taken to follow either:

Route 1: Husband and wife subscribe for, say, 50% of the shares each using their own money. The business is then transferred in using *TCGA 1992, s 165*, to holdover any capital gain.

Route 2: Husband subscribes for all the shares of the new company. The business is transferred in. He then gifts, say, 50% of the shares to his wife.

16.67   If the husband was the original sole trader, again it is necessary to ensure that the wife's dividends are paid to her in her own bank account. She should then be free to spend the proceeds. If the dividends were to go to a joint account, an argument may loom as to what has changed and the whole arrangement constitutes a settlement.

16.68   Incidentally, either route 1 or route 2 will involve a transfer of value for inheritance tax purposes. This is of no significance where husband and wife are involved, since it would be an exempt transfer, assuming both are UK domiciled. More care is needed where children etc. are involved. Route 1 would lead to an immediately chargeable transfer (see **13.9**) though this may only amount to an erosion of the parent's nil rate band. Route 2 would lead to a PET. The possible effects of the death of the proprietor within seven years should be considered.

16.69   One must, in any case, be wary of such situations where the underlying intention of the arrangement is to transfer part of the earning capacity of one spouse to the other. Suppose that the husband is a consultant whose business consists essentially of selling his time and expertise. A company is formed in which the wife takes a substantial shareholding. The husband takes only a modest salary and then large dividends are paid. Effectively, the wife gets a significant slice of what would otherwise be the husband's earnings (very probably utilising her basic rate band when he would otherwise be taxed at the higher rate).

On the face of it, this would seem to be a settlement within *ICTA 1988, ss 660A–G* and the wife's dividend will be taxed on the husband. The exclusion in *s 660A(6)* for an outright gift of property between spouses, which is property from which income arises, is unlikely to apply. Even though she may take fully participating ordinary shares, there is no underlying capital base and what is transferred is substantially a right to income.

The Inland Revenue *Trusts Settlements and Estates Manual para 4210* instructs Inspectors to look at the whole arrangement. An example given demonstrates that an arrangement such as this would be challenged.

Neither the legislation, nor the Revenue's expressed attitude to it are new. However, exchanges on the *Accountingweb* in March 2003 seem to suggest that Inspectors are adopting a harder line. Whether this is sustainable may be questionable and one foresees litigation on this point before too long. *Malcolm Gunn* gives a more reasoned analysis, which again doubts the correctness of the Revenue's stance, in *'All Very Unsettling'* in *Taxation, 13 March 2003.*

Jointly held shares

16.70   If the object of the exercise is to get income to a non-working spouse, a very simple device is often overlooked.

There is a statutory presumption in *ICTA 1988, s 282A(1)* that income arising to property held in the joint names of husband and wife belongs to them in equal shares. It does not therefore matter whose business it is, who subscribed for the shares etc. If the shares are registered in joint names, the dividends will be taxed as to 50% on the husband and 50% on the wife.

Salaries

Too much

16.71   As a general principle, the company (being a Schedule D trader) cannot deduct expenses which are not wholly and exclusively laid out for the purpose of the trade when arriving at the profit for tax purposes. These expenses will include salaries paid to directors. A director, on the other hand, thinking that the business is his, may be inclined to draw a salary of whatever amount he wishes; is this an insoluble paradox? Can the proprietor draw whatever amount he wishes from the company?

Historically, the Inland Revenue has sought to challenge what it perceives to be excessive salaries. The leading case is *Copeman v William Flood Ltd (1940) 24 TC 53* where the controlling director arranged for large salaries to be paid to his son and daughter (one of whom was a minor) with the result that the company made a loss. Although the General Commissioners found that they could not interfere with the company's decision to pay such remuneration as it thought fit, the High Court decided that the amounts were excessive and not paid wholly and exclusively for the purposes of the trade.

16.72   Despite having case law on its side, the Inland Revenue does not normally pursue this point these days. Inland Revenue *Inspector's Manual para 1042* indicates that, where a company's payment of remuneration is matched by an equivalent amount assessable as remuneration of the director/employee, any disallowance under *ICTA 1988, s 74(1)(a)* would result in a double tax charge. For this reason, disallowance is only appropriate in exceptional cases.

However, regard must be had to family relationships, especially where minor children are involved. In *Dollar (t/a I J Dollar) v Lyon [1981] STC 333*, a husband and wife in a farming partnership paid relatively substantial amounts to their four minor children for doing odd jobs around the farm. The amounts paid were held not to be deductible in arriving at the trading profit because of the close family relationship (the payments were really pocket money) and especially bearing in mind that the three younger children could not legally be employed.

16.73   The other weapon in the Inspector's armoury in these circumstances is again the settlements legislation in *ICTA 1988, ss 660A–660G*. Payments to close family relations may have no commercial meaning and are a ruse to use their personal allowances, basic rate bands etc. The arrangement would constitute a settlement and any such payments are taxed on the settlor who is the controlling director/shareholder. The commentary in *Inspector's Manual para 1042* does continue to say that a challenge on this basis might be considered.

16.74   The timing of payment is also important. Unless actual payment has been paid at an earlier stage, the remuneration of a director who is an office holder under the *Companies Act* is normally approved at the annual general meeting. Unless the remuneration is approved at the AGM and paid within nine months of the end of the accounting period to which it relates, *FA 1989, s 43*, precludes a deduction in arriving at the trading profits for that period. If the remuneration is paid 'late', then it is not allowable until the accounting period in which actual payment is made.

Too little

16.75   Possibly the day of the consistently high salary may be past. The tax advantages of dividends are just too compelling. So, can the Revenue challenge salaries which are very low? Anecdotal evidence seems to suggest that that the PAYE Employer Compliance Teams in particular are trying to do so.

Can a close company director simply switch between salary and dividend at will? With suggestions that senior employees in some companies should be given shares so that they can enjoy the bonanza, what needs to be done?

16.76   A director may be engaged in one of two ways:

• As an office holder appointed under the *Companies Act*. The remuneration for such office may be determined from time to time as the parties think fit and is usually approved by the members of the company at the AGM. As it is necessary to determine the level of remuneration annually, there is no reason why the amount should not fluctuate from time to time (so as to satisfy the personal pension basis year rules for example; see **4.34**). Any amounts drawn during the year will be advances on account of the director's fee to be agreed.

• As an employee. Service contracts for directors in family companies are rare, but more common in owner managed companies where the parties are otherwise at arm's length. Whether express or implied, a salary will be due under that contract. Where this is the case, more care should be taken over determining the amount to be paid.

16.77   Many will want to take minimal salary and high dividends. Where the director is an office holder, there should be no problem. Where there is also a service contract, it may be more difficult. Perhaps the service contract should be renegotiated to reflect a much smaller salary (though do not forget, in this case, the constraints of the national minimum wage legislation; see **12.7**). It is more difficult then to get high remuneration for a personal pension basis year, though a bonus could be voted occasionally. Alternatively, some part of the salary could be waived in favour of dividends. As with dividend waiver (see **16.52**), waivers of salary should be properly constructed and used sparingly to avoid arguments that a settlement has been created.

At least in theory, the tax credit issue discussed at **16.58** could be relevant here too.

16.78   To be valid for tax purposes, the entitlement to remuneration must be given up before it is treated as employment income. Once the director or employee is treated as receiving cash emoluments:

• income tax is due under PAYE and NIC must be accounted for;
• he is liable to tax on employment income;
• the employing company is entitled to a deduction in the computation of the profits of its trade, subject to the usual rules.

An individual is treated as receiving emoluments at the *earliest* of the following [*ITEPA 2003, ss 18, 31; ICTA 1988, s 202B*]:

• when actual payment is made;
• when the person becomes entitled to payment;
• where the person is a director and sums on account of the emoluments are credited in the company's accounting records;
• where the person is a director and the amount of the emoluments is determined before the accounting period ends, the end of the accounting period;
• where the person is a director and the amount of the emoluments is determined after the accounting period has ended, the time when the amount is determined.

If any of these events have passed, any cash payment is treated as taxable under Schedule E. Note that the Inland Revenue takes the view (at least for an ordinary employee) that entitlement to salary accrues on a daily basis. Also note the subtle distinction of this test from the time of payment for PAYE purposes in *ITEPA 2003, s 686; ICTA 1988 s 203A* (see **16.40**).

16.79   Alongside the small salary, there is a payment of substantial dividends. There is evidence to suggest that the Inland Revenue might be trying to allege that such dividends are tantamount to a salary. This is not the case and any such argument should be strongly refuted.

A dividend is paid to a shareholder as a return for his investment in the company. A salary (or fee as office holder) is paid to the director for acting in such a capacity. The two are unconnected even if the same individual acts in both capacities. To strengthen the argument, the correct procedures for declaration, payment and recording of dividends must be followed.

Even then, an illegally declared and paid dividend (perhaps because the company has inadequate distributable reserves) cannot be reclassified as salary. Possible action by the Inland Revenue seems to stem from the historic view of the Contributions Agency. In 1994, the Contributions Agency wrote to the ICAEW and other professional bodies admitting that it took the view that disproportionate dividends (whatever that might mean) were not genuine dividends, but earnings. The note goes on to say that an unlawful dividend will be regarded as earnings, but there seems to be no justification for such a stance. In any case, following the transfer of responsibilities from the old Contributions Agency to the Inland Revenue National Insurance Contributions Office, the point seems to be covered by Inland Revenue *National Insurance Manual para 12012*. This says that directors receive dividends as shareholders in the company and not in their capacity as directors. Dividends are therefore not earnings for the purposes of NIC. If a company pays an unlawful dividend to its directors, or any other shareholder, the money is returnable to the company [*CA 1985, s 277*] and is not reclassified.

The company's remedy for an illegal dividend is to seek repayment. If this does not happen, which might especially be the case with a family company, the result must be a loan to a participator whereupon a s 419 tax charge will arise. The amount is clearly not taxable as employment earnings and no NIC is due.

16.80   Perhaps the Inland Revenue attack is in cases where the salary waiver has not been validly effected, perhaps combined with incorrect declaration of a dividend. To avoid the challenge, get the paperwork right.

Planning points

- Section 419 tax is due nine months after the end of the accounting period and must be self assessed (**16.16**).
- Repayment of the loan before the due date removes the charge (**16.19**).
- Take care in offset where loans arising at different times are partially repaid (**16.22**).
- Loan write off may be a useful alternative to dividend payment (**16.25**).
- Make sure dividends are validly declared (**16.31**).
- Loans totalling no more than £5,000 attract no benefit in kind charge (**16.36**).
- Beware of debiting remuneration type items to director's loan account if intended clearance is by way of a dividend (**16.42**).
- Note that PAYE is due when salary is credited to director's loan account (**16.43**).
- Interim dividends must be paid in cash (**16.45**).
- Ensure dividend waivers are valid (**16.52**).
- Consider lettered shares to spread income around the family (**16.63**).
- Jointly held shares spread the income automatically between spouses (**16.70**).
- An illegal dividend alone is not salary (**16.79**).

Chapter 17

Employment Status

The personal service company

17.1   There is a good deal of misconception and perhaps, even, paranoia concerning the *FA 2000* provision of services through an intermediary legislation (the so called IR35 rules). Many small businessmen are reluctant to incorporate their businesses because they have heard of the IR35 problems and think that they will be affected. In fact, IR35 has very little to do with trading in the corporate medium. The crux of it is employment status, i.e. the differentiation between an individual who is self employed and one who provides his services as an employee.

The rules deserve some scrutiny, if only to demonstrate that they will not apply in the vast majority of cases. Also, for those of a negative disposition, could this be a taste of what might be to come should the Government decide to launch a counter attack on the current flood of small incorporations?

Employed or self employed

17.2   The personal service company legislation is to be found in *ITEPA 2003, Part 2, Chapter 8; FA 2000, Sch 12*. It acquired the nickname IR35 after the numbering of the Inland Revenue press release which announced the measures following the 1999 Budget. Although most relevant to companies, that is by no means exclusively the case. The intermediary may be a partnership or another individual, just as much as a company.

The legislation applies where:

- an individual (the worker) personally performs services for the purposes of a business carried on by another person (the client);
- the services are provided not under a contract directly between the client and the worker, but under arrangements involving a third party (the intermediary);
- the circumstances are such that, if the services were provided under a contract directly between the client and the worker, the worker would be regarded for income tax purposes as an employee of the client.

[*ITEPA 2003, s 49; FA 2000, Sch 12 para 1(1)*].

17.3 Employment Status

If the worker supplies his services to the ultimate customer in circumstances which would normally treat him as an employee, then these rules apply. If he would not be an employee, then they do not.

17.3 Employment status is a complex subject, a complete analysis of which is beyond the scope of this work, though it is necessary to look at the basics in order to set the IR35 rules in context. One great concern of the Inland Revenue was the number of individuals, in the mid to late 1990s, who apparently left full-time employment on Friday only to return on Monday providing their services to the same employer through a limited company. Often they sat at the same desk, doing exactly the same job. So what had changed? Other high profile cases, such as John Birt, the apparently self employed director general of the BBC, did not help.

17.4 There is no simple test to establish whether a particular worker is employed or self employed. Certainly it is impossible for the engager to say 'You will be treated as self employed'. This is simply an attempt to negate his responsibilities as employer.

Over the years, many tests have been deduced from common practice and case law, but it is not just a matter of going through a checklist of questions and reaching an arithmetical conclusion. Some tests will be more important than others, with the relative balance perhaps changing from one engagement to another.

17.5 In very broad terms, one might recognise that an employee would:

- work regular hours;
- be paid a fixed sum, irrespective of performance (though good work might attract a bonus);
- be subject to a high degree of control over what to do, when to do it, etc. if not exactly how to do it;
- do the work personally;
- expect continuity of work;
- be subject to dismissal procedures;
- have no financial risk;
- be part of the employer's business;
- have a relatively long period of engagement.

17.6 By contrast, it might be expected that a self employed worker would:

- by agreement with the customer, work when and where he desires;
- be paid on invoice for tasks completed;
- supply his own tools and equipment;
- have to correct poor work for no additional pay;
- have the right to send a (suitably qualified) substitute, rather than do the work himself;
- make a greater profit through efficient work;
- not get holiday pay or sick pay;

- carry on his own business as distinct from that of the customer;
- tend to undertake many small, short-term engagements, perhaps more than one at the same time.

17.7 The important point to make is that none of these issues is conclusive and it is essential to examine the facts.

Faced with interpretation of literally hundreds of case law decisions, relating not only to tax matters but also NIC and employment protection issues, following a checklist approach seems an easy answer. Faced with difficult situations though, there is no substitute for going back to first principles.

17.8 The Inland Revenue view is set out in basic form in leaflet *IR56: Employed or Self Employed*. In the mid-1990s, categorisation of building industry subcontractors (for more of which see below) prompted an article in Inland Revenue *Tax Bulletin 28, April 1997*. The IR35 problem spawned a longer article in *Tax Bulletin 45, February 2002*. Both of these contain several examples of typical situations.

Additionally the Inland Revenue *Employment Status Manual* is now in the public domain and has undergone extensive revision to meet the demands of IR35. Do bear in mind though that all of this material is written with an Inland Revenue slant. It is somewhat notorious for 'overlooking' case law decisions which it lost (for example, *Special Eyes (Optical Services) Ltd* – admittedly unreported – and *McManus v Griffiths [1997] STC 1089*).

17.9 Those who have fallen foul of the IR35 legislation may be highly skilled, intelligent and articulate, but their activities are focussed elsewhere. Many work in the field of information technology but there are also engineers etc. Unfortunately, they do not understand, perhaps until recently have never encountered, the concept of employment status.

They tend to get sucked into the importance of the contract. There are many firms and organisations who offer so called 'IR35 proof' contracts. The author takes the view that there is no such thing, though there are certainly bad contracts which make the application of IR35 almost inevitable.

Many personal service companies do not find work directly, but rather do so through an agency. Where this is the case, the agencies tend to have contracts of a standard form. There are, frankly, some pretty awful ones around. They will typically require the personal service company to provide the services of a specified worker, at the client premises, work standard hours, be paid an hourly or daily rate (often with the addition of expenses) and be subject to a high degree of control. This is an absolute disaster.

But you cannot necessarily tip the scales the other way by having a better worded contract. At the crux of the issue are the facts of the engagement. A nicely worded contract is no use if it does not adequately reflect the way in which the parties behave.

17.10 *Employment Status*

17.10   If an individual, or his adviser, is unsure about his employment status in an engagement of this type, the Inland Revenue can be asked to give a ruling. This will be based on the substance of the actual (signed) contracts and not drafts. Inland Revenue leaflet *IR175: Supplying Services through a Limited Company or Partnership* makes it clear that it will review the facts if necessary by talking to the worker and others. The crux of it is thus what the contract means in terms of actual arrangements as opposed to what it might say.

17.11   It is, of course, perfectly possible that the company may have some contracts which fall within IR35 and some which do not.

17.12   In summary, what IR35 is about is one man companies which provide services to a limited range of customers in circumstances which would appear to be employment. The vast majority of small companies will have an independent business of their own, many customers, appropriate financing and their own infrastructure. They have no need to fear IR35. If a self employed sole trader could not have been deemed to be an employee of his clients for income tax purposes then incorporation, of itself, will not render the company subject to IR35.

Incidentally, some seem to think that the answer to IR35 is the umbrella or composite company. This is almost certainly not the case. The first condition of liability under these provisions is that the worker has a material interest in the intermediary company [*ITEPA 2003, s 51(1)(a); FA 2000, Sch 12 para 3(1)(a)*]. 'Material interest' broadly means ownership of, or the ability to control, 5% of the ordinary share capital of the company. This clearly catches the majority of one man companies providing 'offending' services. However, it seems to be widely overlooked that there is an alternative test leading to liability. This is that the payment received by the worker from the intermediary can reasonably be taken to represent remuneration for services provided by the worker to the client [*ITEPA 2003, s 51(1)(b); FA 2000, Sch 12 para 3(1)(b)*]. Thus it matters not that the worker has no material interest in the company (an umbrella or composite company is set up with the intention that they should not). If a payment received from the personal service company amounts to remuneration for services provided by the worker to the ultimate client, which it must, then the arrangement is still caught.

Effect of the legislation

17.13   First, it has to be said that there are some quasi-employers out there, rubbing their hands with glee. The operation of PAYE is an obligation of the employer. If he engages an individual to provide services, it therefore behoves the engager to decide whether the worker is employed or self employed. If there is failure to account for PAYE and a status dispute ensues, perhaps during an employer compliance visit by the Inland Revenue, then it is primarily the putative employer's responsibility to account for the outstanding tax and NIC. In practice, where the situation is long-standing and the worker has accounted for tax under Schedule D, the Inland Revenue will often permit this to be offset in arriving at the outstanding liability.

17.14 Putting a personal service company in place changes all this. The IR35 provisions place the prime liability on the personal service company. So, amazingly, the engaging company is off the hook. No longer does it have to consider status and weigh up the risks as to whether it should operate PAYE. It is now someone else's problem. Great news. Though it must be commented that the original draft legislation following the 1999 Budget announcement was intended to place the prime responsibility on the engaging company. For many reasons, this was thought to be unworkable but why the balance of responsibility should shift away from the ultimate client is not clear when the PAYE consequences of direct engagement of an employee fall squarely there. The modified proposals, subsequently enacted, place all the responsibilities with the personal service company. For the majority of one man companies, this means that the buck stops with the worker.

17.15 The author does note, from personal experience, a distinct change in attitudes to IR35. From its announcement to implementation, there was a general hue and outcry. The system was alleged to be unfair, unworkable etc. It was even suggested that it could be the death knell of the UK information technology industry. In 2000/01, the rules had to be examined and deemed payment calculations made in appropriate situations. From then on, it seems to have gone relatively quiet. A surprisingly large number of personal services companies have ceased to trade – and their proprietors have got jobs, often with their major clients. The remainder seem to have faced up to the IR35 system as being a fact of life.

Deemed payment

17.16 The company, which is caught by the IR35 rules, has two choices:

- pay out everything (and this does mean virtually everything – not just the net corporate profit) by way of salary;
- pay an additional tax liability on a deemed payment.

The deemed payment is what might be termed a statutory fiction. It does not actually have to be paid but tax is due under PAYE, along with the relevant NIC, whether it is paid or not. In administrative terms, affected companies will be faced with a reconciliation every year, as at 5 April, to check whether they have paid out all of the profits from relevant engagements (i.e. those caught by these rules) as salary or benefits in kind and, if not, will be deemed to make a payment of salary on 5 April to clear the difference.

17.17 There is a specific and detailed calculation of the deemed payment set out in *ITEPA 2003, s 54; FA 2000, Sch 12 para 7*. The full process is not set out here but particular features to note are:

- From the total of the income from relevant engagements may be deducted an allowance of 5%. This is intended to cover all the expenses of running the company, including accountancy fees and *Companies Act* filing fees. In the deemed salary calculation there is no need for the intermediary to show how this expenditure has been laid out, or even that it has.
- Travelling expenses may be claimed as if the worker were an employee of the intermediary and all relevant engagements arise from a single employment. This means that expenses will be deductible following the normal permanent and temporary workplace and 24-month rules [*ITEPA 2003, s 339; ICTA 1988, Sch 12A paras 4, 5*]. Shorter engagements will attract full travelling expense deductions.
- Where the company has several sources of income, consisting of both relevant engagements and other work, the latter will need to be segregated. At least in theory, the company could pay dividends from that income stream, enjoying the advantages of any other company.

17.18   The resulting payment is treated as though it were a payment of salary and PAYE and NIC are due on 19 April following the year of assessment. In practice, the Inland Revenue recognises that many affected companies will not be able to deal with this process in such a short time. It is therefore prepared to accept a realistic payment on account with the balance to be paid on or before 31 January following. Interest runs on any outstanding balance from 19 April.

17.19   The director involved must declare the deemed payment on his personal self assessment return, whether it was paid out or not.

17.20   The deemed payment is treated as an emolument of the employment and is therefore deductible in arriving at the company's profit for corporation tax purposes. The notional 5% deduction for expenses in arriving at the deemed payment is not a corporation tax deduction and must be substituted by actual expenses. Because of the fiction, there is no connection with the real corporate expenses, which may far exceed the notional amount. It is quite likely therefore that the company will find itself in a loss making position.

17.21   Unless the company's accounting date is co-terminous with the fiscal year, there may be some mismatch between the IR35 rules and the relieving of expenses for corporation tax purposes. The deemed payment is deductible on the cash basis. For this reason, the world's worst accounting date for an IR35 company is 31 March. 5 April is ideal and 30 April probably acceptable.

17.22   Whilst the normal deemed payment calculation is required as at 5 April, it must be advanced where the worker is a member of the company and ceases to be such a member, where he holds an office with the company and ceases to hold such office, or where he is an employee and ceases to be employed [*ITEPA 2003, s 57; FA 2000, Sch 12 para 12*].

17.23   What happens next is perhaps even more curious. The whole ethos behind IR35 is to prevent disguised self employment and incorporation which reduces the amount of income tax and NIC flowing to the exchequer. Once the company has been through the deemed payment process, one might think it reasonable to assume that the payment of PAYE and NIC might be available to frank a later payment of actual salary. But that is not the case. If there is an ensuing real payment of salary, then that must be subject to the usual PAYE processes. In that event, the deemed payment of tax is a real additional liability.

17.24   There is a way of getting relief, but that is by means of paying a dividend. Hang on a minute; paying a dividend? Isn't that what this legislation was trying to stop? Where the intermediary company makes a claim, the amount of any subsequent dividend may be reduced to the extent that it reflects amounts already charged to income tax under the deemed payment process [*ITEPA 2003, s 58; FA 2000, Sch 12 para 13*]. The recipient then has no need to return the amount of such distribution.

Clearly, this is very woolly thinking on the part of the Inland Revenue. Salaries are paid to directors and employees as a reward for their services to the company. Dividends are paid in respect of the participators' investments in the company. The two should be unconnected even if, in the vast majority of such cases, the shareholders and directors are identical. But the effect of the relief is almost to encourage the payment of dividends. Surely, it would have been far more logical to set the tax on the deemed payment against an actual payment of salary.

17.25   Which probably takes this section full circle. The only way out is to pay a full salary. This may prove to be impossible if (as seems likely) the company's expenses are above the notional 5% permitted. At least by this means the timing and impact is within the control of the parties and not at the direction of the legislation.

A taste of the future?

17.26   In a couple of places, the author has alluded to close company apportionment (see **1.2** and **16.8**). Indeed, horror of horrors, he is actually old enough to remember its application.

It stemmed from a time when income tax rates were very high (up to 98%) but corporate rates never exceeded 52%. Further, capital gains tax was levied at a flat 30%. There was an obvious incentive to retain funds in the corporate sphere and to achieve realisation by capital transactions rather than income ones. The apportionment provisions countered this for close companies by deeming an acceptable level of distribution. If actual distributions did not reach this level, then tax was levied on the participators as if such distributions had been made.

In some ways, one can see the same logic coming through in the IR35 rules. Either the company pays an acceptable level of salary, or the Inland Revenue will treat it as having done so and levy an appropriate amount of tax anyway.

The pessimists feel that the current free and easy attitude to incorporation cannot last. Small close companies and their proprietors especially have virtually total freedom to name their own tax liability. It remains anybody's guess whether the Government will launch a counter attack and, if so, what it will be.

Some commentators suggested that new measures, announced in the 2002 Budget to encourage incorporation of small businesses, might cost the Government £2.5–£3bn. This is a loss that it presumably cannot afford. Suggested counter measures from several commentators include a return to some form of close company apportionment. Could we see introduction of an acceptable standard of salary payment for close companies, with an extension of the IR35 principles to those that do not pay enough?

Advantages in the personal service company

17.27 If all this seems doom and gloom, is it actually possible to be worse off with a personal service company? This, of course, assumes a free choice. The overriding reason that many of them remain is that the ultimate client wants a corporate contractor (and will not deal with any other medium).

17.28 In theory, it could be possible that the arrangement makes the parties worse off, since the personal service company is liable not only for income tax under PAYE and the primary Class 1 NIC (both of which are recoverable from the individual if actual payment is made), but also the secondary NIC. However, contract prices often reflect this. The author recalls advising a personal service company proprietor in specific circumstances; the tax problem was soluble but a residual liability to NIC remained. The proprietor went to the client and the contract price went from £180,000 to £200,000 almost overnight.

17.29 Many see the 5% expense allowance as restrictive. It has to be said that in some companies this could be the case. In practice, many small personal service companies will only incur accountancy costs and statutory filing fees, which may be well below the prescribed amount. The amount of 5% is deductible whether it is incurred or not.

17.30 There are advantages over employment as regards travel expenses. The worker's actual employment is with the intermediary company so that the client's office may be a temporary workplace. Travel to it may therefore be a deductible expense subject to the 24-month rule. If the worker were to undertake a series of short term employments direct for the clients, this would not be the case.

17.31 The personal service company may undertake other work which does not fall within IR35 and attracts the usual advantages.

17.32 Shares in the personal service company should be business assets for taper relief purposes, though this may be a theoretical rather than a real advantage since they are unlikely ever to be of significant value.

17.33   The real answer is to know the rules and to operate around them. So far as possible, endeavour to establish that engagements undertaken by a company of this type do not amount to quasi employment of the worker.

Nanny companies

17.34   Until an announcement in the 2003 Budget, the IR35 rules only applied where the worker performs services for the purposes of a business carried on by another person [*ITEPA 2003, s 49(1)(a); FA 2000 Sch 12 para 1(1)(a)*]. If the ultimate consumer of the services was not in business or, at least, did not use the services in a business capacity, then the personal service company rules did not apply. This is at least one reason why many small companies would not be caught by IR35 anyway – their customers are not in business and consume the services provided in a domestic capacity.

Some sought to apply this positively. Where the service is a wholly domestic arrangement, why not go for a service company that could not be caught by the rules (and save money).

Enter the nanny company. Persuade the nanny (or gardener, housekeeper etc.) to incorporate. A fee is paid to Nanny Co Ltd and its profits are drawn largely by way of dividend. The tax liabilities would be minimal and there would be no NIC at all, leading to some (proportionately) huge savings.

Clearly this cut no ice with the Chancellor who, in the 2003 Budget, announced that the intermediaries legislation would be extended to domestic workers who provide their services through a company [*Finance Act, s 136*]. This had immediate effect (applying to all services provided after 9 April 2003) for income tax but secondary legislation will be required for NIC purposes.

Thus, any such company continuing to trade in 2003/04 will have different deemed payment calculations for income tax and NIC. In practice, most will have ceased to trade shortly after the Budget announcement.

Construction industry subcontractors

17.35   The problems of employment status are widespread. In most instances they will not impinge on issues of incorporation. The IR35 problem is very specific since, in most cases, the intermediary is a company. That apart, we actually need a bona fide business before we can consider the issues of incorporation. If the employment status of the proprietor is doubtful, then maybe there is no business to incorporate at all.

There is, however, one further area in which employment status is a perpetual problem and in which incorporation may now be very relevant. This is the construction industry which has its own, very specific, tax treatment. The labour only subcontractor has been a feature of the building industry since an arrangement known as 'the lump' 40 years or more ago.

Present position

17.36 There is really a two stage process to go through:

- first, ask the question: is the arrangement one of self employment?;
- second, if so, follow the construction industry scheme.

17.37 The first step may often be conveniently overlooked. There is nothing different in the building industry from any other. One can apply the tests of employment or self employment (for a summary see **17.5–17.6** above) to a building worker just as much as to a worker in any other industry. This is the first hurdle. If the terms of engagement are such as to render the worker an employee of the contractor, then income tax must be deducted under PAYE and NIC accounted for in respect of all payments in exactly the same fashion as they would be with any other employee. To emphasise this point, the Inland Revenue has even issued an industry specific leaflet *IR148 'Are your Workers Employed or Self Employed? A Guide for Tax and National Insurance for Contractors in the Construction Industry'*.

Only if it is possible to clear that hurdle is it necessary to consider the specific construction industry scheme of tax deduction. To counter perceived abuses in the past, a system of subcontractor registration and certification was introduced in 1971. The rules have gradually been tightened over the years, with the last major revamp in 1999. Even so, the Chancellor's pre-Budget statement in November 2002 included proposals to undertake a consultation process regarding major changes to the construction industry scheme, including status. Press Notice PN6, following the 2003 Budget, indicated that a revised scheme would come into operation in April 2005.

Outline of the current scheme

17.38 Contractors and subcontractors can be companies, sole traders or partnerships. Contractors can also include local authorities and other organisations, but not private householders. Contractors can also be subcontractors and vice versa, thereby having a joint responsibility.

17.39 Subcontractors must hold a certificate or registration card to get paid at all, unless of course they are taken on as an employee. To fall within the scheme at all, they must be genuinely self employed.

Contractors and subcontractors must register with the Inland Revenue, obtaining a certificate enabling payment to be made gross, provided they meet certain conditions; payment should be made net of tax if only a registration card is held.

17.40   The scheme applies to all construction operations carried on in the United Kingdom. Construction operations are defined in *ICTA 1988, s 567*. The Inland Revenue view of matters included and excluded from the scheme is given in Inland Revenue leaflet *IR14/15 Construction Industry Scheme*.

17.41   Where tax deductions from payments are necessary under the construction industry scheme, the deductions are made on the labour charges, together with any expenses payments, excluding VAT and after deducting any materials purchased by the subcontractor. The rate of deduction is currently 18%.

17.42   The first stage to entering the scheme is to obtain a registration card. This facilitates payment by a contractor to a subcontractor under deduction of tax for self employed work. The subcontractor needs to complete an application form, supply a photograph and attend an identity check with the Inland Revenue. From September 2002, a registration card may be held for 12 months (or, in certain cases, 36 months) and there is the possibility of a renewal.

17.43   The primary legislation governing the specific tax regime for the construction industry is contained in *ICTA 1988, ss 559–567*. The specific rules concerning certification etc. are contained in *Income Tax (Sub-contractors in the Construction Industry) Regulations 1993, SI 1993/743*.

Obtaining a certificate

17.44   Most subcontractors will wish to receive gross payments, if for no other reason than to improve the cash flow to their businesses. An application form has to be completed at which time the applicant must satisfy three tests (business, compliance and turnover tests).

17.45   To fulfil the business test, the applicant must be carrying out construction work or supplying labour in the UK, running the business through a bank account, maintaining proper records and have proper business premises, stock, equipment, facilities etc.

17.46   To fulfil the compliance test, the applicant must have met various conditions for a period of three years up to the date of application. All tax returns must have been completed on time and all information requested by the Inland Revenue must have been supplied. All tax and NIC must have been paid on time in the individual's capacity as an employer or contractor, as well as in respect of his own self assessment. To verify that the compliance test has been met, the Inland Revenue needs to know what the applicant has been doing in the three year period. He must be prepared to provide documentary evidence of any periods of self employment, absences abroad and periods of full-time education. An employment or self employment history for this period must be demonstrated.

17.47   To fulfil the turnover test, the applicant must demonstrate what the turnover has been (i.e. gross amounts actually received from construction work, less materials and excluding VAT) for a specific period. The amounts vary for sole traders, partnerships and companies and the standard test is a period of three years or more. A six month test is applicable where the business has only recently commenced. Certificates normally last three years before the whole process needs to be repeated. Most certificates issued are CIS6, but a CIS5 certificate can be issued to companies with a turnover of at least £1m or, if they can make a business case for requiring such a certificate; this might include administrative needs such as a high turnover of vouchers or considerable time spent travelling to contractors simply to present certificates before payments can be made.

17.48   Where a certificate is held, the contractor must examine this on the occasion of the first payment to the subcontractor and record certain information, the contractor may make payment gross and should supply a voucher to the subcontractor.

Effect of incorporation

17.49   There are very many small subcontractors making a modest living on payments of perhaps £15,000–£20,000 p.a. However, as we have seen, it is possible to effect significant tax and NIC savings, even at this sort of level of profit. As the author writes this particular chapter (early 2003), there is news of the construction of a new terminal at Heathrow Airport and a suggestion that skilled tradesmen engaged on the project will be paid £55,000 p.a. Assuming that such individuals are self employed within the construction industry, then incorporation would seem to be advisable. Incorporation brings with it an administrative burden for the business but then, so too does the operation of the construction industry scheme.

17.50   The change of tax status from sole trader or partnership to company requires the cancellation of the existing certificate(s) and the application for a new one. It should be borne in mind that the application process usually takes about six weeks. This lead time must be considered in relation to the overall mechanics of incorporation, otherwise there might be a hiatus during which payments cannot be obtained. Careful planning should facilitate an overlap period and the continuation of contract.

17.51   Each relevant person must complete a fresh application for a new certificate, bearing in mind the usual business, compliance and turnover tests. For a sole trader, incorporating the business and running the company by himself as the director, the Inland Revenue will simply look at the various tests relating to his past three years history and will accept his turnover as a sole trader as fulfilling the turnover test. In principle, incorporation of a small partnership should be similar, though bear in mind where there are multiple directors, the business and compliance tests have to be certified for each of them, which requires a coordination of the applications and their processing.

17.52   If the forming of the company is a complete business takeover, involves multiple directors or is generally anything other than the transfer of a sole trade or partnership to the same individuals running the company, there will be a fresh turnover test:

- a standard test of £30,000 turnover p.a. for each of the relevant persons for three years in the four years to the date of application;
- alternatively, a six month test of £21,000 per relevant person for six consecutive months in the twelve months to the date of application;
- a turnover of £200,000 p.a. for the company over a three year period in the four years to the date of application.

The relevant persons are the directors of the company or, if it is a close company, the shareholders. A shareholder who is also a director counts as one.

17.53   Overall, incorporation of the business should not cause insuperable problems but the parties must recognise the construction industry scheme compliance procedure and ensure that this is built in to the scheme of incorporation.

Planning points

- IR35 is about employment status. If the worker would be self employed if engaged direct then the IR35 rules are irrelevant (**17.2**).
- A 'good' contract will not solve the IR35 problem (**17.9**).
- If a deemed payment is taxed, payment of a dividend is the only way to withdraw funds from the company without a further tax charge (**17.24**).
- A service company may help in relieving travel expenses (**17.30**).
- When incorporating a construction industry subcontractor, remember that a new gross payment certificate will be required (**17.50**).
- Build in a lead time to ensure that the business is not left without a gross payment certificate during the incorporation (**17.50**).

Chapter 18

Taper Relief

18.1   No self-respecting book on a tax-related subject these days can possibly be complete without a mention of taper relief. Introduced in 1998 by a Chancellor of the Exchequer who said that he proposed to simplify CGT, experience to date has demonstrated that this has done anything but. For starters, taper relief is only available to individuals and trustees. The former regime involving indexation allowances is still in place for companies. How replacing one system with two can possibly be simplification puzzles this commentator at least.

Bearing in mind that we are concerned here with incorporation of a business, we have to consider the position of both the individual shareholder and the company. It is therefore necessary to know both systems. It is assumed that the reader is familiar with the basics of CGT computations, though we will begin with a very brief recap of the basics of taper relief.

Some see taper relief as the ultimate answer to withdrawal of profit from a company at minimum tax cost. This proposition will be explored. Start with a warning. If you are a professional adviser reading this book, do not under-estimate the complexity. Taper relief is not easy. There are plenty of pitfalls to trap the unwary. The author's usual question for those of a cavalier attitude is to ask whether they understand the difference between the qualifying holding period and the relevant period. Think you do? Read on to find out.

It does not help that, in its very short lifespan, there have already been two substantial tinkerings with taper relief. These came in *FA 2000* and *FA 2002*. Just as you think that you are getting to grips with one set of rules, they change slightly.

The basics

18.2   Let it be emphasised that there is not room here to cover all aspects of taper relief. Those who need to know more might do well to consult *Tolley's Taper Relief.*

Broadly, taper relief is to be taken as a deduction from every chargeable gain arising on disposal of an asset [*TCGA 1992, s 2A(2)(a)*]. It is generally the last relief to be given apart from the annual exemption.

18.3

In establishing the rate of relief applicable, business assets are distinguished from other assets. The rates of relief for disposals on or after 6 April 2002 are:

Business Assets

Number of whole years in qualifying holding period	Percentage relief given on gain
1	50%
2 or more	75%

Non-Business Assets

Number of whole years in qualifying holding period	Percentage relief given on gain
1	nil
2	nil
3	5%
4	10%
5	15%
6	20%
7	25%
8	30%
9	35%
10 or more	40%

For non-business assets only, where the asset was held before 17 March 1998, the number of years according to the table may be increased by 1 (the bonus year).

18.4   The qualifying holding period for a business asset is:

'The period after 5 April 1998 for which the asset had been held at the time of its disposal.'

[*TCGA 1992, s 2A(8)(a)*].

Note that:

- whilst the qualifying holding period might involve part years, only complete years count in establishing the applicable rate of taper relief;
- except where you start counting on 6 April 1998, at the commencement of the relief, the qualifying holding period does not have to be co-terminous with a tax year.

18.5   For non-business assets, the qualifying holding period is the same, except where the bonus year applies, in which case see *TCGA 1992, s 2A(8)(b)*.

There is further explanation of the bonus year and an example at Inland Revenue *Capital Gains Manual para 17902*.

18.6   Since we are concerned here with the incorporation of a business, the remainder of this chapter concentrates on business asset taper relief. A brief examination of the tables will show that this is far more valuable than the relief available for non-business assets. With a maximum of 75% and a marginal tax rate of 40%, this equates to an effective tax rate of 10% on the net gain (an astonishing 5% for a basic rate taxpayer). On the other hand, non-business asset taper relief only gets to 40% after ten years. Note for direct comparison that a non-business asset gets no taper relief at all after a two year qualifying holding period (when a business asset is already at its maximum relief). There is therefore a significant advantage in having a business asset.

Business asset taper relief

18.7   What then is a business asset? The answer is to be found in *TCGA 1992, Sch A1*, and this is where the complications begin. The legislation distinguishes shares [*para 4*] and other assets [*para 5*].

Other assets

18.8   So far as an individual is concerned, an asset is a business asset if, at the time of disposal, it was being used wholly or partly for one or more of the following:

* the purposes of a trade carried on at that time by the individual, or by a partnership of which he was a member;
* the purposes of a trade carried on by a company which, at that time, was a qualifying company by reference to the individual;
* the purposes of a trade carried on by a company which, at that time, was a member of a trading group, the holding company of which was a qualifying company by reference to the individual;
* the purposes of any office or employment held by that individual with a person carrying on a trade.

[*TCGA 1992, Sch A1 para 5(2)*].

18.9   There is what appeared to be a strange lacuna in relation to an asset that is used by a qualifying company, the meaning of which is examined at **18.15** below. The definition of qualifying company no longer has an ownership test. Prior to the *FA 2000* changes, a minimum shareholding in the company had to be maintained by the owner of the asset used by the company. This has now gone, so an individual can let an asset to a qualifying company (anybody's qualifying company) and obtain business asset taper relief on a later disposal. However, it is now apparent that this was no mere accident of fate. New rules flowing from *Finance Act 2003, s 160* are intended to extend the availability of business asset taper relief to any asset which is used by a UK trader whether incorporated or not. This will take effect from 6 April 2004.

18.10   The asset does not need to have been a business asset throughout its period of ownership to attract business asset taper relief. The period of ownership is deemed to be:

'The period which –
(a) begins with whichever is the later of 6 April 1998 and the time when the asset disposed of was acquired by the person making the disposal; and
(b) ends with the time of the disposal on which the gain accrued.'

[*TCGA 1992, Sch A1 para 2(1)*].

18.11   Where business use has not continued throughout, it is necessary to examine the relevant period of ownership and the parts thereof during which business use subsisted. The gain is then apportioned according to the fraction of business use periods to the total relevant period [*TCGA 1992, Sch A1 para 3(3)*]. Business asset taper relief is given for the business portion and non-business asset taper relief for the remainder as if there were two separate gains [*TCGA 1992, Sch A1 para 3(5)*].

The relevant period is:

'Whichever is the shorter of –
(a) the period after 5 April 1998 for which the asset had been held at the time of its disposal; and
(b) the period of ten years ending with that time.'

[*TCGA 1992, Sch A1, para 2(2)*].

18.12

Example 18.12

Sue has owned a property since before 17 March 1998. From 6 April 1998 to 5 September 1999, it was unoccupied. She then uses it for her business until she sells it on 6 August 2003 realising a gross gain of £50,000.

Relevant period	6 April 1998 to 6 August 2003	5 years	123 days
Business use	6 September 1999 to 6 August 2003	3 years	335 days

Gain apportioned to business use:

$$£50,000 \times \frac{3 \text{ years } 335 \text{ days}}{5 \text{ years } 123 \text{ days}} \qquad\qquad £36,704$$

Gain apportioned to non-business use:

£50,000 – £36,704   £13,296

258

Taper Relief	Business Asset	Non-Business Asset
Apportioned gains	£36,704	£13,296
Qualifying holding period business asset 5 years (75%)	(27,528)	
Qualifying holding period non-business asset 5 years + bonus (20%)		(2,659)
Tapered gains	9,176	10,637
		9,176
Taxable gain (subject to annual exemption)		£19,813

18.13   Make sure that you understand the difference between the qualifying holding period and the relevant period. They may be compared and contrasted as follows.

Qualifying holding period:

* must be computed for all assets, whether they qualify as business assets or not;
* is the period used to extract the appropriate percentage from the taper tables;
* part years are ignored;
* may sometimes include a bonus year;
* can exceed ten years but there is no credit in the taper tables for longer periods.

Relevant period:

* is applicable only to business assets;
* has no relevance to the taper tables;
* can include part years;
* never attracts a bonus year;
* is limited to a maximum of ten years.

Shares

18.14   So far as an individual is concerned, shares are a business asset if they are shares in a company which is a qualifying company [*TCGA 1992, Sch A1 para 4(2)*]. It is not limited to ordinary shares and may include preference shares.

18.15   Again, so far as an individual is concerned, a qualifying company is now defined as:

18.16   *Taper Relief*

'(a)   ... a trading company or the holding company of a trading group, and
(b)   one or more of the following conditions was met –
    (i)   the company was unlisted.
    (ii)   the individual was an officer or employee of the company or of a company having a relevant connection with it, or
    (iii)   the voting rights in the company were exercisable, as to not less than 5%, by the individual.'

[*TCGA 1992, Sch A1, para 6(1)*].

18.16   This is the second definition of a qualifying company since taper relief commenced on 6 April 1998. It was substituted by *FA 2000* with effect from 6 April 2000. Previously there had been minimum holding requirements for all companies; now the 5% test only applies to a quoted company.

Since 6 April 2000, all holdings of shares (however small) in unlisted trading companies qualify for business asset taper relief. Previously, it was necessary to hold 5% of the voting rights and be a full time working officer or employee of the company or, otherwise, hold 25% of the voting rights.

18.17   It will rapidly be seen that some small shareholders of unlisted shares will have held a non-business asset from 6 April 1998 to 5 April 2000 and a business asset thereafter. Through no action of their own, merely a change in the legislation, on disposal they would be forced into the apportionment calculation of *TCGA 1992, Sch A1 para 3(3)* as demonstrated at **18.12** above.

Example 18.17

Lisa owns 20% of the shares in her family trading company. She does not work in the business. She has owned the shares since 6 April 1998 and sells them on 6 April 2003 realising a gross gain of £100,000.

| Relevant period | 6 April 1998 to 6 April 2003 | 5 years |
| Business use | 6 April 2000 to 6 April 2003 | 3 years |

Gain apportioned to business asset: £60,000

$$£100,000 \times \frac{3 \text{ years}}{5 \text{ years}}$$

Gain apportioned to non-business asset:

£100,000 – £60,000   £40,000

Taper Relief	**Business Asset**	**Non-Business Asset**
Apportioned gains	£60,000	£40,000
Qualifying holding period		
Business/non-business asset		
5 years (75%/15%)	(45,000)	(6,000)
Tapered gains	15,000	34,000
		15,000
Taxable gain (subject to annual exemption)		£49,000

18.18   So much for the Chancellor's promise in the 2002 Budget that he was reducing the holding period for maximum business asset taper relief to two years. So he was, but not for many small company shareholders who had held the shares for a number of years.

This situation has been nicknamed 'tainted taper'. Lisa in the above example, would not get maximum business asset taper relief unless she held the shares until 6 April 2010. The relevant period would then be 6 April 2000 to 6 April 2010 [*TCGA 1992, Sch A1 para 2(2)(b)*] throughout which the shares were always a business asset. Before that date, apportionment within the relevant period will always be necessary. The qualifying holding period has no influence on this part of the calculation. When considering such circumstances, it is vital to distinguish the qualifying holding period and the relevant period.

It does seem perverse that, had Lisa acquired the shares on 6 April 2000 and had a much shorter period of ownership, she would have got the maximum business asset taper relief on 6 April 2002. As it is, she would have to wait for a period of ownership of not two, not even ten, but twelve years in order to get the maximum benefit from taper relief.

Incorporation

18.19   Taper relief is given in respect of the gain arising on disposal of an asset by an individual. The qualifying holding period is for an asset.

A sole trader (or partner) will have a collection of assets used in a business. On incorporation, he will dispose of some or all of these to the company. With a very small business, taper relief may be sufficient to reduce the gain to such an amount that no tax is payable (see **9.48–9.49**).

18.20   Larger businesses will usually need to rely on the holdover relief afforded by *TCGA 1992, s 165*, or the rollover relief in *s 162*. The problem is that taper relief is applied to the chargeable gain.

The effect of a claim under *s 165* is to defer the chargeable gain which would otherwise arise. Accordingly, it is the gross gain which is held over and the benefit of any accrued taper relief is lost. The company shares are a new asset and a new qualifying holding period must be established for them.

18.21 Likewise, *TCGA 1992, s 162*, gives a relief by deduction from the chargeable gain. The Revenue view is that (certainly in the case where the consideration is only an issue of shares in the new company) no gains fall into charge and therefore no taper relief is due.

This does beg the question of what happens when there is consideration other than shares. The gain remaining in charge is a proportion of the whole and not attributable to any specific asset (see the example at **9.16**). In practice, the Inland Revenue will allow allocation in any reasonable way [Inland Revenue *Capital Gains Manual para 65821*].

Given that the wording of *s 162* (which is dissimilar to *s 165*) requires the calculation of a chargeable gain, there is a view that taper relief should be given. This view is not shared by the Inland Revenue. The company shares are a new asset and a new qualifying holding period must be established for them.

Further, one commentator has suggested another alternative. *TCGA 1992, Sch A1 para 14* treats assets derived from other assets as having been acquired at the earliest time that any asset giving value to the disposed asset was acquired. Arguably, where every asset of the trade is transferred into the company, the shares themselves are derived from the underlying assets and taper relief should continue uninterrupted. Whilst this appears to be a tenable construction, it is untested.

Where incorporations under *TCGA 1992, s 162*, are concerned the potential problems have been overtaken by events, being partially solved by *s 162A* which permits disapplication of *s 162* where so desired. This could be used to maintain the benefit of accrued taper relief where a sale is in prospect shortly after incorporation.

Trading company

18.22 This is where the going starts to get really difficult. The first requirement of a qualifying company in *Sch A1 para 6(1)(a)*, is that it should be a trading company or the holding company of a trading group. Being concerned here with incorporation, we shall only explore in detail the circumstances of a single company.

In the short life span of taper relief there have already been two definitions of a trading company. The initial one was in *Sch A1 para 22*, and lasted from 6 April 1998 to 16 April 2002. The second is in *Sch A1 para 22A*, inserted by *FA 2002* and applies from 17 April 2002.

The first definition was somewhat obscure, but it took the Inland Revenue until *Tax Bulletin 53, June 2001*, more than three years after the introduction of taper relief, to provide an explanation of what it understood the definition to mean. The author remains to be convinced that the second definition is any better, though explanations in *Tax Bulletin 62, December 2002*, did come rather quicker.

Since this is a fundamental concept and may impinge on some peoples' view of profit withdrawal from a small company, it deserves close scrutiny.

First definition

18.23 What *TCGA 1992, Sch A1 para 22* originally said was:

'Trading company means a company which is either –

(a) a company existing wholly for the purpose of carrying on one or more trades; or

(b) a company that would fall within para (a) above apart from any purposes capable of having no substantial effect on the extent of the company's activities.'

18.24 There are two legs to the test. First that the company must exist wholly for the purpose of carrying on one or more trades. The objects clause of many company memoranda is so widely drawn that the company may be authorised to engage in a wide variety of activities, including investment. Some commentators were inclined to the extreme view that this would breach the wholly trading test and almost no companies could ever satisfy the test. The Inland Revenue took a more pragmatic view in *Tax Bulletin, June 2001*, deducing that a company's purpose could be inferred from its current activities. If all it did at one point in time was to carry on one or more trades, then trading was its purpose. This would also be the case for a company not actually trading, but actively seeking or preparing to do so.

The Inland Revenue also took the view that trade for this purpose means anything which is a trade, profession or vocation within the meaning of the Income Tax Acts and is conducted on a commercial basis and with a view to the realisation of profit. It also includes any Schedule A business (within the meaning of the Taxes Acts) which consists in the commercial letting of holiday accommodation as defined in *ICTA 1988, s 504*. It also includes activities, such as farming, which are treated as a trade by *ICTA 1988, s 53*.

18.25 However, there is a second leg to the test which envisages that a company may actually do something other than trade. A company would continue to qualify if its other activities were not capable of having a substantial effect on the extent of the company's activities. This is doubly problematic; what does 'capable' mean and what does 'substantial' mean?

Whilst the *Tax Bulletin* article touches on the influence of capable, it does not satisfactorily answer it. The Inland Revenue takes it as an objective assessment at any given moment in time. Small speculative investments which are theoretically capable of having an enormous impact in the future are ignored.

18.26   Substantial is more objective and it is a shame that, even today, there is no statutory definition. The word also appears in *ICTA 1988, s 293(3B)* and *s 297* in relation to the Enterprise Investment Scheme. Inland Revenue *Venture Capital Schemes Manual para 17040* in that context treats substantial as more than 20% by any reasonable measure in the circumstances, e.g. turnover or capital employed.

The *Tax Bulletin* article follows the EIS usage and, in the current context, the Inland Revenue again takes substantial as meaning more than 20%. This begs the obvious question, 20% of what? It then goes on to cite various tests obviously drawn from the judgment in the inheritance tax case of *Farmer (Farmer's Executors) v IRC [1999] STC (SCD) 321*, without actually naming the case. Thus, the relative influence of the following factors on trading and non-trading activities should be considered:

- turnover;
- asset base;
- expenses incurred or time spent by officers and employees of the company in various activities.

The Inland Revenue considers that the relative influences vary according to the facts (though it is not indicated how or why). There is no demonstration that all relevant factors should be considered in the overall context of the business, as was the conclusion in the inheritance tax case.

18.27   If all else fails, the *Tax Bulletin* article concludes that once an accounting period has ended, the Inland Revenue will respond positively in expressing a view on the company's status for the period where requested to do so. The author's experience of such requests has been to get answers which are, at best, lukewarm and give no real confidence.

Second definition

18.28   With effect from 17 April 2002, *TCGA 1992, Sch A1 para 22A* defines a trading company thus:

'. . . means a company carrying on trading activities whose activities do not include to a substantial extent activities other than trading activities.'

18.29   Notice that the two legs of the original test have been rolled together and the purpose bit has gone. The company must actually carry on trading activities though this is extended to mean:

'. . .trading activities means activities carried on by the company –

(a) in the course of, or for the purposes, of a trade being carried on by it
(b) for the purposes of a trade that it is preparing to carry on
(c) with a view to its acquiring or starting to carry on a trade, or
(d) with a view to its acquiring a significant interest in the share capital of another company that is a trading company . . .'

[*TCGA 1992, Sch A1 para 22A(2)*].

Also gone is the capable bit of the substantial test. So it appears that current non-trading activities should not be substantial.

18.30   The date of the change will be problematic in itself. A year or so on, we might just remember that 17 April 2002 was the date of the Budget in that year. Will we still remember in five years time? What would have been wrong with making the change as of 6 April 2002? Would that have been a disastrous example of retrospective legislation?

Some explanation of the change is given in *Tax Bulletin 62, December 2002*. At the outset, this says that the definitions described in *Tax Bulletin 53, June 2001*, now apply only for periods of ownership before 17 April 2002 even where the disposal takes place on or after that date. However, it goes on to say that the changes to the wording in the definition of trading company aligns the statute with existing practice. It is not intended to alter the substance of the original definition or to have different meanings before and on or after 17 April 2002. In the author's view, this is somewhat weasily worded. Has the definition changed, or has it not?

Example 18.30

Consider Terry's Universal Trading Co Ltd. For many years it carried on a manufacturing trade. On 1 October 2001, it received an offer it could not refuse and sold its trade and assets to a third party. As a result, it had £1m cash in the bank and no trade, though it made efforts to find a new business to acquire and eventually did so on 1 March 2003.

From 1 October 2001 to 16 April 2002 it had no trade, though one could argue that because of its past history and its attempts to find a new business it was a trading company (the old definition required its purpose to be to carry on a trade – which appears to be satisfied).

From 17 April 2002 to 28 February 2003, it had no trade. Is it still a trading company? The new definition has lost the purposive test and replaced it with a factual one. Or is *TCGA 1992, Sch A1 para 22A(2)(c)* enough?

18.31   Remember why we are considering all of this. We need to know whether the shares in the company are a business asset for the purposes of taper relief. We have already seen that apportionment can be necessary because of a change in definition of a qualifying company on 6 April 2000. If the old definition of trading company and the new definition cannot be interpreted identically, then surely apportionment will be necessary pre and post 17 April 2002.

Extraction of profit from the company

18.32   It has been acknowledged that one of the great rationales for incorporation of a business has been the potential tax savings. These are derived from the ability to take profits out of the company in the most tax efficient manner.

So far, this book has considered the many aspects of dividends as against salary (see **Chapter 4**) and the alternative of taking tax efficient benefits in kind, rents, interest etc. (see **Chapter 15**). Many commentators seem to perceive that there is another way, namely capital transactions.

18.33   First, one has to consider the aspect that this is going to kill the goose that lays the golden egg. To get money out of the company by a capital transaction requires, broadly:

- sale of the shares;
- liquidation of the company;
- company purchase of own shares.

It is basically a one-off. Once you have done it, you have done it. It cannot be repeated. Though it has to be admitted it might have occasional uses, e.g. on the retirement of the business proprietor.

18.34   The possible advantages are easy to perceive. Once a qualifying holding period of two years has been established, business asset taper relief is available at 75%. Remember, though, that may not apply to the whole gain unless the company has been a qualifying company throughout the relevant period (see **18.11**). Apply a marginal personal tax rate of 40% to the remaining 25% of the gain and this gives an effective tax rate on the gross gain of only 10%. Most business proprietors seem to find this acceptable and no longer seek to apply more exotic schemes to minimise the liability further.

Remember that the company will have borne tax on its profits before retention. At **4.9** is a comparison of the overall effective tax rate where £10,000 gross is taken out of the company by way of dividend. If there were to be a capital transaction, the overall effective rate is as follows (assuming maximum business asset taper relief and the proprietor is in the higher rate band for CGT):

Company CT rate	Effective tax rate on profit withdrawn
0%	10%
23.75%	31.38%
19%	27.1%
32.75%	39.48%
30%	37%

All of which assumes that maximum business asset taper relief is available. To get that, we need a qualifying company which, in turn, must be a trading company.

18.35   From the preceding sections, this requires a company that actually trades and whose other activities are not substantial. Whilst the holding of cash temporarily surplus to the needs of the trade might be ignored (Inland Revenue *Capital Gains Manual, para 17919*), an investment activity which grows to exceed 20% of the total (however measured) prejudices the availability of business asset taper relief. If the company maintains a cash hoard, with a view to realisation by liquidation, then this seems almost inevitably the case. Depending on the duration and extent of this, business asset taper relief will become tainted (through the apportionment calculation to periods when it was a qualifying company or non qualifying company) or, in the worst case, lost altogether.

18.36   If business asset taper relief is not available at all, the overall effective rate of tax on extraction by a capital transaction (with the same assumptions as **18.34** above) becomes:

Company CT rate	Effective tax rate on profit withdrawn
0%	24%
23.75%	42.1%
19%	38.4%
32.75%	48.9%
30%	46.8%

These rates are scarcely below the level of extraction by way of dividend. If you fancy extraction of profit by way of a capital transaction, make sure you understand the meaning of a trading company and ensure the rules continue to be satisfied.

18.37   Finally, do not forget the somewhat draconian anti-avoidance provisions in *TCGA 1992, Sch A1*. Where a close company either started to carry on a business of holding investments, or that business increased significantly in size during a period of twelve months, the effect of *para 11* was to stop taper relief running at all. This was not simply a change from business asset taper relief to non-business asset taper relief. The qualifying holding period started again from scratch at the time of change. With effect from 17 April 2002, *para 11A* has been substituted to give the more expected apportionment to periods of qualification as a business asset and non-business asset (periods when the company has no activity at all are ignored).

Capital transaction

18.38 One should perhaps backtrack slightly. If extraction of profits from the company by way of a capital transaction is a viable option (and in the previous section it has been suggested that business asset taper relief might be prejudiced) then, at the risk of stating the obvious, make sure you have a capital transaction. There are three possibilities for disposing of shares:

- sale;
- liquidation;
- company repurchase of own shares.

Only the first of these can be guaranteed to give a capital gain which might be relieved by business asset taper relief.

Liquidation

18.39 For the most part, distributions in liquidation will be treated as giving rise to a capital gain. However, liquidation is undoubtedly a transaction in securities within the meaning of *ICTA 1988, s 703*. This is not a point that the Inland Revenue usually takes in respect of an ordinary liquidation (for further commentary on liquidations and the Inland Revenue view of ordinary, see **21.51**). One wonders though, where there has been deliberate retention of profits with a view to realisation in this fashion, whether it is a point which might be taken. The result would of course be treatment as a distribution, an income tax charge and, therefore, no business asset taper relief. There is a clearance procedure in *ICTA 1988, s 707*, and it would be wise to take this course of action if the liquidation process is, in effect a distribution of a large amount of retained profit. Note that, should an informal striking off procedure (without formal liquidation) under *Companies Act s 652* or *s 652A* be invoked, the distribution is strictly one of income within *ICTA 1988, s 209*. Only if the assurances in *ESC C16* are given will the Inland Revenue treat the transaction as giving rise to a capital distribution. In such circumstances, a formal liquidation might be a wiser move.

Purchase of own shares

18.40 On the face of it, the repurchase of own shares by a company falls to be treated as a distribution and subject to income tax. Where the various conditions laid down in *ICTA 1988, s 219* et seq are satisfied, then the transaction may be treated as giving rise to a capital gain. The company can seek clearance to this effect under *s 225*.

One wonders whether it is possible to get beyond the first hurdle. *ICTA 1988, s 219(1)(a)* requires that the repurchase of shares does not form part of a scheme or arrangement, one of the main purposes of which is to enable the share owner to participate in the profits of the company without receiving a dividend or the avoidance of tax. If history shows the accumulation of retained profits within the company, then it is difficult to see how this condition could be satisfied. If that is the case, then clearance is likely to be denied and, again, the payment will be treated as a distribution with a corresponding income tax charge and the scope for business asset taper relief lost.

Business asset taper relief for an investment company

18.41   As the taper relief legislation was originally drafted, it may have been difficult for ordinary employees of large public companies to establish whether their holding of shares in the company qualified for business asset taper relief. The difficulty is in establishing whether or not it satisfied the requirements as a trading company. Banks, insurance companies etc. do trade, but have extensive investment activities too. It could be well nigh impossible for the ordinary employee to find out whether the company might meet the very stringent business asset taper relief trading company tests.

FA 2000 therefore extended the definition of a 'qualifying company' to include one where:

- the company was a non-trading company or the holding company of a non-trading group;
- the individual was an officer or employee of the company, or of a company having a relevant connection with it; and
- the individual did not have a material interest in the company or in any company which, at that time, had control of the company.

[*TCGA 1992, Sch A1, para 6(1A)*].

18.42   So the ordinary employee is now well catered for. If his employer company is trading, a disposal of shares in the company would give rise to a capital gain attracting business asset taper relief under *para 6(1)*; if the company is non-trading, then he would still get relief under *para 6(1A)*.

18.43   *TCGA 1992, para 6(1A)* deserves a closer look though. If the company is non-trading (an investment company perhaps – though it might be a company carrying on a trade but which fails the trading company test) and the individual shareholder is an employee then, if he does not have a material interest, business asset taper relief is still available.

The meaning of 'material interest' for this purpose is given by *para 6A* and means possession of (including any holdings of connected persons):

- more than 10% of the issued shares in the company of any particular class;
- more than 10% of the voting rights in the company;
- the entitlement to more than 10% of the company's income were it to be distributed among the participators;
- entitlement to more than 10% of the assets of the company on a winding up.

So, given reasonably diverse holdings, the shares in an investment company may also attract business asset taper relief, provided that the shareholder is also an employee of the company.

Taper gets everywhere

18.44   Had you been minded to make a gift of company shares in 2002/03 or earlier, then you would most probably have relied on *TCGA 1992, s 165*, to hold over the capital gain arising. The assets covered by this relief do indeed include shares or securities of a trading company where the shares are not listed on a recognised stock exchange, or the company is the transferor's personal company [*s 165(2)(b)*]. This relief does not have its own definition of trading company and, until 5 April 2003, borrowed the one in *TCGA 1992, Sch 6*. This is simply that a trading company means a company whose business consists wholly or mainly of the carrying on of a trade or trades [*Sch 6 para 1(2)*]. There is still no definition of 'mainly' which is taken to have its customary usage meaning, i.e. more than half.

However, *TCGA 1992, Sch 6* was, of course, the retirement relief legislation and that relief disappeared at 5 April 2003. With effect from 6 April 2003, *FA 1998, s 140(4)*, directs that the taper relief definition of trading company should be used. Given the announcement five years beforehand, not many people will have remembered that one.

So, *TCGA 1992, s 165*, now requires a company whose trading activities are not substantial (more than 20%). This is a significant restriction when, until so recently, it was only necessary that the trading company should be able to demonstrate that its non-trading activities were less than 50% of the total. Without any fuss or complaint, the range of shareholdings which might attract the holdover relief has suddenly been drastically reduced.

Planning points

- Property let to a qualifying company always gets business asset taper relief (**18.9**).

- Apportionment of the gain is necessary where business use of an asset does not continue throughout the relevant period (**18.11**).

- Distinguish the relevant period and the qualifying holding period (**18.13**).

- Watch for tainted taper due to the change in definition of a qualifying company (**18.16–18.18**).

- Accrued taper relief is generally lost on incorporation (**18.20–18.21**).

- If business asset taper relief is available, a one off capital transaction may be an effective way of drawing accrued profits (**18.34**).

- Business asset taper relief can be achieved for an investment company if it has reasonably diverse shareholdings (**18.43**).

Chapter 19

Sale of Business

19.1 Can there be advantages or disadvantages of incorporation at or about the time of sale of a business? There is, of course, no right answer. It depends how you do it. The effects are perhaps best demonstrated by a series of examples.

Sole trader/partnership

19.2 On the sale of a business, a sole trader (or a partner, to the extent of his share in the assets) will realise a capital gain against which, hopefully, can be set business asset taper relief reducing the effective rate of tax on the gain to 10%.

Example 19.2

In the summer of 2003, Philip wishes to sell his insurance broking business. It is worth about £250,000, largely representing goodwill. The base cost is nil as he started the business from scratch in the late 1980s.

Sale proceeds	£250,000
Cost	–
Gain	250,000
Business asset taper relief Qualifying holding period 5 years = 75% (see **18.3–18.4**)	(187,500)
Tapered gain	62,500
Annual exemption	(7,900)
	£54,600
Tax due @ 40%	£21,840

The actual rate of tax suffered is slightly below 10% because of the effect of the annual exemption.

We can now test the effect if the business has just been incorporated.

Company

Incorporation under *TCGA 1992, s 165*

19.3   First of all, let us suppose that, shortly before disposal (within one year so that no further taper relief accrues) the business had been incorporated by the transfer of the assets at under value, holding over the gain under *TCGA 1992, s 165*.

Example 19.3

In September 2002, Philip incorporated the business taking a payment of £31,200 and holding over the gain under *TCGA 1992, s 165*. He subscribed £100 for the shares in the company. In the summer of 2003, as alternatives: (a) he sells the company shares for £250,000; or (b) the company sells the business for £250,000.

(a) Sale of company

Sale proceeds		£250,000
Cost		(100)
		249,900
Taper relief		
Qualifying holding period <1 year = 0%		nil
		249,900
Annual exemption		(7,900)
		£242,000
Tax due @ 40%		£96,800

(b) Sale of business from company

Proceeds		£250,000
Cost market value	£250,000	
– less gain held over	(218,800)	(31,200)
		£218,800
Tax due @ 19%		£41,572

19.4   Thus, if Philip sold the shares in the company, he would be considerably worse off. This is in the sense of having paid more tax; at least having sold the shares he has cash in hand (if the company sold the business, the money would be locked inside). This shows the dramatic effect of the loss of business asset taper relief when using this means of incorporation (see **18.20**). He can do nothing but wait in order to restore the original position. At least, with 75% business asset taper relief now accruing after a qualifying holding period of only two years, he would not have to wait too long. When taper relief was first introduced, it took ten years to reach this position.

19.5 Alternatively, if the business were to be sold, the gain would be realised by the company. Again, it has no significant base cost because of the held over gain on incorporation, though the tax is less because of the company's much lower effective rate. The proceeds are locked into the company. This may not necessarily be bad news – see **19.9** below.

Incorporation by this means just before sale of the business therefore seems to be bad news.

Incorporation under *TCGA 1992, s 162*

19.6 The alternative position is that there was an incorporation under *TCGA 1992, s 162*.

Example 19.6

In September 2002, Philip incorporated the business under *TCGA 1992, s 162*. He subscribed £100 for the original shares in the company. 250,000 more shares were issued in exchange for the business. In the summer of 2003 he sells the company shares for £250,000.

Sale of company

Proceeds		£250,000
Cost – Initial shares	£100	
– Further shares	250,000	
– Less deferred gain	(250,000)	(100)
		249,900
Annual exemption		(7,900)
		£242,000
Tax @ 40%		£96,800

This is essentially the same result as an incorporation under *s 165* followed by a share sale.

19.7 On this occasion though, there is an alternative. Philip could restore the gain on transfer to the company by making an election under *TCGA 1992, s 162A*, to disapply the deferral procedure of *s 162*, leaving no gain on disposal of the company.

He could therefore pay the tax (with the benefit of business asset taper relief) in respect of the gain arising on incorporation. The shares would then carry no deferred gain and there would be no further gain on their disposal. This effectively puts him back in the pre-incorporation position. Payment of the tax in this example would be advanced by one year though.

19.8   The real magic comes at the end. What a corporate purchaser might really want is the assets of the business (largely goodwill) for which it can get a tax deduction under *FA 2002, Sch 29*, (see **6.18**).

If the company sells the business now, the computation of its gain is as follows:

Example 19.8

Philip incorporated in September 2002 under *TCGA 1992, s 162*. The purchaser really wants to buy the goodwill. In the summer of 2003 the company sells the business for £250,000.

Sale of business from company	
Proceeds	£250,000
Base cost (= market value on incorporation)	(250,000)
Gain	nil
Tax due	nil

This is because the incorporation was a connected party transaction and market value must be imputed. Philip's gain on incorporation is reflected in the depressed value of his shares but this does not stop the company's value of the assets being their market value. There is no capital gain and, therefore, no tax to pay.

If the sale of an unincorporated business is envisaged to realise a substantial gain, incorporation by the route afforded by *TCGA 1992, s 162* has to be strongly recommended. It should ensure that little or no gain arises on the disposal.

19.9   Of course, the sale proceeds are now locked into a company. Extracting them will have other tax consequences. However, if Philip wishes to invest in a new business, he can do so through the medium of the company, having the full gross proceeds to utilise. Alternatively, if the sale was made in anticipation of retirement, Philip could take up to a salary of £4,615 plus dividends of £27,450 in each of the next six years, clearing out all the company's funds and paying no tax himself. This is because (assuming no other income) he does not get into the higher rate band and has no more tax to pay on the dividends.

Planning points

- If a business sale is in prospect, incorporation under *TCGA1992, s 165* can make the position worse (**19.4**).
- An incorporation under *TCGA 1992, s 162* can be a means to sell a business with little or no tax (**19.8**).

Chapter 20

Investment Businesses

Is it possible to incorporate?

20.1 During the course of the last year or so, the author has been asked on countless occasions whether it is possible to incorporate an investment business. To which the obvious answer has to be, yes, why not? There are, after all, many existing investment companies.

What the querists really mean to ask is whether it is possible to incorporate an investment business without any adverse tax consequences. To which the answer is almost certainly no.

Usually the nature of the investment business concerned is the letting of property. Whilst for income tax purposes the receipt of rents from property is treated as a Schedule A business [*ICTA 1988, s 15(1)*], the real problem with the tax legislation is that there is no satisfactory definition of what is a 'business'. At the start of **Chapter 9**, the author suggested his own definition of a business, namely a collection of assets, actively managed with a view to deriving income therefrom (see **9.1**). The inheritance tax legislation even hedges its bets by defining a business to include a certain sort of business and exclude another type of business (all of which is without actually saying what a business is) [*IHTA 1984, s 103(3)*].

There is abundant case law on activities in the nature of a trade, but nothing on activities in the nature of a business. It is clear that a business is rather wider than (but includes) a trade, as well as a profession or vocation.

Active management is a characteristic of a business, as is the profit motive.

Outside the confines of a trade, profession or vocation, what can actually be managed with a view to profit? Whilst there is no doubt that some individuals will actively manage a portfolio of stocks or shares, it is extremely unlikely that this amounts to a business unless it is ancillary to a trade such as stock-broking. Much as the individuals might like to think that they have a business, they would no doubt shy away from the possibility that any profits generated are chargeable to income tax rather than capital gains tax.

20.2 Why, in any case, would anyone want to incorporate such an activity anyway? The possibility of either business asset taper relief for capital gains tax purposes, or business property relief for inheritance tax purposes, in respect of shares in the company seems remote. Against this is the potential double tax charge of corporate operation. The company pays tax on its gain; the share-holder pays tax on extraction of the profit. Such companies do exist and many of them are largely historical relics. Anyone wishing to create one today should think carefully about the potential disadvantages against any perceived tax saving.

Which leaves us really back at property letting. An unincorporated property letting business will derive gross rents against which may be set various expenses to arrive at a net Schedule A profit. An individual receiving this will be chargeable to income tax at his highest marginal rate as it arises. Getting the profits into a company has the obvious attraction of the ability to withdraw profits by way of dividend rather than salary, just as with any trading company.

20.3   At that point we return to the fundamental problem for any business. That is getting the assets of the business into the company in the first place. Almost inevitably, with recent meteoric rises in property prices, this leaves a proprietor facing a large capital gain on incorporation.

There are two traditional routes of relieving the capital gains arising on incorporation of a business. These use either the general relief for gifts of business assets in *TCGA 1992, s 165*, or the specific incorporation relief in *s 162* (see **Chapter 9**).

20.4   *TCGA 1992, s 165* is a non-starter. This permits the holdover of a capital gain where an asset is transferred at undervalue and the asset is used for the purposes of a trade, profession or vocation. Whatever property letting may be, it is not a trade, profession or vocation.

20.5   Therefore, to succeed, we would have to rely on *s 162*, which provides a mandatory rollover of the gain where a person who is not a company transfers to a company a business as a going concern, together with the whole assets of the business.

This must take us back to the beginning: what is a business? As already noted, there is no definition in the *Taxation of Chargeable Gains Act*, for this or any other purpose of CGT.

At *paras 65712–65715*, the Inland Revenue Capital Gains Manual tries to extract a meaning from various pieces of case law. *Para 65713*, rather unhelpfully, says it is a question of fact whether a particular activity does constitute a business. It is not easy to draw the line. It does, however, go on to say that the Inland Revenue will resist claims that the passive holding of investments or an investment property amount to a business. At least we have got that far then.

In relation to *s 162, Tolley's Roll-over, Hold-over and Retirements Reliefs 12th edition* says, at *para 13.3*:

> 'The section refers to a "business" and not to a trade. Thus it is not only trades which are capable of being transferred to obtain the benefit of

section 162. In rare situations there may be a transfer of a profession or vocation. It must, however, be questioned whether the transfer of a property investment undertaking can also be included. Whilst the matter is not free from doubt, the possibility seems rather unlikely. In this respect, it is a requirement that the business must be transferred as "a going concern"; an expression which does not readily illustrate the activity of holding investment properties in return for rental income.'

There are other references in the Inland Revenue Manuals. Particularly, *para 63250* of the Capital Gains Manual notes that *TCGA 1992, Sch 6 para 12(2)* (fundamentally retirement relief, but provisions of this Schedule are picked up elsewhere in the capital gains legislation) defines a business asset as one which is used for the purposes of a trade, profession, vocation, office or employment. The same paragraph then draws the, perhaps illogical, conclusion that, in practice, business means trade, profession or vocation. That comment is still in place despite the abolition of retirement relief on 6 April 2003. It might be interesting to note what alternative is substituted in due course.

20.6   As hearsay evidence, one might consider the case of *Burkinyoung's Executor v IRC [1995] STC (SCD) 29*. This concerns inheritance tax and it may be dangerous to rely on precedents created for one tax as giving some sort of definitive view for another. However, *IHTA 1984 s 105* does define 'relevant business property' for the purposes of IHT business property relief initially as 'consisting of a business or interest in a business'. Mrs Burkinyoung let a number of properties and, on her death, her executors claimed IHT business property relief. In reaching his decision, the Special Commissioner noted that it was common ground (between the executors and the Inland Revenue) that Mrs Burkinyoung's owning and letting activity consisted of a business and, therefore, met the first test of relevant business property – though the claim failed on other grounds. The decision usefully referred to the case of *Customs & Excise Comrs v Lord Fisher [1981] STC 238*. Off we go to another tax.

That case noted that, for the purposes of VAT, there was no definition of business, but went on to demonstrate six criteria for determining whether an activity is a business:

1. whether the activity is a serious undertaking, earnestly pursued;
2. whether the activity is an occupation or function actively pursued with a reasonable or recognisable continuity;
3. whether the activity has a certain measure of substance, as measured by the quarterly or annual value of taxable supplies made;
4. whether the activity was conducted in a regular manner and on sound and recognised business principles;
5. whether the activity is predominantly concerned with the making of taxable supplies to consumers for a consideration;
6. whether the taxable supplies are of a kind which are commonly made by those who seek to profit by them.

20.7   These digressions into inheritance tax and VAT appear to conflict with, for example, the judgment of Lord Diplock in *American Leaf Blending Co v Director General of Inland Revenue [1978] STC 561.*

> 'In the case of a private individual it may well be that the mere receipt of rents from property that he owns raises no presumption that he is carrying on a business.'

The author's personal view is that *actively managed* letting of property probably is a business. However, there is much hearsay evidence to the contrary.

That contrary view has been reinforced by the very recent Special Commissioners' Decision in *Rashid v Garcia [2003] STC (SCD) 36.* This is a NIC case in which the appellant sought to pay Class 2 contributions in respect of 'earnings' from property letting. The Special Commissioner held that, whilst it was not free from doubt, the arrangements did not amount to a business. Rather, it was an investment which, by its nature, required some activity to maintain it.

20.8   Going back to *TCGA 1992, s 162,* this not only requires transfer of the business but of the business 'as a going concern'. It is difficult to see how the letting of property could be a going concern. This predicates something more than transfer of a mere collection of assets. There must be an active infrastructure to go with it. It follows that, almost certainly, a property letting business could not be transferred to a company with the benefit of the relief in *s 162.*

20.9   There is a limited exception to all of this. This is the possibility that the properties concerned meet the conditions to be treated as furnished holiday lettings [*ICTA 1988, ss 503, 504*]. This is the case where:

- there is a commercial letting of property with a view to the realisation of profit;
- the letting is of furnished accommodation;
- the accommodation is available for commercial letting to the public generally as holiday accommodation for a period of not less than 140 days in a twelve month period;
- the accommodation is actually let for at least 70 days;
- for a period comprising at least seven months it is not normally in the same occupation for a continuous period exceeding 31 days.

The effect of this is that, for certain purposes, furnished holiday lettings are treated as a trade. In particular in the current context, *TCGA 1992, s 241,* invokes *s 165.* Therefore, it is possible to transfer a property used for furnished holiday letting at under value (to a company) and hold over any capital gain arising by making a claim under *s 165.* In other words, it is possible to incorporate a Schedule A business which consists entirely of furnished holiday lettings without triggering a taxable capital gain.

In some ways, this is justification for the author's view that incorporation of an ordinary property letting business by *s 162* is not possible. The furnished holiday lettings reliefs include holdover by *s 165*, but not rollover under *s 162*. This compounds the view that property letting cannot be treated as a business which is akin to a trade.

20.10   Finally, one should bear in mind the impact of stamp duty. Where land and buildings are transferred to a company which is connected with the transferor, stamp duty is charged by reference to market value (see **10.13**) [*FA 2000, s 119*]. A significant stamp duty liability may therefore arise should it be desired to transfer properties to a company.

New projects

20.11   With very limited exceptions therefore, it will prove impossible to transfer existing investment activities to a company without incurring significant capital gains tax liabilities. Where properties are involved, there will also be stamp duty to pay.

This is not to say that an investment business cannot or should not operate through the medium of a limited company. As already noted, if we are concerned with a property letting business, most of the usual advantages of a trading company can be enjoyed. These include:

- The benefit of lower corporate rates of tax on income as it arises.
- The ability to use the company as if it were a moneybox. The business may develop using retained profits which have suffered lower rates of tax. Often the investment business will be the proprietor's secondary activity. When already suffering the higher rate of income tax on income from a trade or profession, carried on personally or through another company, one of the major desires can simply be to reduce the tax on investment income.
- The facility to pay out dividends rather than salary to the proprietor. Indeed the ability to pay a salary may be severely restricted. It is unlikely that the duties of a director in relation to such a company will be extensive, so the size of salary which meets the wholly and exclusively test is limited. In other words, this is not a means of converting investment income into earned income.
- The ability to smooth the flow of income.
- It makes a more divisible business to facilitate estate planning. It is easier to transfer shares in a company rather than proportionate shares of a property.

20.12   However, the shares in the company will never qualify for business asset taper relief as it will not be a trading company. Nor will the shares attract business property relief as the business of the company will consist of dealing in land or buildings, or making or holding investments.

In the absence of business asset taper relief, a capital transaction to terminate the arrangement is unlikely to be of any benefit. This is especially the case where properties are held inside the company. Their realisation, by whatever means, will lead to a significant chargeable gain in the company. Distribution of the funds to the shareholders engenders a further liability.

20.13 The next problem will be financing the business. Large share capitals are not a regular feature of small private companies. There is no great advantage in financing the company this way. Like a trading company therefore, an investment company is likely to have a relatively small share capital.

There are two ways of introducing more funds. Either the company itself must borrow, or the proprietor must do so. Where it is possible, the former alternative might ensure greater availability of tax relief whatever the company's activities. Example 20.16 does demonstrate that this is not exclusively the case.

20.14 If this is a property letting company, then the profit for tax purposes must be computed as a result of the Schedule A business. In effect, nowadays, this means that the profit is computed in accordance with the general principles of Schedule D case I [*ICTA 1988, s 21A*]. Any interest paid by the company on its own borrowings to purchase let property may therefore be deducted in computing the profit, so long as it is incurred wholly and exclusively in generating that profit. It is more than likely that any bank funding such an arrangement would require a personal guarantee from the director/shareholder.

If the activity of the company were something other than a trade or property letting, it is still at an advantage as compared to an individual. Relief of interest generally for a company now falls within the loan relationship rules of *FA 1996, s 80* et seq. In particular *s 83* deals with non-trading deficits on loan relationships. Where the company makes a claim, this may be set against the company's profit (of whatever description). In other words, the company may relieve any interest it pays against investment income.

20.15 On the other hand, if the director/shareholder were to incur any borrowings personally then the tax relief available is more specific and limited. In particular, *ICTA 1988, s 360* deals with interest incurred in relation to a close company (if the company is not close – which is probably unlikely, then no relief is available at all).

Where the borrower has a material interest (very broadly, the ability to control 5% or more of the ordinary share capital in a close company) then he may claim relief for interest paid on a loan applied in purchase of ordinary share capital in the company. Equally, relief may be claimed where the money borrowed is lent on to the company and the company uses it in its business.

In either case, the company must comply with the requirements of *ICTA 1988, s 13A(2)*. This concerns close investment holding companies, which are dealt with separately below. Suffice it to say here that the requirement is either for the company to carry on a trade, or carry on a business of investing in land (including buildings) which is let to third parties.

20.16   So a property letting company may be financed by borrowings made by a shareholder provided that he has a material interest in the company. The result is actually more than satisfactory as the following example demonstrates:

Example 20.16

John and Sarah are thinking of venturing into the buy to let market. They propose to buy a house for £150,000, borrowing £120,000. They anticipate rents of £10,000. Interest payable is £6,000. John is a higher rate taxpayer; Sarah basic rate.

(a) They buy the property in joint names.

		John	**Sarah**
Rents	10,000		
Less: Interest	(6,000)		
Profit	4,000	2,000	2,000
Tax	(1,240)	(800)	(440)
Net income	2,760	1,200	1,560

(b) Suppose they create a company owned 20% John : 80% Sarah. John incurs all the borrowings and lends the money on to the company. The company pays no tax on its income of £10,000 which is paid out as a dividend.

		John	**Sarah**
Interest paid		(6,000)	
Less: Tax relief		2,400	
		(3,600)	
Dividends	10,000	2,000	8,000
Tax on dividends		(500)	
Net income	5,900	(2,100)	8,000

Not only has the net income more than doubled, it is actually more than the net profit on the rentals (£10,000 income less interest £6,000 = £4,000). Curious, but true.

20.17   So a corporate structure can be created and satisfactorily financed for new investment activities, especially property letting. Short-term advantages may not be the overriding factor. Long-term capital gains should also be borne in mind. Personal holding might still be preferred for a range of smaller properties where gains might be mitigated by taper relief and the annual exemption.

Also watch that there is no deleterious effect on other business activities through creation of an associated company.

The company after a trade sale

20.18   The other circumstance in which an investment company might arise is from a former trading company. The company has had a trade and then disposed of it. This might be because of:

- retirement of the business proprietor from active involvement without a need or intention to pass on the business to younger family members;
- deliberate action to mitigate capital gains tax on the disposal of a business. Prior incorporation via *TCGA 1992, s 162*, can achieve this (see **19.8**).

Either way, this leaves the company with a stack of cash. At this point, liquidation of the company is one option, but not very creative especially if it was deliberately formed to mitigate the gain in the first place.

Unlike the previous scenario, there is no need to fund the business. It is more a question of what to do next. This is down to the proprietor's personal preferences and the usual investment decisions.

Whatever means of investment is chosen, this leaves the company in receipt of investment income. This suffers tax at corporate rates which may be lower than personal tax rates. Of course, this depends on the respective financial situations of the parties. If the proprietor has just retired, his income may have reduced significantly, leaving the lower rate and basic rate bands unused. In this circumstance, the company's effective tax rate may not be lower.

Depending on the circumstances, all the usual opportunities, recapped in the previous section, apply:

- the corporate moneybox;
- lower rates of tax;
- use of dividends;
- smoothing the flow of income.

The downsides are that, once trading has ceased, business asset taper relief ends. The longer the company exists, the lower the effective rate of taper relief becomes because of the apportionment required by *TCGA 1992, Sch A1 para 3(3)* (see **18.11**). Additionally, there will be no business property relief in respect of the value of the shares held in the proprietor's estate on death. Either way, long-term estate planning is required.

Close investment holding companies

20.19   This chapter has so far been slightly evasive as to the rate of tax which might apply to the corporate profits and whether this is, indeed, lower than the personal tax rates applying to the proprietor.

This is for a good reason. Some of these investment companies could be close investment holding companies. Perhaps one should start on the footing that all close companies are close investment holding companies (and then exclude the ones that are not).

20.20 The close investment holding company is any close company, other than one which exists wholly or mainly (throughout the accounting period under consideration) for one or more of the following reasons:

- carrying on a trade or trades on a commercial basis;
- making investments in land and property for letting to unconnected persons;
- acting as a holding company, i.e. holding shares and making loans to one or more trading or property investment companies in the same group (the other group companies must also satisfy one of the first two tests);
- co-ordinating the administration of two or more trading or property investment companies in the same group (with the same proviso as before for each group company);
- providing services to other companies in the same group to enable them to carry on a trade or to invest in land and property for letting to unconnected persons.

[*ICTA 1988, s 13A(2)*].

Thus, trading companies are not close investment holding companies, neither are property investment companies (unless the properties are let to connected parties). All other close companies are.

20.21 The close investment holding company rules took effect for accounting periods beginning on or after 1 April 1989, i.e. they followed on from the repeal of close company apportionment (see **16.8**).

20.22 The only current effect of being a close investment holding company is that the rate of corporation tax applied to profits is the mainstream rate of 30%. Application of the small companies rate is precluded by *ICTA 1998, s 13(1)*, and the starting rate by *s 13AA(8)*.

20.23 Therefore, one only needs to be really wary in respect of long-term investment companies which exist wholly or mainly to invest in assets other than property (e.g. stocks and shares, money market deposits etc.). The Inland Revenue's view of 'wholly or mainly' in this context is given by *Corporation Tax Manual para 8163* as really a purposive test. The actual level of trading and other income at any point in time may not give a true picture. What is the intention and what are the levels of activity, to what uses have assets been put? Crucially, what do minutes of meetings and other documents reveal?

Where a pure investment company does exist, then it must suffer an effective corporation tax rate of 30%. This raises the overall effective rate of tax on a dividend withdrawn from such a company to 47.5% (the comparative rate for a trading company suffering the small companies rate of corporation tax being

39.25% – see **4.9**). One must consider whether the other advantages of maintaining an investment company outweigh this downside.

20.24 For the sake of completeness, it should be mentioned that there used to be a limitation on the tax credits which could be recovered by a shareholder in a close investment holding company. These rules only applied where there was an attempt to gain a tax advantage either by use of dividend waivers, or different classes of share capital. Obviously, this fell by the wayside with the end of repayable tax credits from 6 April 1999. However, commentators who suggest that some form of close company apportionment may limit the advantages of incorporation, will no doubt point to this as additional ammunition for their arguments.

Planning points

- The conventional capital gains tax incorporation reliefs do not apply to investment businesses (**20.4**, **20.8**).
- A furnished holiday letting business can be transferred to a company without triggering a gain (**20.9**).
- Setting up a new property letting business in a company, using personal borrowings, has a surprisingly beneficial result (**20.16**).
- Pure investment, but not property letting, companies suffer corporation tax at the full rate of 30% (**20.22**).

Chapter 21

What if it All Goes Wrong?

21.1   The decision to incorporate a business is a complex one with many factors to consider. However, there is no doubt that at the present time many business proprietors and professional advisers are letting one matter alone override all the others. This is especially true at the bottom end of the market – that is to say businesses showing profits of less than, say, £40,000 for a sole trader (or a multiple thereof for a partnership).

The potential for tax saving is so attractive under the present regime that there almost has to be an argument that every business should be incorporated. In the case of the very smallest, the additional professional fees of carrying out the process and maintaining ongoing compliance are likely to outweigh the tax saving.

The common thread recurring throughout, and addressed in various aspects in several chapters of this book, is the ability of the corporate business proprietor to take remuneration by way of dividends. This suffers lower effective rates of tax and no NIC, as compared to either the Schedule D case I profit of an unincorporated trade or drawing by way of salary. The corporate profits themselves attract lower rates of tax than personal profits – in some cases, down to zero.

It all sounds too easy. The pessimist has to offer some caution and say what could go wrong. Consider:

- is it possible to swap salary for dividends at will?
- is it excessively naive to think that there is no NIC on dividends?
- will the Government realise the tax leakage that is going on and do something about it?
- will the corporate business survive?

These and associated issues are addressed below.

Salary for dividend swap

21.2   For the newly incorporated business, this should not present a problem. If a prime objective in the process is the saving of tax, then arrangements should be put in place from the start of trading in the company to ensure that a minimal salary can be taken. Substantial dividends are then drawn when the company profits permit. Do consider carefully the factors involved in declaring and paying a dividend (see **11.68–11.73**).

21.3 Depending on the size of the business, it may not always be possible to take a minimal salary. Many business proprietors will want to fund private pension arrangements. If this is by way of a personal pension plan, then premium payments are limited to a percentage of net relevant earnings. This may dictate an occasional large payment of salary. With the present basis year rules, this may need to be at least every six years (see **4.38**). This could be achieved by payment of a bonus on top of the director's fee, at appropriate occasions but would limit the tax advantages in those years. Again, for the smallest of businesses, this process may not be necessary. Almost all individuals can pay a contribution to a stakeholder scheme up to the earnings threshold of £3,600. For younger people, earning up to about £20,500, this is adequate without resorting to the percentage net relevant earnings limit.

21.4 What then of the more established business? The attraction of taking a dividend rather than a salary sounds good. But is it that easy? Can one simply abandon salary and take a dividend instead?

A director of an established company has been used to taking a salary of, say, £30,000 p.a. Assuming all other things are in place (appropriate shareholdings etc.), can he just decide to drop to a salary of £4,615 and then take a dividend of £22,847 (which would give him the same gross income as before the change)?

First move. He has to get rid of the salary. At this point, readers should backtrack to **16.76–16.78** where there is drawn the distinction between a director appointed as an office holder under the *Companies Act 1985* and one who has a contract of employment. The manner in which they are remunerated is different and, in the latter case, a formal waiver may be necessary to reduce the amount of the salary. This too is addressed at **16.77–16.78**.

Next move. Pay a dividend. This sounds easy, but is strictly regimented by *Companies Act 1985*. Again, see **11.68–11.73**. A dividend that does not meet these requirements will be illegal (in the sense of being contrary to the *Companies Act*). See **16.78**. There may be especial difficulties in this respect should interim dividends be required and the management accounting of the company leaves something to be desired.

So the short answer to the fundamental question, is it possible to swap salary for dividend at will, is that there can be a straight swap provided that care is taken over the exact process followed and with appropriate documentation.

It should be noted that *Social Security (Contributions) Regulations SI 2001/1004, Reg 30* permits a direction charging NIC where there is an abnormal pay practice. 'Abnormal' is not defined, though it is reasonably clear that it relates to the type of employment rather than individuals. Given the official view that dividends are not earnings, it seems unlikely that the substitution of dividends for salary could amount to an abnormal pay practice. Even the Inland Revenue *National Insurance Manual para 8220* admits that proving a pay practice is abnormal is difficult. Consequently, directions under *Reg 30* are very rare (the author has never seen one).

21.5   Without due care, this may not always be the case. If there is a residual entitlement to salary under a contract of employment, then there might be an argument to say that any cash payment made by the company to the individual is in satisfaction of this entitlement. If the payment is an invalid dividend, then it appears not beyond the bounds of possibility that the Inland Revenue could argue that this amounts to the salary foregone. This should not be the case and is defensible if the correct process is followed. However, it is known that Inland Revenue Employer Compliance Teams are looking closely at the relevant paperwork where they discover close company directors whose former salaries have dropped markedly, supposedly to be replaced by dividends.

An additional defence to mount is that salaries and fees are payable to employees and directors. Dividends are payable to shareholders. This ought to break any connection but, when the director and the shareholder are one and the same, it may not be easy to see in what capacity any payment is made, especially if the documentation is inadequate.

The obvious answer to any possible challenge is to ensure that the paperwork stands up to scrutiny.

National insurance on dividends

21.6   Supposing we can get over the hurdle in the previous section. Any rights to salary have been validly waived and the dividends are properly declared and paid. There really is a genuine right to a small salary and a large dividend.

Could someone (the Inland Revenue) still spoil the party?

Think why many small businesses are incorporating. Partially because the effective rate of tax in small and very small companies is significantly lower than unincorporated businesses of the same size. But, more importantly (given that all profits are likely to be withdrawn), because differing tax treatment favours dividends over remuneration (whether the latter be by way of profits, salary, bonus or whatever).

What if, though, the dividends were to be taxed as if they were salary? Heresy, I hear you cry, but please read on.

21.7   There is clear evidence of Inspectors of Taxes who might like to treat dividends as 'salary in disguise'. Assuming all the paperwork was in order, if they tried that on, would they have justification in doing so? You might like to draw comfort from:

- The personal service company legislation in *ITEPA 2003, Part 2, Chapter 8; FA 2000, Sch 12*. If the Inland Revenue could treat dividends as if they were remuneration, why was such convoluted legislation enacted to counter the perceived abuse?
- Articles such as the reader's query *'Salary or Dividend'* in *Taxation* dated 21 June 2001. Basically, the querist asked whether the Inland Revenue had any authority to deem a dividend to be salary. For various reasons, the respondents seemed to think not. One ventured to suggest that there was neither legislation nor case law to support such an attack. The author is inclined to the view that this was not a properly considered answer.

A more recent question on *Accountingweb* was in similar vein. One respondent said that the Inland Revenue had successfully challenged a family company where 'the wages were a pittance' but dividends were high – implying, but not specifically saying, that the dividends were eventually taxed as salary. Pause for thought. If we are about to go down this route, thousands of times over, between us, might there be any merit in the Revenue's argument? Or is this an unnecessary panic?

Well, first it is true that there is no specific legislation, or there may not be. We have to begin at:

- *ITEPA 2003, ss 6(1), 7(2), (3)* which charge tax on employment income and general earnings; formerly *ICTA 1988, s 19(1)* which charged tax under Schedule E on emoluments from an office or employment, and
- *ITEPA 2003, ss 10(2), 62(2)* which define taxable earnings and earnings to include any other profit or incidental benefit; formerly *s 131(1)* which told us that emoluments include salaries, fees, wages, perquisites and profits whatsoever.

21.8   *ITEPA* 2003 is too new to have specific commentary in the Inland Revenue Manuals or elsewhere. However, it does include 'other profits' in earnings, broadly equivalent to the old 'profits whatsoever'. So, it's magical mystery tour time; what is a 'profit whatsoever'?

The Inland Revenue *Schedule E Manual* at *paras SE520* et seq, gives the official view on emoluments and, especially at SE610, important principles. Whilst this exemplifies what may or may not be emoluments, nowhere does it mention dividends – so there is nothing either positive or negative to go on.

21.9   At some point, you need to go off at a tangent. We are concerned not only about income tax but also NIC. Various authorities have suggested that the Department of Social Security/Contributions Agency would not (could not?) levy NIC on a validly declared dividend. More than one suggests that this would not be the case for a dividend which was not validly declared in accordance with company law. The author is not convinced. The remedy for an illegal dividend is repayment to the company (see **16.78**). NIC is now in the care of Inland Revenue National Insurance Contributions Office and you may draw some comfort from Inland Revenue *National Insurance Manual at para 2115* (revised in September 2001) which says that:

'Dividends are derived from a shareholding and not employment. They cannot therefore be classed as earnings and do not attract NICs.'

It even goes on to say:

'... even if the dividends do not meet these conditions [lawful declaration], this is a matter which can only be taken up by the shareholders themselves under company law. . . . The fact that a dividend has not met the requirements of company law does not make it earnings for NIC purposes.'

21.10   It was suggested above that there was neither legislation nor case law to support treatment of a dividend as remuneration. Well, the legislation has got us half way there. If a dividend is a 'profit whatsoever', then it could be remuneration. What does case law tell us on this point? This is where it begins to go downhill.

- In *Recknell v IRC, (1952) 33 TC 201*, Mr Recknell held a number of 'A' shares in the company which employed him. These were available only to employees of the company and there was no obligation on the employees to purchase them. He received a dividend of £450 (a lot of money at the time, this was 1948) and declared it as investment income. The High Court found that the dividends attached to property derived from the employment and were therefore earned income. This was not his only remuneration – he received a salary of £2,287 as well.
- In *White v Franklin, (1965) 42 TC 283*, a number of shares in the employer company were settled on Mr Franklin in such terms that he was entitled to the income therefrom, so long as he continued to be engaged in the management of the company. The dividends received were held to be remuneration of an office or employment (again, he also received a substantial salary and bonus).

21.11   So, if the Inland Revenue has case law on its side, why does it not at least 'try it on'?

- ignoring NIC, up to 6 April 1999, there was no difference in the taxation treatment of salary and dividends;
- until 6 April 2001, any company director wishing to provide for a pension would want reasonable remuneration anyway;
- notwithstanding the attractions of dividends, many small company directors/shareholders seem to take a reasonable remuneration anyway.

Therefore, the amounts at stake have been small and the numbers of companies involved low. However, we are now past the housewarming party and into the realms of a massive rave. The general press have got wind of the idea and there was a suggestion in *The Times* after Budget 2002 that the tax leakage from incorporation of small businesses could be in the region of £2.5–3bn (equivalent to about 2 percentage points on the basic rate of income tax). When the Government gets wind of that, surely they must try to stop it.

21.12   Possible suggestions for amending legislation come in the next section below. Many take the view that it is 'worth a go' for a year or two anyway. Is this a naive assumption; could a clued up Inspector of Taxes try an attack – treating dividends as remuneration that is.

Where might he start? Probably not with those companies where sensible management remuneration is paid. If the salary is at a reasonable level, rewarding the individual's services, then the dividend really must be the 'super profit' for the proprietorial interest. It is to be noted that the cautious replies to the reader's query in *Taxation* did suggest:

(a) there should be a realistic salary;
(b) dividends should be declared no more than quarterly;
(c) attention should be paid to company law aspects, correct declaration, payment and ensuring that there were distributable reserves to be certain that the dividends were valid.

21.13   This will still leave a great raft of 'mini-companies' at risk. Most proprietors will not have an employment contract but remember that *ITEPA 2003, s 5; ICTA 1988, s 19(1)*, applies to offices too. A director appointed by the Companies Acts does hold an office (if there is an employment contract, do not forget the impact of the national minimum wage legislation as well). The £20,000 p.a. businessman spends all he earns; when incorporated, he will not live on an annual salary of £4,600 say. He still needs the balance. It's his earnings. It's what he lives on. It's not the company 'super profit'. The author might give the Inland Revenue a sporting chance of winning that argument if the balance is distributed by way of dividend, especially if the paperwork is defective.

21.14   Do not forget the possible influence of non-proprietorial interests. Can a company give non-voting 'A' shares to its senior managers? The senior manager waives part of his salary and gets a dividend. Ignoring the tax consequences of the share transfer in the first place, this ought to be approached with due caution.

21.15   If this is a significant risk, what defence mechanism might be employed. This has to be in taking a realistic attitude. Many commentators and, indeed, examples throughout this book, illustrate the advantages of dividends over salary by taking an extreme view. That is reducing salary to the minimum which will give continuing entitlement to benefits; in other words, a figure around the basic income tax personal allowance. But, that is perhaps too extreme. It gives the ultimate tax advantage but greater risk. Perhaps consider instead taking reasonable remuneration for duties as a director, say a salary of £20,000–£25,000, and then build the dividend on top of that.

If an attack along the lines suggested is possible, stop and consider why the point does not seem to be taken. Indeed, the NIC guidance seems to shy away from it. Also reconsider the provision of services through intermediaries legislation; if NIC could be charged on dividends anyway, why was this necessary?

The author does have his fingers firmly crossed.

Government changes

21.16 Is incorporation the future of all small businesses? If the commentary in many professional journals throughout 2002/03 is anything to go by, the answer must be an unequivocal yes. It is not just the immediate tax savings which have a major influence. Every time the Chancellor of the Exchequer gets to his feet in a Budget and announces more help targeted at small businesses, he always seems to mean companies. There appears to be a mind set in Westminster that small business directly equates with company.

Perhaps that is deliberate. There is concern over the tax lost through the black economy, much of which must derive from phantom sole traders. Companies are much easier to control. They have to be registered, their existence is known to the Inland Revenue and, for the most part, their activities can be tracked. If all businesses were operated through companies, perhaps it would indeed make the jobs of departments like the Inland Revenue easier.

21.17 The tax advantages have arrived piecemeal. There seems no clear, consistent policy to the changes which have taken place, especially since 6 April 1999. Has anyone in a position of power in the Government stopped to think of the overall effect of the various, apparently unconnected, changes (if readers have forgotten at this point what they are, please back track to **Chapter 1**). Does anyone actually understand? The author remembers an occasion several years ago when a Parliamentary question asked the Chancellor what was the highest marginal rate of income tax (it was then 45.5%). The Financial Secretary to the Treasury replied that the higher rate of income tax was 40%, clearly missing the point of the question.

21.18 Might the Government come to its senses:

- Will it notice the loss of tax? This is clearly dependent on the actual number of companies created and how extreme their dividend/salary policies are. Many estimates in the immediate aftermath of Budget 2002 put the figure at £2.5–£3bn. Surely the Chancellor will notice a hole like that in his coffers, or will it be masked by wider influences of the economic downturn in 2002/03.
- Might the man in the street lobby his MP? Fred earns £15,000 working for a builders merchant. He pays tax and NIC of about £3,200. Bill is a labourer on the building site up the road; he earns £15,000 too and pays tax and NIC of about £2,900. Joe is a bricklayer; he earns £15,000 and pays tax of just

£91. The difference? Fred is an employee and Bill is self employed. Joe was self employed too, but his accountant has just advised him that he should incorporate his business and he now operates through the medium of a small private company.

The author does not consider himself a political animal, but does have a view that people earning the same amount of money should pay the same amount of tax (even if he does earn a living ensuring that some pay less!). Will the Freds and Bills of this world lobby their MPs as to the inequity of their position compared with Joe?

- Will someone in the Inland Revenue say 'hang on a minute'. Talk to local office staff and find out how they are struggling to cope with the administration for the rafts of new companies being formed. How will it then deal with the additional compliance issues next year? One Inspector of Taxes referred to the author as having some 50,000 self employed taxpayers in his district and about 9,000 companies, but 'at the rate you lot (i.e. the tax-profession) are going' it will soon be the other way round. Can they actually cope with all these companies? And that is before all the ancillaries, such as the number of new PAYE schemes which will be required.

21.19   Inevitably, there are those who will continue to be taxed by inertia. That is to say, those who cannot or will not think company for whatever reason. Indeed, if you are a professional adviser reading this book, could you be guilty of professional negligence if you do not at least mention the possibility of incorporation to all your business clients? That apart, is incorporation the future, or will someone spoil the party?

Extension of National Insurance Contributions

21.20   If existing case law is not enough to justify the levying of NIC on dividends, what are the odds on specific legislation. This seems to be the favourite in the minds of most commentators as a countermeasure to the incorporation bonanza.

The vast majority of the mischief in tax saving through dividends will come from close companies. If an attack comes, then they have to be the prime target.

There seem to be two choices. The first would be to redefine earnings in *SSCBA 1992, s 3*, to include dividends from close companies. They would then fall within the scope of Class 1 NIC.

Alternatively, a new class of NIC could be created (might this be 1C or 5?) specifically charging contributions in respect of dividends from close companies. In this case, one would expect the amount to be comparable with Class 1.

For the time being, it has to be speculation as to whether this might happen and, if so, when. In the meantime, keep on planning.

Return of close company apportionment

21.21 In its former existence, close company apportionment was there to prevent private companies being used as moneyboxes in times of very high personal tax rates. The effect was to treat certain amounts of profit as being distributed from the close company whether they were or not. Such amounts were apportioned to the participators pro rata to their shareholdings and the individuals were taxed as if they had received dividends of that amount.

Some commentators suggest the return of some form of close company apportionment as a means of combating the use of dividends to gain a tax advantage. Clearly close company apportionment in its former guise would not help. That treated the amounts apportioned as if they were dividends; now it is the use of dividends that causes the problem (if problem it be).

21.22 'New close company apportionment' would have to create a minimum standard of distribution by way of salary, so that the amounts in question would be charged to income tax at effective rates of 10%/22%/40% rather than Nil/25%. Both employers' and employees' NIC would also be due.

Have we not heard this before? In reality, is this not what *ITEPA 2003, Part 2, Chapter 8; FA 2000, Sch 12*, (the IR35 rules) does? In effect, that says that the company earnings are the directors' earnings and the latter should be taxed on them. One hopes that, should such an approach be considered for all close companies, it would not be so simplistic. There is no mischief in the trade of most close companies; it is the manner of distribution of the profit which could trouble the authorities.

Could we therefore see an IR35 type calculation applied to an acceptable standard of profit distribution by way of salary (50%, 75%, 90% – who knows, name your own figure). Unless and until this happens, the present advantages can continue undisturbed.

Return of investment income surcharge

21.23 Until 1984/85, differential rates of income tax applied to earned and investment income. This was effected by levying a surcharge on investment income above a certain threshold.

At present, one could almost regard the present system as applying an earned income surcharge. This is because investment income suffers only income tax but earnings suffer both income tax and NIC. Logically, this does show, at least, a degree of inequity.

It might be fairly neat, simple and effective to reintroduce an investment income surcharge. If this were applied across the board to all forms of investment income then it might provoke some howls of anguish. However, if dividends taken from close companies are perceived to be an abuse of the system, maybe such an impost could be limited to them.

Disincorporation

21.24   The application of NIC to dividends, by whatever means, could well reverse the perceived tax advantages of incorporation. An IR35 type of close company apportionment certainly would. So, there we are with a company that is no longer tax-efficient.

One should also consider the possibility that the company ran into trading difficulties, or had served its purpose. Its useful life was ended.

What happens next?

21.25   Any business proprietor heading for incorporation must understand and appreciate that he may have a one-way ticket. In principle, all the considerations for incorporation, such as the cessation of trade, capital gains, VAT, inheritance tax etc. apply to disincorporation. The problem is that, whilst there are reliefs to ease the way into the company, there is precious little to help on the way out. Perhaps the biggest single problem is capital gains tax. *TCGA 1992, s 162* and *s 165* are there to defer capital gains arising on the incorporation of a business. There is no equivalent to deal with such liabilities on the way out. Bear in mind that these could be enormous with inflation, development of the business inside the company and understanding that the underlying assets may have a low base cost because of deferred gains when the company was incorporated.

21.26   The Government appears to have paid lip service to the potential problems of disincorporation. However, much of this stems from a time when the developing business would traditionally have headed for the corporate sphere and not the other way round. The need to move the other way was either not recognised or not considered significant. The last comment of note came from the Financial Secretary to the Treasury in 2000, when it was recorded that the Government had no plans to change the tax rules applying to disincorporation (Question: What tax rules? – is that not the whole point; none exist). So it looks like, for the time being at least, we are stuck with what we have got.

21.27   For the sake of completeness, it is necessary to address the fundamental issues, though a complete analysis of disincorporation could well be almost as lengthy as that of incorporation and is clearly beyond the scope of this work. One should think about:

- cessation of trade;
- losses;
- close investment holding company status;
- extracting the business as a going concern;
- extracting cash from a solvent company;
- liquidation;
- striking off.

All of the foregoing assume a solvent company at the end of its useful life. There may be failed companies giving rise to alternative considerations. These are briefly addressed at **21.44–21.47** below.

Cessation of trade

21.28   The cessation of trade in a company will bring about the end of its current corporation tax accounting period [*ICTA 1988, s 12(3)(c)*]. This means an advance in the date for payment of any corporation tax due for the last period.

21.29   Computational adjustments will include consideration of the price at which stock should be sold. There will be a deemed disposal of plant and machinery leading to a balancing adjustment for capital allowance purposes. Cessation of the trade will not itself trigger a balancing adjustment on industrial buildings, though no writing down allowances are available where industrial use ceases. Disposal of an industrial building will lead to a balancing adjustment; if this generates a balancing charge, any unused trade losses may be offset.

21.30   Disposal of the company's chargeable assets may produce capital gains. As suggested above, this can often lead to significant liabilities. The disposal will usually take place after cessation of the trade. This precludes the offset of any trading losses which will have accrued in an earlier corporation tax accounting period.

21.31   If the company was loss making at the cessation of trade, this may give rise to an additional problem. Losses for the final corporation tax accounting period of trade may be offset against the profits of the period [*ICTA 1988, s 393A(1)(a)*]. Any surplus can be carried back and set against the total profits of the previous three years [*s 393A(1)(b), (2A), (2B)*]. That is all that is available. The losses cannot go forward, especially against any gains in a later corporation tax accounting period as noted above. They certainly cannot be transferred with the trade to a successor.

Close investment holding company status

21.32   Once the company has ceased to trade, it will almost certainly become a close investment holding company [*ICTA 1988, s 13A*]. The consequences of this are considered at **20.19–20.24**. Largely it means that any profits arising will be taxed at the mainstream rate of 30%.

21.33   However, if the company is not a close investment holding company throughout the corporation tax accounting period which ends on the commencement of winding up, it will not be a close investment holding company for the next corporation tax accounting period [*ICTA 1988, s 13A(4)*]. This is probably of limited value where trading has already ceased. The company is quite likely to have become a close investment holding company before liquidation even commences.

Extraction of the business from the company

21.34   If the proprietor(s) want to take the trade out of the company as a going concern, it is still necessary to consider all the influences of the cessation of trade in the company. Pay especial attention here to the capital gains arising. This will be a connected party transaction, requiring the use of market value in calculating the gain. However, in the absence of a third party sale, there will not be any cash proceeds to pay the tax. This may influence the manner of extraction.

21.35   If the company is needing funds with which to pay any capital gains tax due, this almost certainly forces the proprietor to buy the assets of the business from the company. This is quite probably a situation that he will not have envisaged. The payment does not need to be of the full market value (even though that will be imposed in order to calculate the gain) but simply sufficient to leave the company with adequate funds to pay the tax.

21.36   Alternatively, if the company has adequate cash reserves to ensure that it can pay its own tax liabilities consequent on the transfer, the business may be paid to the shareholders as a dividend in specie. This is a distribution within *ICTA 1988, s 209(4)* with the consequence that the shareholders suffer higher rate income tax on the grossed up value of the business transferred.

Remember: there is a double charge. The company has a liability on any realised or deemed gains (or trading profit on cessation of trade) and the individual has a liability on his receipt.

21.37   Where the proprietor buys the business at under value to provide the company with funds to meet its tax liability, it is to be hoped that the excess of market value over the actual consideration given is also to be treated as a distribution under *ICTA 1988, s 209(4)*. The author has seen comment to the effect that a liability under *ICTA 1988, s 419*, could arise, though this seems unlikely as the transaction is a permanent transfer of the business assets and not a loan.

Extracting cash from the company

21.38   If the company was adequately funded then, after extraction of the trade (or perhaps its sale to a third party), there remains the problem of getting any remaining cash out of the company.

This is no different to the usual considerations and really is a special case of the company after a trade sale (see **20.18**).

The choice is probably a straight decision between:

- dividend;
- a capital distribution on liquidation.

A dividend may be useful if the amounts are small and the shareholders are not higher rate taxpayers. Otherwise, tax will be due at an effective rate of 25%.

The capital distribution may enjoy the benefits of business asset taper relief (watch whether the company is still a trading company; its status may have changed on the cessation of trade and apportionment of the gain may be necessary – see **18.35**). See also the comments in Inland Revenue *Tax Bulletin 61, October 2002* as regards whether the company is active or inactive for the purposes of *TCGA 1992, Sch A1 para 11A* during the course of winding up. The capital distribution may be effected during liquidation and specifically gives rise to a capital gain under *TCGA 1992, s 122*. Any personal capital losses and the annual exemption may also be offset.

Liquidation

21.39   Formal liquidation of the company may prove to be a long and costly process. The members of a solvent company can proceed to wind it up, but this must be dealt with by a licensed insolvency practitioner.

The commencement of winding up proceedings terminates the company's current corporation tax accounting period and a new one begins. Any corporation tax liabilities which arise in the course of winding up are an expense or disbursement of the liquidation.

The liquidator must also take account of any pre-liquidation tax liabilities. Some of these, including outstanding tax under PAYE and NIC for the twelve months prior to the liquidator's appointment, are preferential.

Striking off

21.40   The expense and complexity of a formal liquidation may seem excessive when dealing with a close company which is no longer required and which has only modest reserves. Strictly, capital distributions are only seen after the appointment of a liquidator. Otherwise, the distribution of funds to the members of a company, even prior to its dissolution, is strictly an income distribution under *ICTA 1988, s 209*.

21.41   There is a far simpler procedure for disposing of an unwanted company. The company may apply to the Registrar under *Companies Act 1985, s 652*, to be struck off the register. The directors must meet the stringent requirements in *s 652A* to notify all shareholders, employees, creditors etc. of the intention to invoke this process. Additionally, the application cannot be made until at least three months after the company has ceased trading. The first move in this process, assuming that the company's business has not been sold, is to deal with its extraction as above. A solvent company may be dissolved as a result of its name being struck off the register.

21.42   Under *ESC C16*, the Inland Revenue is prepared to accept that distributions made prior to such a dissolution have been made under a formal winding up. In other words, they should be treated as capital and not income distributions. Application of the concession requires that the company and its members give certain assurances to the Inland Revenue. These include that:

- the company does not intend to trade or carry on business in future;
- the company intends to collect its debts, pay off its creditors and distribute any balance of assets to its shareholders (or has already done so);
- the company intends to seek or accept striking off and dissolution;
- the company and its shareholders will supply such information as is necessary to determine, and will pay, any corporation tax liability on income or capital gains;
- the shareholders will pay any capital gains tax liability in respect of any amount distributed to them in cash or otherwise as if the distributions have been made during the winding up.

21.43   The author has heard comment to the effect that, since the implementation of corporation tax self assessment, the Inland Revenue will delay clearance for the application of the *ESC C16* procedure. The logic is seemingly that the process foreshortens the time available to enquire into the company's return for the last corporation tax accounting period of trading. However, this is not the author's personal experience and requests to apply *ESC C16* are granted without undue delay. Indeed, clearances have been given even where it has been stated that the clearance is required to allow an interim distribution to use up the annual CGT exemption.

21.44   An interesting exchange on this issue took place in the Tax Faculty Newsletter *TAXline* during Autumn 2002. The first correspondent pointed out that technically under *ESC C16* the company is not actually in liquidation. Notwithstanding the Inland Revenue acceptance for tax purposes, company law actually forbids distributions of anything in excess of the company's distributable reserves. This leaves the share capital (including any share premium) to pass to the Crown bona vacantia under *Companies Act 1985, s 654*. One respondent took the view that, the Inland Revenue having given clearance under the extra statutory concession, this point is not pursued. Others were not so sure. In most cases, the share capital will be minimal and this seems a point which is not normally worth arguing about. If the share capital is large, the solution would seem to be to go for a formal liquidation.

Failed companies

21.45   The processes of disincorporation, liquidation and striking off assume that there is something in the company worthy of sale or recovery.

What is the position, though, if the company has simply ceased to trade and has no significant assets or is insolvent.

Bear in mind that, if a sole trader business fails, then bankruptcy is the only obstacle to the proprietor picking himself up and starting again. There is no statutory bar to trading.

By contrast, an incompetent director can be banned from acting in such capacity in other companies and future options may be limited to sole trader without the tax advantages of a company that this book discusses. In a very small family company, it may be wise to ensure that husband and wife are not both directors of a company. If one is barred from acting in this capacity, then maybe the other can continue.

21.46   In the case of insolvency, enforced liquidation is still a possibility. This presumes, though, that the creditors perceive prospects of recovery to invoke the formal procedure. This does not always happen; some companies just die. It should be noted that the company cannot just be abandoned if no longer required. *Companies Act* filing requirements must still be met even if the company has no transactions and no activities.

The shareholders are left with what, to all intents and purposes, is an empty shell. This may have cost them money in terms of purchase of the share capital or loans to the company.

21.47   In these circumstances, a members' voluntary liquidation to effect disposal of the shares and crystallise a capital loss seems unlikely. However, a capital loss may still be claimed by a negligible value claim under *TCGA 1992, s 24(2)*. The shareholders must demonstrate to the Inspector of Taxes that the shares are of negligible value, which should not be difficult if the company has ceased to trade and has no assets. A claim is then made, the effect of which is to treat the shares as disposed of and immediately reacquired. The disposal value will be nil, with the cost being the original subscription price or purchase price. The loss arising may then be set against any other capital gains realised by the shareholder. The claim may specify an earlier date for negligible value treatment, though it cannot be more than two years before the claim.

21.48   Where the shares were originally acquired by subscription, *ICTA 1988, s 574* provides a useful extension to give relief for the loss against income. The shares must be in a qualifying trading company as defined in *s 576*. This invokes many of the provisions of the Enterprise Investment Scheme legislation, thus prohibiting the relief where the company had any significant activity other than a trade. The loss must be computed in accordance with capital gains principles (which can include a negligible value claim under *TCGA 1992, s 24(2)*). A claim may then be made that the capital loss arising is set against income of either the same tax year as that in which the loss arose, or the preceding year.

21.49   Lastly, the company may not have been financed entirely by share capital. There may also have been loans. Where a person lends money to a UK trader (which includes a company) and the funds are used in the borrower's trade then, if the loan becomes irrecoverable, a claim may be made that the amount lost should be treated as a capital loss [*TCGA 1992, s 253*]. There are connected party provisions limiting relief but, curiously, these do not include a company and its shareholders/directors. So a participator who has loaned money to a trading company may claim relief for the capital loss if the company fails. Note that the Inland Revenue interprets the provision in *s 253(3)* that the loan has become irrecoverable very strictly. If funds were put into an ailing company to 'prop it up' so to speak, then there is an argument that there was never any realistic prospect of recovery and relief would be denied.

Phoenix companies

21.50   As we have seen throughout this work, classical tax planning for profit extraction by the proprietor of a private company often encompasses the establishment of a balance between salary and dividends so as to achieve an optimum tax liability. Since the proposals for accrual of maximum business asset taper relief (BATR) after only two years, confirmed in *FA 2002*, the author has heard suggestions that there is a third way. The bulk of profits might be accumulated in the company. After two years, the company is liquidated; the proprietors suffer an effective capital gains tax rate of only 10% on the distributions in liquidation and the business carries on in a new company (the phoenix) which takes over from the old. The proprietors of the new company are identical, or at least very similar, to those of the old company.

21.51   In talking about a 10% capital gains tax rate, there appears to be a presumption that the shareholders and the company have satisfied all the conditions for business asset taper relief so that 75% taper relief will be applied to the gain arising from the distributions in liquidation.

Is this right? Many thousands of words have been written about taper relief since its inception yet it would be a brave tax practitioner who could say that he understood all its nuances. The crux of the matter here is whether there is a trading company.

A 'trading company' for this purpose is now defined in *TCGA 1992 Sch A1 para 22A*. The Inland Revenue gave its views in the, now notorious, *Tax Bulletin* article of June 2001 which, in turn, has spawned extensive comment. Fundamentally, the company must carry on trading activities and anything else that it does must not be substantial. A detailed analysis of the ramifications of this, and the previous definition, together with the Revenue commentary thereon, is contained in **Chapter 18** (see **18.22–18.31**). One must ask oneself why the company is retaining a large amount of undistributed profits. If it is simply building up cash reserves so the shareholders can liquidate it with the full benefit of taper relief (rather than pay an effective rate of income tax of 25% on dividends) then it may have established another business purpose.

If that is the case could one be unequivocally certain that business asset taper relief is available.

21.52 But, there is potentially a bigger problem. Remember that in the absence of a formal liquidation or application of *ESC C16*, distribution of accumulated reserves in a company is actually an income distribution. There is established case law, from days long before taper relief was ever dreamed up, concerning the cessation of trade in one company only for it to recommence in another. In *IRC v Joiner [1975] STC 657*, the Revenue argued that a distribution of assets in a winding up was a transaction in securities within what is now *ICTA 1988, s 703*. In other words it could be taxed as income, not a capital gain. In a case with similar circumstances, *Addy v IRC [1975] STC 601*, the Chancery Division upheld a *s 703* notice served by the Inspector.

21.53 Following the *Joiner* decision, the Board of the Inland Revenue issued a statement to the effect that *s 703* would not be applied to an 'ordinary liquidation'. That latter phrase is taken to mean the bona fide winding up of the business as a discrete entity, whether it comes to an end or is taken over by some other concern which is under substantially different control. The Board does not regard as 'ordinary' a liquidation which is part of a scheme of reconstruction which enables the old business to be carried on as before with substantially the same shareholders.

In the circumstances envisaged here, there has to be a significant risk that the Inland Revenue would take the *s 703* point. This seems to be borne out by the commentary in the Inland Revenue *Inspectors' Manual* at *para 4519*. Of course, the shareholders could make a clearance application under *s 707* but one has to question how they could demonstrate that obtaining a tax advantage was not one of the main objectives.

21.54 Any suggestions that this scheme might be employed should therefore be tempered with a degree of caution.

Planning points

- Existing salary can probably be swapped for dividends if the correct process is followed and appropriate documentation created (**21.4–21.5**).
- Be sensible with management remuneration to limit any argument that dividends paid amount to salary (**21.15**).
- Understand that disincorporation can be expensive (**21.35–21.36**).
- Consider the *ESC C16* procedure for striking off an unwanted company (**21.42**).
- Income tax relief can be obtained for losses incurred on shares originally subscribed for in a trading company (**21.48**).
- The business asset taper relief phoenix company almost certainly does not work (**21.54**).

Worked Example of Possible Savings

The following is based on the text of an article written by Roger Jones and published in Tolley's Practical Tax Newsletter on 19 July 2002. Whilst the measures taken are rather extreme for the purposes of illustration, the principles hold good and combine many of the techniques considered in the main body of the text to demonstrate how tax liabilities may be reduced.

I wrote 'A Painless Extraction' (TPT 29 March and 12 April 2002) long before the Chancellor presented his 2002 Budget. In that article I demonstrated the comparative effects of taking profits from a small company in different ways. I looked at dividends as against salary or benefits or the long-term effect of a capital transaction. At the end of the day, one needs to strike a compromise giving the optimum result for a particular business proprietor's needs.

I thought then that it would be nice to play a little game and let tax considerations override everything else. Just how low could the tax bill go? Since then, of course, we have had a Budget which has brought the matter of incorporation into even sharper focus. In particular:

- the differing tax treatment of dividends and salary becomes even greater with the NIC 'surcharge' applicable from 6 April 2003;
- the availability of a nil rate band on profits up to £10,000 favours a company;
- relief for intangibles such as goodwill is only available to a company;
- the removal of stamp duty on transfers of goodwill extinguishes a previous disincentive to incorporation.

For these, and other, reasons incorporation is *the* planning manoeuvre of the moment. If tax is the overriding factor (and who doesn't want to save money?) then there has to be an argument that every small business should incorporate. One questions whether this is actually a good move. Is the business consistently profitable? How good is the bookkeeping? Will the owner treat the company's money as if it were his own? Do I detect a rash of *ICTA 1988, s 419*, and illegal dividend problems waiting to happen? In the 'real' world such businesses would be far better advised to remain as sole traders.

In my hypothetical real world, though, I have a presumption that two individuals earning similar amounts would pay roughly the same amount of tax and NIC. However, with recent Government policy, this is anything but the case. Without getting too political, is it a policy at all? Have the Treasury and the Inland Revenue actually thought through the real effect of recent changes

Appendix 1 Worked Example of Possible Savings

or are we simply seeing the combination of a series of 'accidents' benefiting a significant minority of the population?

Do not forget that the vast majority of the working population are 'ordinary' employees. They have little scope to reduce their tax liabilities. But a growing number of the self employed can do so. Who can blame them for taking advantage? When the Government realises what it has done (and I have seen the cost to the Exchequer of the many forthcoming 'micro incorporations' put at £2–3bn) will it take action to prevent the leakage?

At this point, for those who have not met him before, let me introduce Ivor Goodhuise. He is a senior manager with a well-known firm of accountants. His salary is £50,000 and he is provided with a 2 litre Rover 75 which originally cost £18,500. His total tax and NIC bill for 2003/04 would be £17,661 leaving him net spendable income of £32,339.

Example 1

Salary	£50,000
Car BIK; Rover 75 OLP 18,500, CO_2 228g/km	5,365
Tax thereon	14,575
Class 1 NIC	3,086
Net spendable (50,000 – [14,575 + 3,086])	32,339

Ivor does quite a lot of consultancy work and is heavily involved in training and lecturing. He has thought for a while about going it alone and thinks now is the time to try it. His business plan shows that his first year profit, after all expenses, will be £50,000. Okay, this may not be quite the real world but it makes my later comparisons easier. He anticipates continuing to use a car like the Rover which will cost a little under £8,000 for 15,000 total mileage (about two thirds of this is private). His projected tax and NIC bill for 2003/04 is now £16,956 and net spendable income is £33,044.

Example 2

Profit	£50,000
Add car expenses, private	5,300
Tax thereon	14,549
NIC (Class 4)	2,30
NIC (Class 2)	104
Net spendable (50,000 – [14,549 + 2,303 + 104])	33,044

He has saved a modest £705. Perhaps this is close to my ideal – the employee earning £50,000 pays similar tax to the self employed man with a £50,000 profit.

Everyone knows that the self employed can offset more expenses than the employee though. Ivor's first move would be to pay his wife a salary. She does not otherwise work and will do some typing for him and act as a point of contact for the business when he is out. He will pay her £4,615 or a little less. This is below the income tax personal allowance and the NIC primary threshold so no tax or NIC is due. However, it reduces his profit and therefore the tax and NIC bill.

Example 3

Profit	£50,000
Add car expenses, private	5,300
Less wife's salary	(4,615)
Tax thereon	12,703
NIC (Class 4)	2,257
NIC (Class 2)	104
Net spendable (50,000 – [12,703 + 2,257 + 104])	34,936

His net spendable income is now £34,936, a useful £2,600 higher than if he remains an employee.

Having advised so many clients on the benefits of incorporation, how can he possibly use any other medium for his business? In Example 4, I have assumed he forms a company as sole shareholder. He takes management remuneration for himself of £25,000, still pays his wife £4,615 and the company provides a car like the original Rover. The company's net profit is all distributed as a dividend. The corporation tax payable is £1,684, secondary Class 1 NIC and Class 1A is £3,296 and he has personal liabilities of £10,454.

Example 4

Profit	£50,000
Less salaries (25,000 + 4,615)	(29,615)
Less NIC (Class 1 secondary [25,000 – 4,615] @ 12.8%)	(2,609)
Less NIC (Class 1A 5,365 @ 12.8%)	(687)
Corporation tax (on net profit 17,089; 10,000 @ nil, 7,089 @ 23.75%)	1,684
Salary	25,000
Car BIK	5,365
Tax thereon	5,430
NIC (Class 1)	2,242
Net profit distributed as dividend	15,405
Higher rate tax thereon	2,782
Net spendable (50,000 – [1,684 + 2,609 + 687 + 7,672 + 2,782])	34,566

His net spendable income is £34,566, usefully £2,200 up on where we started but nearly £400 down on the pre-incorporation position. This demonstrates that it is possible to incorporate and get it wrong. If much of the profits are taken as salary or taxable benefits there is nothing to be gained.

Ivor knows that the real advantage is in taking dividends. So he creates a structure to maximise this route. In Example 5, Ivor and his wife are 50:50 shareholders. Ivor takes no salary but retains the use of the company car. His wife has a salary of £4,615 and the whole of the company's net profit is distributed by way of dividend. The corporation tax payable is £8,241 along with £687 Class 1A NIC. Ivor has a tiny tax liability on the car benefit.

Example 5

Profit	£50,000
Less salary	(4,615)
Less NIC (Class 1A)	(687)
Corporation tax on net profit (44,698; 10,000 @ nil, 34,698 @ 23.75%)	8,241
Salary covered by PA	
Dividends fall in basic rate band	No tax
Car benefit £5,365, tax thereon	75
Net spendable (50,000 – [687 + 8241 + 75])	40,997

The net spendable income is now £40,997, a whopping £8,658 up on the starting position and nearly £6,500 up on the previous example.

Last, but not least, the creative bit:

1. FA 2002 provides 100% first year allowances on the least polluting cars (those emitting no more than 120g/km CO_2). Looking down the list of those qualifying, Ivor decides on an Audi A2 TdiS. The original list price is £14,100 and it emits only 119g/km. Assuming capital allowances on the 'dirty' car would have been £3,000, this gives a useful additional deduction of £11,000. Better still, his personal benefit in kind is reduced to £2,538 (18% – remember 3% diesel addition – of £14,100).
2. His daughter has been pestering him for a computer to help with her homework. He was thinking of buying one personally but now the company could acquire it. At a cost of £2,000 it gets 100% first year allowances on information, communications and technology expenditure and Ivor has no personal benefit.
3. The family makes quite a lot of private telephone calls. Ivor proposes that the company gets a couple of mobile phones and meets all the costs estimated at £1,000. The cost is written off and there is no personal benefit.

So, in Example 6, having reduced the car benefit, Ivor can take £2,000 salary. Items 1–3 reduce the company profit by £14,000; the corporation tax is reduced to £4,527 and the Class 1A NIC to £325. Again the net profit is distributed as dividends so there is no personal liability.

Example 6

Profit	£50,000
Less car FYA (net of original capital allowances)	(11,000)
Less computer cost	(2,000)
Less phone costs	(1,000)
Less salaries	(6,615)
Less NIC (Class 1A)	(325)
Corporation tax on net profit (29,060; 10,000 @ nil, 19,060 @ 23.75%)	4,527
Salary, car BIK, dividends all covered by PAs or fall in basic rate band	No tax
Net spendable (50,000 – [4527 + 325])	45,148

The net spendable income is now £45,148, no less than £12,800 more than Example 1, an increase of almost 40%.

Not many businessmen could or would take the last step but incorporation and care in profit extraction can produce enormous savings. Even a £10,000 p.a. business can save nearly £1,500 (more than enough to cover the cost of incorporation and the additional compliance cost for the first year alone). At £20,000 the saving doubles to £3,000. The savings reach a peak near £40,000 after which higher rate income tax liability kicks in on the dividends. The progression is not smooth with breakpoints as corporation tax rates, personal tax rates etc. change. For a detailed analysis of these effects, I would refer readers to Mike Thexton's article *'The Burning Question'* in *Taxation, 16 May 2002*, but see also the rider in *Feedback* in the *13 June 2002* edition.

Finally, will it last? Who knows? If the policymakers really get a grasp of what they have done, surely it cannot. The obvious counter attack would be the imposition of NIC on close company dividends but it has to be at least a year before that comes. I have seen suggested as an alternative a return to some form of close company apportionment (hands up those old enough to remember that one).

The success of this form of planning lies essentially in the differing treatment of dividends as against salary. I might actually venture to suggest that existing legislation and case law is adequate to counter this. But, if I am right, why was such convoluted legislation introduced to meet the perceived abuse by personal service companies?

Looks like we keep on planning (for a while anyway).

Footnote: Yes, I do realise that in Examples 5 and 6 Ivor's salary has dropped below the NIC lower earnings limit so he no longer maintains a contribution record for National Insurance Retirement Pension. In the real world I would not recommend this but we do seem to be operating in 'Alice's Wonderland' at the moment.

An Incorporation Checklist

This appendix should not be taken as a comprehensive guide to the steps required to incorporate a business. There is no single correct way. The process to follow may vary according to the nature of the business, the requirements of the proprietors, the capital assets involved and their destination, together with many other factors.

Rather, the items listed out are those which may need to be considered in the majority of incorporations. Not all of them need to be addressed in every situation. Equally, some businesses may exhibit unusual features which do need to be addressed, but are not mentioned here.

They are clustered under generic headings, not in the order that they should be approached. It should be noted that it is necessary to deal with items from different lists simultaneously. For example, issues connected with income tax or capital gains tax may need to be tackled at the same time as some of the legalities.

It is not a resume of the main text. As far as possible, there is a reference to the main body of the text where commentary on the point begins. However, this may not be the totality of the comment. Some checklist points impinge on more than one tax, or a tax plus some other issue, and the full text should be consulted.

Professionals should note that incorporation is perhaps one of the ultimate examination questions. It brings together so many diverse tax problems in one transaction. Add on the company law and practical issues and good advice in this area should be seen as a high value product.

Business proprietors should recognise the complexity of the operation. Getting it right involves a lot of work. Skimping on the process will leave open many gaps inviting a challenge by the Inland Revenue.

Good luck and do recognise the following.

Before you start

- If you are a professional advising on the incorporation transaction, do the terms of your engagement letter cover it?
- Is this an established business?
- Is it consistently profitable?

- Does the proprietor live within his means?
- Is this a business that might be caught by the IR35 provisions? (**17.2**)
- Will the nature of the business and the proposed share structure cause potential problems under the settlements legislation? (**16.69**)
- Are there any associated companies which might limit the tax advantages? (**2.74**)
- Estimate the income tax and NIC savings. Consider the additional costs of operating the business through a company. Is there a saving? (**4.29**)
- Ensure that the business proprietors are aware of the implications of incorporation. The tax savings may be nice, but the additional administrative burdens of running the company correctly are significant. Do the proprietors realise that the company's assets are not their assets?
- Is the proprietor sure that he wants to proceed – this may be a one way ticket; disincorporation is difficult. (**21.25**)
- Does incorporation fit in with the business plan?
- Is the business record keeping of a good and reliable standard?
- Will the Companies House filing requirements, leading to a certain loss of privacy, cause problems?
- Consider peripheral issues such as landlord and tenant matters, constraints of professional bodies, agricultural herd basis, agricultural quotas and premium payments, grants of all types, agricultural set aside payments, environmentally sensitive area payments, construction industry subcontractors scheme.
- Obtain valuations of significant assets to be transferred, especially land and buildings.
- Establish the nature of any business goodwill, consider whether it is transferable and obtain a valuation of it. (**14.6**)
- In the small family situation, consider whether both husband and wife should be directors of the company. In the case of financial difficulty, they might both be disqualified from acting in this capacity, inhibiting future actions and invoking personal guarantees. (**21.45**)

Legalities

- Confirm the company name. (**11.6**)
- Obtain the names and personal details of the directors and company secretary. (**11.6**)
- Agree the registered office address. (**11.6**)
- Agree the accounting reference date (the default is the end of the month of incorporation). (**11.38**)
- Consider the content of the memorandum and articles of association. Think about pre-emption rights, and exit route for the shareholders, who is to hold the casting vote, the classes of share and funding. Is a shareholders' agreement required? (**11.4, 11.5, 11.20**)
- If electronic facilities exist, incorporate the company direct with Companies House; otherwise use *Jordans* or a similar agent, or acquire a ready made shelf company. (**11.8**)

- Agree the number of shares to be issued (the ratio of which should normally be in the profit sharing ratio of the unincorporated business). (**11.16**)
- After incorporation hold a board meeting, particularly to agree to appointment of the company bankers. Prepare minutes of that meeting. (**11.10**)
- Set up the statutory books. (**11.11**)
- Display the company's name at the registered office and the place of business. (**11.12**)
- Ensure that the business and asset transfer to the company is adequately documented. If there is not to be a comprehensive incorporation agreement, consider what evidence is required concerning the transfer of items such as stock, plant and machinery etc. (**11.31**, **11.32**)
- Ensure that employment law requirements are satisfied where employees are transferred from the unincorporated business to the company. Is a new contract of employment required? (**12.28**)
- Consider whether a contract of employment is required for the directors. Do not forget the constraints of the National Minimum Wage requirements. (**12.7**)
- Prepare forms CT41G and 64–8 for the Inland Revenue. (**12.28**)
- Set up a PAYE scheme. (**12.28**)

Income tax

- Consider the current year basis closing rules as regards the income tax liability of the ceasing unincorporated business and the date of payment. (**7.2** et seq)
- Consider the impact of overlap/transitional relief. (**7.6**, **7.8**)
- Consider the most appropriate date of incorporation (note particularly the influence on capital allowances). (**7.12**, **8.22**)
- Consider the price at which stock is to be transferred. Prepare any election which might be necessary. (**7.20**)
- Estimate the income tax and NIC on the final profit. Provide for this in the closing accounts of the business. (**7.16**)
- If the unincorporated business has a terminal loss, consider how this will be relieved or whether it can be carried forward and set against amounts received from the new company. (**3.14**, **3.15**)
- Consider the transfer of assets to the company and any benefit in kind implications which may arise in respect of future private use. (**15.24**)
- If the proprietor's car is to remain outside the company, consider whether authorised mileage allowance payments will be sufficient to cover the cost of business mileage and, if not, how the shortfall will be funded. (**15.8**)
- Make sure arrangements are in place for recording business mileage if the proprietor's car remains outside the company.
- Ensure that the proprietor is aware that the company's funds must not be used for private expenses. (**16.29**)
- Make arrangement for paying rent on assets which are held outside the company. (**14.23**)

Capital allowances

- Consider whether the incorporation will lead to a loss of allowances in respect of plant and machinery, particularly first year allowances on any recent capital expenditure. (**8.16**)
- Adjust the final period of trading, if necessary, to minimise any loss of allowances. (**8.21**)
- Consider the amount which the company should pay for plant and machinery in order to engineer a balancing adjustment of appropriate magnitude. (**8.25**)
- Prepare an election under *CAA 2001, s 266*, to carry the plant and machinery forward at tax written down value if appropriate. (**8.19**)
- For industrial buildings, consider whether the relevant interest should be transferred to the company and, if so, whether there needs to be an election to override the balancing adjustment. (**8.39**)
- With agricultural buildings, consider whether an election should be made to invoke a balancing adjustment. (**8.51**)

Capital gains tax

- Check whether any assets carry deferred gains. (**9.3**)
- Consider whether all assets will be transferred to the company.
- Consider the price to be paid for assets to create loan account balance in the company to facilitate drawings at minimum tax cost. (**9.31**)
- If all assets will be transferred to the company, consider the implications of *TCGA 1992, s 162*, where the entire business is transferred to the company in exchange for an issue of shares. (**9.10**)
- Consider whether *TCGA 1992, s 162*, should be disapplied by an election under *s 162A*. (**9.20**)
- Where not all the assets will be transferred to the company, consider the implications of gifting assets or selling them at under value and relieving the gain under *TCGA 1992, s 165*. (**9.25**)
- Prepare an election to hold over the gain where appropriate. This must be on form IR295. (**9.29**)
- Consider the Enterprise Investment Scheme CGT deferral provisions as an alternative to the two more conventional routes. Bear in mind that this is complex and not tried and tested. (**9.40**)
- If shares in a trading company are to be sold, is the business asset taper relief tainted?
- Consider whether a capital transaction can be a valid means of extracting accumulated profit from a company. (**18.32**)

Value added tax

- Register the company with Customs & Excise. (**12.30**)
- Consider whether the incorporation transaction is a transfer of a going concern. (**12.33**)

- Consider whether to transfer the unincorporated business's existing registration which also transfers its history and any liabilities. (**12.35**)
- After incorporating, cancel the registration of the old business. (**12.36**)

Stamp duty

- Consider whether a document of transfer is required. It will be where intangibles such as goodwill require to be transferred, or where capital gains are to be deferred by the route afforded in *TCGA 1992, s 162*. (**10.1, 11.31**)
- Ad valorem duty will be charged on dutiable assets transferred by a document. (**10.4**)
- To minimise the duty, do not transfer debts of the old business; the company may collect these as agent. (**10.22**)
- Where the consideration is required to be apportioned, make a return on form Stamps 22. (**10.18**)

National Insurance Contributions

- Consider the impact of Class 1A contributions on benefits in kind. (**5.12**)
- Cancel arrangements for payment of Class 2 contributions.
- Make arrangements to record earnings for Class 1 contribution purposes if the amount is between the lower earnings limit and the primary threshold. (**5.23**)

Inheritance tax

- Consider whether the route to incorporation will lead to a transfer of value for inheritance tax purposes. (**13.9**)
- Consider the potential loss of business property relief on assets which are held outside the company. (**13.26, 14.34**)
- Consider the increased flexibility on future transfers of the business which is afforded by incorporation.
- Be wary that transfer of business or asset to an existing company could create an immediately chargeable transfer. (**14.35**)

Non-tax issues

- Notify all parties having dealings with the business. (**12.28**)
- Arrange new stationery. (**12.29**)
- Get new banking facilities in place. (**11.10**)

After the event

- Ensure that the business proprietors understand that the company assets are not their assets.
- Ensure that the accounting procedures are adequate to cope with the split of business and private expenditure and benefit in kind implications.
- Ensure that procedures are in place for taxing all withdrawals of funds from the company.
- Ensure that a PAYE scheme is in place. (**12.28**)
- Ensure that procedures are in place to declare and pay dividends. (**11.66**)
- Ensure that the statutory registers, minute book etc. are set up. (**11.11**)

Index